"THE HIGHER CHRISTIAN LIFE"

SOURCES FOR THE STUDY OF THE HOLINESS, PENTECOSTAL, AND KESWICK MOVEMENTS

A forty-eight-volume facsimile series reprinting extremely rare documents for the study of nineteenth-century religious and social history, the rise of feminism, and the history of the Pentecostal and Charismatic movements

Edited by
Donald W. Dayton
Northern Baptist Theological Seminary

Advisory Editors
D. William Faupel, *Asbury Theological Seminary*
Cecil M. Robeck, Jr., *Fuller Theological Seminary*
Gerald T. Sheppard, *Union Theological Seminary*

A GARLAND SERIES

HOLINESS TRACTS DEFENDING THE MINISTRY OF WOMEN

with a Preface by
Donald W. Dayton
Northern Baptist
Theological Seminary

Garland Publishing, Inc.
New York & London
1985

For a complete list of the titles in this series
see the final pages of this volume.

The facsimiles of *Woman's Right to Preach the Gospel*
and *Women Preachers* have been made from copies in
the Library of Congress; that of *Female Ministry*
is from a copy in the New York Public Library.

Preface copyright © 1985 by Donald W. Dayton

Library of Congress Cataloging-in-Publication Data
Main entry under title:
HOLINESS TRACTS DEFENDING THE MINISTRY OF WOMEN.

("The Higher Christian life")
Reprint of works originally published 1853–1905.
1. Women clergy—Addresses, essays, lectures.
2. Holiness churches—Clergy—Addresses, essays,
lectures.   I. Series.
BV676.H65   1985   262'.14   85-20909
ISBN 0-8240-6411-9 (alk. paper)

The volumes in this series are printed on
acid-free, 250-year-life paper.

Printed in the United States of America

Contents

Preface
Donald W. Dayton

Woman's Right to Preach the Gospel
Luther Lee

Ordaining Women
B. T. Roberts

*Female Ministry; or,
Woman's Right to Preach the Gospel*
Catherine Booth

Women Preachers
Fannie McDowell Hunter

PREFACE

Though it has been little recognized outside the movement, one of the most consistent themes throughout most holiness circles has been the advocacy of the ministry of women. Often, though not always, this has been combined with feminist convictions. Indeed, one could argue that the holiness churches pioneered the ministry of women and that the history of feminism in the United States will not be complete, nor even fully understood, until this fact is taken into account.

The holiness movement was born in the period of the rise of feminism in antebellum America and became one of its major carriers. There have been various efforts to explain the rise of feminism in this period: industrialization and the rise of the urban family, which freed women from traditional duties; a mid-nineteenth-century feminization of American culture and religion; the extension of modern ideas birthed in the Enlightenment; and so on. Little attention has been given to the role of perfectionism in this period and the manner in which it supported a form of feminism. Yet perfectionism is the clue that unlocks many mysteries of this period.

The history of the role of women in the Western Christian traditions is complex, but it is possible to correlate openness to the ministry of women with certain theological themes. Modern currents of thought like Enlightenment egalitarianism have led to the ministry of women. Thus we get the irony that it was the holiness movement, Quakerism, and Unitarianism that in antebellum America were most open to the ministry of women. This is in part because all were variously in protest against the traditional church and its hierarchies and, like the newer religious movements of the period (Mother Ann Lee among the

Preface

Shakers, Ellen White among the Seventh-Day Adventists, and Mary Baker Eddy among the Christian Scientists) were able to incorporate this new theme into their religious life.

Experiential religious traditions have also been especially open to the ministry of women because in such contexts religious authority is grounded in religious experience and not in traditional patterns of education or ecclesiastical structures. Thus many famous mystics have been women, and experiential movements like Pietism have to a certain extent been more open to the ministry of women. Also those movements that have emphasized the role of the Holy Spirit have tended to be more open to women. Thus Quakerism has a long history of the ministry of women and involvement in the feminist movement—because in such contexts the Holy Spirit has the autonomy to call and use persons apart from normal patterns of authority.

But the theme of perfectionism has also been a powerful impulse to the ministry of women and feminism within the Christian world. Feminist theologies generally emphasize the extent of the new that is created in the Christian dispensation and identify patriarchal patterns with the old. Thus those theologies that are the most optimistic about the change that is possible in human life are the most likely to accept feminist principles. In antebellum America, therefore, conservative and traditional theologies emphasized that the subordination of women was a part of the sinful state that was not to be overcome in this life, while the perfectionist theologies tended to see the subordination of women as part of the sinful state out of which redemption was being effected. For the former traditions the subordination of women was prescriptive; for the latter, it was merely descriptive of the sinful state in which we find ourselves and without any normative value.

The holiness movement brought all these currents together, and the cumulative effect was an explosion of the ministry of women. Its "gospel egalitarianism" was not unrelated to the modern Enlightenment ideas—and was a sort of populist counterpart to the more intellectually elite patterns of egalitarian thinking. The increasing "free church" orientation of the movement and the increasing polemic against traditional church hier-

PREFACE

archies opened up the ministry to laity, both men and women, in ways not common in the mainstream churches. Such tendencies were accentuated by the experiential orientation and the increasing emphasis throughout the nineteenth century on the Holy Spirit. And finally the doctrine of Christian perfection with its social correlates of the admitted focus on personal experience led to the claim that a new era was dawning in which the subordination of women would be overcome.

The cumulative effect of these dynamics was profound, and the extent to which the holiness movement lies behind many of the events in the history of nineteenth-century feminism is not yet well recoignized. Thus it was the revivalism of evangelist Charles Grandison Finney that created controversy in the churches by encouraging women to pray and speak in public. It was Oberlin College, where Finney taught theology and articulated a form of "Oberlin Perfectionism," that was the first coeducational college and the *alma mater* of many nineteenth-century feminists (see volume 15 in this series on the history of early Oberlin College). Antoinette Brown, the first woman to be ordained to the Christian ministry was a Congregationalist but a disciple of Finney and a graduate of Oberlin. Her ordination sermon was preached by Luther Lee, a founder of the perfectionist and abolitionist Wesleyan Methodist Connection (see volume 25 in this series for Lee's *Autobiography*). The first woman's rights convention of 1848 was held in the Wesleyan Methodist Church in Seneca Falls, New York. Phoebe Palmer, usually described as the major force behind the antebellum holiness revival, offered an exposition of her holiness teachings in *The Promise of the Father* (see volume 33 in this series), which was essentially a defense of the ministry of women and implicitly of her own role in the movement.

The tracts in this volume illustrate how this practice was defended within the movement. The case was variously made. In many Christian contexts in antebellum America feminism was an extension of the new antislavery interpretation of the Bible. Those persons who concluded that the spirit of the Bible was antislavery even though the letter of some passages seemed to condone slavery found that the form of the argument allowed them to make a similar case that the spirit of the Bible was for the

PREFACE

liberation of women. Indeed the classical text, the *magna carta* of the antislavery movement, seemed to lead inevitably in that direction: There is neither Jew nor Greek, there is neither slave nor free, there is neither male nor female; for you are all one in Christ Jesus (Galatians 3:28). It was this abolitionist and perfectionist context that produced the most distinctly feminist of the holiness defenses of the ministry of women.

This position is represented in this volume by two statements. The sermon by Luther Lee (1800–1889), "Woman's Right to Preach the Gospel," was the ordination sermon for Antoinette Brown (1825–1921), who in 1853 became the first woman to be ordained to the Christian ministry. As already indicated Lee was a founder of the abolitionist Wesleyan Methodist Connection that had withdrawn a decade earlier from the Methodist Episcopal Church for its compromise of founder John Wesley's antislavery convictions. Lee and Brown had met earlier when Lee defended the right of women to vote in the conventions of the temperance movement—and he became the natural preacher of her ordination sermon.

Similar in character is the essay *Ordaining Women* by B. T. Roberts (1823–1893), the founder of the Free Methodist Church (see Roberts's defense of the emergence of Free Methodism in *Why Another Sect*, volume 41 in this series). This church, founded in 1860 primarily in opposition to the pew rental system that was increasingly used to finance Methodist churches and was perceived to discriminate against the poor, was like the Wesleyans abolitionist in conviction. Roberts early on developed the feminist convictions revealed in this tract, but was not able to convince his denomination to begin ordaining women. This essay, written a couple of years before his death, was composed in response to General Conference debates and a vote against the ministry of women. The Free Methodist Church did not fully ordain women until the mid-twentieth century—in spite of its founder's views on the question.

In the latter half of the nineteenth century, the holiness movement adopted more and more of the rhetoric of Pentecost—a key development in the emergence of Pentecostalism at the turn of the century. As this took place, the ministry of women was given a new biblical and theological grounding. The new focus on the

Preface

account of the coming of the Holy Spirit upon the church as recorded in the second chapter of the book of Acts brought to the fore the prophecy recorded there that "in the latter days . . . your sons and daughters shall prophesy." Both the holiness and the Pentecostal movements understood themselves to have a special role in the divine providence as the "latter rain" of spiritual blessing that would usher in the end of history. Both expected new spiritual gifts and experiences as a part of this period. Thus Phoebe Palmer (see the several books relating to her life and teachings in this series) would argue in *The Promise of the Father* that the ministry of women was a "neglected specialty of the latter days."

During the period in which Phoebe Palmer was developing this argument and rationale (the mid-1850s) she spent several years of ministry and evangelism in England with her husband. Her public ministry, of course, excited controversy and in Newcastle-upon-Tyne prompted a local clergyman to attack her and the idea of women ministers. Catherine Mumford Booth (1829–1890), who was to become with her husband William a cofounder of the Salvation Army, had already confronted her minister and her husband during their engagement over their views of women. The attack on Phoebe Palmer prompted the pamphlet "Female Ministry" reprinted here. The dependence on the Pentecostal argument for the ministry of women—and indeed the work of Phoebe Palmer herself—is clear. These convictions found expression then in the life of the Salvation Army, making it arguably one of the most consistently feminist organizations in Christian history.

By the turn of the century such convictions had become commonplace in the holiness movement, and such churches as the Pilgrim Holiness Church and the Church of the Nazarene had large contingents of female clergy, at some points as high as a third. The final text in this volume illustrates the situation at the turn of the century. Fannie McDowell Hunter (dates unknown) came out of the Methodist Episcopal Church, South, and moved into the holiness movement through the Vanguard Mission and the New Testament Church of Christ, a group that later merged into the Church of the Nazarene. As her own story, narrated in this volume, reveals, she was an evangelist and musician. In this

Preface

volume she presents a biblical rationale for the ministry of women, answers objections, celebrates the history of the ministry of women, especially as it occurred in variations of the Methodist tradition, and finally presents the testimonies of a number of women ministers in the Church of Christ. It is also worth noting that the volume is introduced by A. M. Hills, the first theologian of the Church of the Nazarene, one of its most prolific authors, and president of several of its colleges and universities.

These tracts defending the ministry of women illustrate the various ways in which the holiness movement argued its case against the churches of the mainstream who still opposed the practice. The Pentecostal movement, which emerged at the turn of the century as a sort of "holiness heresy," continued the practice, defending the ministry of women along the lines of the Pentecostal argument. Even the more moderate Keswick traditions of spirituality cultivated the ministry of women (see especially the work of Hannah Whitall Smith, represented in several volumes of this series).

Donald W. Dayton
Northern Baptist
Theological Seminary

WOMAN'S RIGHT TO PREACH THE GOSPEL.

A SERMON,

PREACHED AT THE ORDINATION OF THE

REV. MISS ANTOINETTE L. BROWN,

AT

SOUTH BUTLER, WAYNE COUNTY, N. Y., SEPT. 15, 1853.

BY REV. LUTHER LEE.

"Help those women which labored with me in the gospel."—PAUL.

SYRACUSE, N. Y.:
PUBLISHED BY THE AUTHOR.
60 South Salina Street.
1853.

SERMON.

"There is neither male nor female; for ye are all one in Christ Jesus."—GAL. III. 28.

THE thinking portion of the assembly have, by this time, reasoned within themselves, "that is a singular text from which to preach an Ordination sermon." This may render it proper for me to remind my hearers, just at this point, that the text is no more unusual, as the basis of an Ordination sermon, than the occasion is unusual, upon which I am called to preach it.

The ordination of a female, or the setting apart of a female to the work of the Christian ministry, is, to say the least, a novel transaction, in this land and age. It cannot fail to call forth many remarks, and will, no doubt, provoke many censures.

For myself, I regard it in the light of a great innovation upon the opinions, prejudices and practices of nearly the whole Christian world. There have been some Christian communities who have allowed females to preach the gospel, but so far as I know, they have not ordained their ministers, male or female, or by any solemn form or service, set them apart to the work of the ministry, as I suppose is intended to be done at the conclusion of this discourse.

It is to be presumed that the parties concerned in this transaction, believe their course to be right, and that they have their reasons for so believing; and I feel assured that there can be no time nor place more appropriate for an exhibition of such reasons, than the time and place of the transaction, which breaks in upon long established opinions and usages. And as I have been called upon to deliver the discourse on the occasion, I should deem it out of place, tame and cowardly, for me to deliver an ordinary sermon setting forth the duties and responsibilities of a Christian minister, without taking hold of the peculiarity of the occasion, and vindicating the innovation which we this hour make upon the usages of the Christian world.

It is with these views, and under these impressions that I have selected the text which I have read as the basis of my discourse. "There is neither male nor female; for ye are all one in Christ Jesus." What does this text mean? and what was the Apostle's design in uttering these words? Whatever the text means, or does not mean, its application is to be limited to what is clearly and specifically Christian. It is in Christ Jesus that there is no difference, and that the sex become one. There may be differences of rights and positions growing out of incidental relations, and conventional rules and usages, in matters which do not affect the fundamental rights of humanity, which I need not discuss; but when we come to consider those rights and privileges, which we claim as Christians, and which belong to us as believers in Christ, there is no difference, we are all one in Christ Jesus. Without even presuming to discuss, on this occasion, the questions of civil and political rights, the text amply sustains me in affirming that in a Christian community, united upon Christian principles, for Christian purposes; or, in other words, in the Church, of which Christ is the only head, males and females possess equal rights and privileges; here there is no difference, "there is neither male nor female; for ye are all one in Christ Jesus." I cannot see how the text can be explained so as to exclude females from any right, office, work, privilege, or immunity which males enjoy, hold or perform. If the text means anything, it means that males and females are equal in rights, privileges and responsibilities upon the Christian platform. I am very frank to confess that I had never very thoroughly investigated the question, until called upon to preach on this occasion, though I have held an opinion loosely on the subject for many years. This call, in my own estimation laid me under obligation to do one of two things, either step forward and assist this church, or decline so to do, for good and satisfactory reasons. I might have evaded the question, by declining for want of time, or some other fictitious reason, but that would not only have been in bad keeping with my general character, but would have been false to Christianity and my brethren. If those inviting me here are right in proposing to ordain a female to the Gospel ministry, they needed my help, and were entitled to it; if they were wrong, they needed my reproof and reasons for it, and it was due to my own fidelity, and to truth, that I should administer it. But to do either, required thought beyond what I had ever bestowed upon the subject. You may then suppose me to have asked myself, "If I decline, what reason can I give for so doing? So far as I know there is no want of moral, or mental or educational qualification on the part of the candidate; if it be right to ordain any female, it is right to ordain this female." At this point, the text which I have selected for the occasion, presented itself to my mind, and I reasoned thus :—"I acknowledge the candidate to be in Christ, to be with me a sister in Christ; if I deny her the right to exercise her gifts as a Christian minister, I virtually affirm that there is male and female, and that we are not all one in Christ Jesus, by which I shall contradict St. Paul, and though he is not among us to reply to me, to know myself at variance with him, would give me more uneasiness than to differ from modern doctors of divinity, and divinity schools. I am then brought to this conclusion, which I will state in the form of a proposition as the sequence of the text.

FEMALES HAVE A GOD-GIVEN RIGHT TO PREACH THE GOSPEL.

I take it upon myself, as my portion of the effort on this occasion, to defend and substantiate the above proposition. To make any distinction in the church of Jesus Christ, between males and females, purely on the ground of sex, is virtually to strike this text from the sacred volume, for it affirms that in Christ there is no difference between males and females, that they are all one in regard to the gospel of the grace of God. If males may belong to a Christian church, so may females; if male members may vote in the church, so may females; if males may preach the gospel, so may females; and if males may receive ordination by the imposition of hands, or otherwise, so may females, the reason of which is found in my text; "there is neither male nor female, for ye are all one in Christ Jesus."

But it will be asked, why this sense of the text has not been discovered before, why has it lain hid until this hour? I answer, it has been discovered and understood, but not practically applied, as has been the case with a great many other truths. Dr. Clarke concludes his comment upon the text in these words. "Under the blessed spirit of Christianity, they have equal *rights*, equal *privileges*, and equal *blessings;* and let me add, they are equally *useful*."

This goes as far as I have gone. But Dr. Clarke was a Methodist, and may be suspected of having been influenced by the usages of his sect or denomination, by which females have been allowed to exercise their gifts in social meetings, composed of both sex. Well, then, hear what a Scotch Presbyterian Divine says on the text. Dr. McKnight gives the following comment:

"In Christ Jesus there is no distinction of persons, as under the law : under the gospel no Jew is superior to a Greek, neither are slaves inferior to free men, nor are males preferred to females, for ye are all one, in respect to dignity and privileges under the gospel dispensation." "Under the law males had greater privileges than females. For males alone bore in their bodies the sign of God's covenant; they alone were capable of the priesthood."

Whether Dr. McKnight designed it or not, he has affirmed, by the most clear and certain implication, that females may be priests or ministers under the gospel. And remember that I am not responsible for his inconsistency in having advocated the opposite opinion in other places, which he has done. Just let me read the two clauses, reversing the order, and see by what logical necessity the mind will be carried to the conclusion that females have an equal right to the Christian ministry with males. The Dr. says, " Under the law males had greater privileges than females. For males alone were capable of the priesthood. In Christ Jesus there is no distinction of persons as under the law, males are not preferred before females, for ye are all one, in respect to dignity and privileges under the gospel dispensation." It is clear then that I have the authority of Dr. McKnight for my construction of the text. And any construction which will make it mean less than I suppose it means, must make it mean nothing.

The general design and scope of the apostle's reasoning, greatly strengthens the view I have taken of the text. The design was to counteract certain Judaizing teachers, and show that Christians were not bound to observe the law of Moses, that the Gentiles need not be circumcised and observe other Jewish rites. To accomplish this he shows that the law is abrogated. Now the law made distinctions between Jews and Gentiles, and between males and females, excluding females from the priesthood, and laid them under other disabilities, and the apostle comes to the conclusion that under the gospel, there is neither Jew nor Greek, that is Gentile, neither male nor female, but that all are one in Christ Jesus.

The Apostle clearly designs to say that females are exempt, under the gospel, from the disabilities imposed by the law, and that they enjoy equal rights with men. There is clearly an extension of their rights and privileges under the gospel, and if so, how far does such extension reach ? The text fixes no limits, prescribes no bounds, names no places, occasions, subjects or duties, but affirms in general and unqualified terms, that there is neither male nor female, but that all are one in Christ Jesus, and this is done by way of proclaiming the abrogation of the Mosaic law, and it of necessity places males and females upon an equal platform of rights under the gospel.

The declaration concerning males and females, is just as full and unqualified as it is concerning Jews and Gentiles, and if it does not place males and females upon an equality, it may be argued with equal force that it does not place Jews and Gentiles on an equal footing. Having said what I judge to be necessary by way of explaining my text, and bringing out its meaning and force, I will proceed further to confirm the doctrine arrived at by other considerations.

1. There were female prophets under the Old Dispensation. "And Miriam, the prophetess, the sister of Aaron, took a timbrel in her hand, and all the women went out after her with timbrels and with dance. And Miriam answered them, Sing ye to the Lord, for he hath triumphed gloriously." Exo. xv. 20, 21.

"And Deborah a prophetess, the wife of Lapidoth, she judged Israel at that time." Judges iv. 4.

Thus have we an account of two female prophets, and one of them judged Israel; yes, a female was both prophet and judge.

I will now call your attention to a more remarkable case. During the reign of King Josiah, the book of the law was found, which appears to have been lost, and it was read before the king, and on hearing the law, the king become alarmed, and commanded his principal officers to go and inquire of the Lord for him, and for all the people, concerning the words of the book that was found. Now to whom did they go to inquire of God ? We have the rest of the history as follows :

"So Hikiah the priest, and Ahikam and Achbor, and Shaphan, and Asahiah, went unto Huldah the prophetess, the wife of Shallum, the son of Tikvah, the son of Harhas, keeper of the wardrobe ; (now she dwelt in Jerusalem in the college ;) and they communed with her. And she said unto them, Thus saith the Lord God of Israel, Tell the man that sent you to me, Thus saith the Lord, behold, I will bring evil upon this place, and upon the inhabitants thereof, even all the words of the book which the king of Judah hath read : Because they have forsaken me, and have burnt incense unto other gods, that they might provoke me to anger with all the works of their hands ; therefore my wrath shall be kindled against this place, and shall not be quenched. But to the king of Judah which sent you to inquire of the Lord, thus shall ye say to him, Thus saith the Lord God of Israel, As touching the words which thou hast heard ; Because thine heart was tender, and thou hast humbled thyself before the Lord, when thou heardest what I spake against this place and against the inhabitants thereof, that they should become a desolation and a curse, and has rent thy clothes, and wept before me ; I also have heard thee, saith the Lord. Behold, therefore, I will gather thee unto thy fathers, and thou shalt be gathered into thy grave in peace ; and thine eyes shall not see all the evil which I will bring upon this place. And they brought the king word again." 2 Kings xxii. 14–20. See also 2 Chron. xxxiv.

This woman, Huldah, was undeniably a public religious teacher, according to the usages of the times in which she lived. She spake for God, in his name, and by his authority, and her words are recorded in the book. " And there was one Anna, a prophetess, the daughter of Phanuel, of the tribe of Azer." Luke ii. 36.

Of this woman and her public labors we have no account, only that she preached publicly in the temple concerning Christ, when he was brought there, an infant in his mother's arms, to be presented to the Lord. The fact that she recognized the Saviour, and spake of him as she did, proves that she was endowed with the extraordinary gifts of a prophet.

This case, though recorded in the New Testament, occurred under the Old Dispensation, where I have classed it. There were other cases of less note, as Nehemiah mentions a prophetess that discouraged him in his work. vi. 14.

Isaiah appears to have had a prophetess for his wife. Chap. viii. 3.

So common a thing was it to have female prophets, that the propagaters of error judged it an object to counterfeit the usage, and hence there were false female prophets, as well as false male prophets. God said to his true prophet, Ezekiel, " Likewise, thou son of man, set thy face against the daughters of thy people, which prophesy out of their own hearts, and prophesy thou against them." xiii. 16.

This proves beyond a doubt, that it must have been common for females to have the true spirit of prophesy, or there would not have been false pretenders. There is never a counterfeit, without a genuine ; and had it not been believed and understood that God did call females to the office and work of prophets, the fact of a female pretending to prophesy in the name of God, would have proved her false. The fact therefore, that there were false female prophets, furnishes strong evidence, not only that there were genuine female prophets, but that they must have been common ; sufficiently so, at least, as not to create suspicion upon its face when one appeared.

2. There were prophetesses or female prophets in the Primitive Church

under the gospel. The fact that there would be, was foretold by the Prophet Joel. "And it shall come to pass afterward, that I will pour out my Spirit upon all flesh; and your sons and your daughters shall prophesy." Joel. ii. 28.

This text most clearly began to be fulfilled at the day of Pentecost, as we learn from Acts ii. 17; where Peter declares the development of that day, to be what was foretold by the prophet. But how was the prediction, that daughters should prophesy fulfilled on the day of Pentecost? The history of the subject answers this question. It is as follows:

In the first chapter, we are told who constituted the assembled Christians. "Then returned they unto Jerusalem from the mount called Olivet, which is from Jerusalem a sabbath-day's journey. And when they were come in, they went up into an upper room, where abode both Peter, and James, and John, and Andrew, Philip, and Thomas, Bartholomew, and Matthew, James the son of Alpheus, and Simon Zelotes, and Judas the brother of James. These all continued with one accord in prayer and supplication, with the women, and Mary the mother of Jeus, and with his brethren." Verses 12-14.

Here we have named the eleven apostles, then "the women," then Mary the mother of Jesus in particular, and lastly "his brethren." By his brethren is probably meant his near relatives. It is probable that there were a number of women in the company, as they are mentioned as forming one portion of the assembly. In the 15th verse we are told that the whole number present was about one hundred and twenty persons. In the fourth verse of chapter two, we are told that they were all filled with the Holy Ghost, and began to speak with other tongues.

Who were filled with the Holy Ghost, and began to speak with other tongues? Most clearly the hundred and twenty persons, consisting of the apostles, the women, and Mary the mother of Jesus, and his brethren. To deny this would be to falsify the plainest portion of the record. The record declares that there were about one hundred and twenty persons assembled together, that this number embraced the women, and that they were all filled with the Holy Ghost, and began to speak with other tongues. Thus did the Holy Ghost, in his first descent, crown females as well as males, with tongues of fire, to speak the wonderful works of God.

But the remarkable prophesy of Joel did not receive its entire fulfillment on the day of Pentecost, for about twenty-seven years afterwards we read, Acts xxi. 9, that Phillip of Cesarea, "had four daughters which did prophesy." As this fact is mentioned only incidentally, and not as a new or strange thing, it appears probable that female prophets were not unusual in the Primitive Church.

This is the proper place to remark that prophesying is not to be understood in the restricted sense of foretelling. A prophet is not exclusively one who foretels, but who explains prophesies, and teaches ; and to prophesy is to explain prophesies and to teach. In this sense every gospel minister is a prophet, and every prophet under the new dispensation is a gospel minister. Here then were four female gospel ministers, daughters of one man. When it is said, "Your sons and your daughters shall prophesy," the meaning is, your sons and your daughters shall become teachers, or gospel ministers.

The Greek word which we translate prophet, is *propheetuo*, and signifies "to foretell, to predict, to explain and apply prophesies." To explain and apply prophesies, was the peculiar work of the first ministers. The Greek word which we translate prophet, is *propheetees*, and signifies "a declarer, a foreteller, a priest, a teacher, an instructor." It was always the work of prophets to labor as religious teachers, and to explain and apply the predictions which had been previously uttered by others, and when we consider that there were whole schools of prophets, we may conclude that but few of the whole number were employed to foretell, and that their principal calling was to labor as religious teachers. That prophets were preachers or religious teachers, is perfectly clear from the use of the words, prophet and prophesy, by the apostles.

The church at Antioch sent Paul and Barnabas to Jerusalem for the settlement of the great question, whether Gentile converts were bound to keep the law of Moses concerning circumcision and other rites. The apostles and the church at Jerusalem, having considered the case, sent back a written answer, and sent also two messengers of their own company, Judas and Silas. "And Judas and Silas being prophets also themselves, exhorted the brethren with many words, and confirmed them." This proves beyond a doubt, that they exhorted, or preached in the common acceptation, by virtue of their prophetic office, and the conclusion is that to be a prophet, is to be a preacher, or public religious teacher. We read again, 1 Cor. xix. 3 : "He that prophesieth, speaketh unto men to edification, and exhortation and comfort." Here the entire pulpit work of a gospel preacher is described as the act of prophesying, which renders it certain that prophets were preachers.

Again, we read Rev. ii. 20, "Nevertheless, I have a few things against thee, because thou sufferest that woman Jazebel, which calleth herself a prophetess to teach, and to seduce my servants to commit fornication, and to eat things offered to idols." This proves two points; first, that the doctrine must have prevailed that women might rightfully be prophets; and secondly, that being prophets, they taught the people. The complaint is not that she was a *woman*, but that she was a bad woman; not that she was a *prophetess*, but that she called herself one when she was not; not that she *taught*, but that she taught false and corrupting doctrine. It is clear that there would have been no false female teachers, had there been no true ones, and that a false female teacher could not have been sustained in the church, had the doctrine prevailed that the gospel forbade females to preach the gospel.

I have now proved that there were a class of females in the Primitive Church called prophetesses, that is, there were female prophets, and these prophets were preachers or public teachers of religion. Here I rest this branch of my argument, and will proceed to introduce another branch of evidence.

3. There were female preachers of the gospel in the primitive church, and some cases in which it appears that females occupied the official relation of minister, or religious teacher, to particular congregations. If this position can be sustained, the whole controversy will be settled, and there is one text, so clear and full on the subject, that I would not fear to rest the whole argument on that alone. Paul says in his Epistle to the Romans, chapter xvi. 1 : " I commend unto you Phebe our sister, which is a servant of the church which is at Cenchrea." The words, "servant of the church," clearly express an official relation. The churches had no servants but officers, and what office did Phebe fill, if not that of preacher, teacher or minister ?

The translation obscures the sense, which will became plain by an examination of other texts where the same word occurs in the original. The Greek word here rendered servant, is *diakonos*. This word occurs just thirty times in the New Testament. In two instances it is translated servant, where it means a common house servant or waiter. John ii. 5, 9 : "His mother said unto the servants," &c. "But the servants which drew the water knew." Here the word is applied to the waiters at a marriage feast. In three instances the word is applied to civil officers. Once by Christ, Matt. xxii. 13 : "Then said the king unto his *servants*, bind him hand and foot, and take him away and cast him into outer darkness." Here it is rendered *servant*, but clearly means an officer of the king.

Paul uses the word twice in the same sense, Rom. xiii. 3, 4 : "Rulers are not a terror to good works, but to the evil. For he is the *minister* of God to thee for good—for he is the *minister* of God, a revenger to execute wrath upon him that doeth evil." Here the same word is twice translated *minister*, and it clearly means a civil ruler or judicial officer. Once it is translated servant, where it means any christian or follower of Christ. John xii. 26 : "Where I am, there shall also my *servant* be." Twice the word is applied to Christ, and is translated *minister*. Rom. xv. 8 : "Now I say that Jesus Christ was a *minister* of the circumcision for the truth of God, to confirm the promises made unto the fathers." Gal. ii. 17 : "But if while we seek to be justified by Christ, we ourselves are found sinners, is therefore Christ the *minister* of sin." In two other texts it is translated servant, where its meaning may be a little doubtful. Matt. xxii. 11 : "But he that is greatest among you shall be your *servant*." This I think clearly means minister, but it is not important. Mark ix. 35 : "If any man desire to be first, the same shall be last of all and *servant* of all." Servant here may mean simply an inferior position, and the text may be a maxim, that ambition will generally defeat itself.

I have now disposed of ten of the thirty texts in which the word *diakonos* occurs, which is rendered servant when applied to Phebe. This leaves twenty other instances of the use of the word, in the Greek Testament, in every one of which it clearly and unequivocally means a minister of the gospel, or religious teacher of some grade. In one case it is applied to false ministers. 2 Cor. xi 15 : "It is no great thing if his (Satan's) *ministers* are transformed into an angel of light." In every other case the word is used to express a true minister of the gospel, or teacher of some grade. In three cases it is rendered Deacon, and clearly means a church officer. The texts are Philip. i. 1 : "Paul and Timotheus to all the saints which are at Philippi, with the bishops and deacons." 1 Tim. iii. 8, 12 : "Likewise must the deacons be grave." "Let the deacons be the husbands of one wife, ruling their children and their own house well." We will not pause here to dispute about what the office of a deacon was, for the word rendered deacon, is so rendered only three times out of thirty.

I have now disposed of four other texts of the thirty, leaving sixteen, and in every one of these the word is translated *minister*. I need not quote all these texts, but will refer to a few of them as specimens.

Matt. xx. 26 : "But whosoever will be great among you, let him be your *minister*."
1 Cor. iii. 5 : "Who then is Paul, or who is Apollos, but *ministers* by whom ye believed?"
2 Cor. iii. 6 : "Who also hath made us able *ministers* of the New Testament." Chap. vi. 4 : "But in all things approving ourselves as the *ministers* of God."
Eph. iii. 7 : "Whereof I was made a *minister*, according to the gift of the grace of God."
Chap. vi. 21 : "Tychicus, a beloved brother and faithful *minister* in the Lord."
Col. i. 23 : "Whereof I Paul am made a *minister*."
1 Thes. iii. 2 : "Timotheus, our brother and *minister* of God."

The above texts are sufficient, the remaining ones are just like them. Here it is seen that the same word which Paul applied to Phebe, to describe her official relation to the church at Cenchrea, is the word which the same writer generally used to denote a minister of the gospel. Take another view of the matter. Out of the thirty instances of the use of the word in the Greek Testament, twenty two of them are in the language of Paul. Note, Paul uses a word twenty two times, and in eighteen cases out of the twenty two, the translators have rendered it *minister*; in three they have rendered it *deacon*, and in the one remaining case they have rendered it *servant*, and that is where it is applied to Phebe. Poor Phebe is made a single exception out of twenty two instances of the use of the word. In eighteen cases it means a *minister*, in three it means a *deacon*, and in one only, where it is applied to a female, it means a *servant*. The translators could not even allow her the subordinate honor of being a deaconess, but because she was a woman, she must be a servant, though Paul, whose language they thus translated, had declared that there is neither male nor female, but that all are one in Christ Jesus. Had it been a man of whom Paul thus wrote, there is not a shadow of doubt that they would have rendered it, "the *minister* of the church which is at Cenchrea." We see then if we conform the translation to the almost undeviating course of the translators, we shall make it read, "I commend unto you Phebe our sister, which is a *minister* of the Church which is at Cenchrea," and so reading as it ought to read, the question of a woman's right to preach the gospel is settled.

But it does not depend upon this one text alone, but I have pushed the argument far enough in this direction, and will only glance at a few texts which speak of female laborers. After commending Phebe, the minister of the Church at Cenchrea, Paul proceeds to name other worthy persons, among whom are a number of females. "Great Priscilla and Aquilla, my helpers in Christ Jesus." Priscilla was a woman, the wife of Aquilla, and they were Paul's helpers in Christ. "Salute Tryphena and Tryposa who labor in the Lord." These were two females, and they labored in the Lord.

"Salute the beloved Persis which labored much in the Lord." Persis was another female laborer, and she labored much in the Lord. Paul says, Phil. iv. 3., "Help those women that labored with me in the gospel." If it were now said of any persons, that they labor in the gospel, it would be understood that they preach the gospel, and it is clear that Paul labored in connection with females, who preached the gospel of the grace of God.

It is a fact worthy of mention in this connection, that women were the first persons employed by Christ, after his resurrection, to tell the story of his triumph over death and the grave. They were last to forsake him when his enemies triumphed, first to visit his grave amid the gray dawn of the first morn after the Sabbath was past ; and first to go and tell the glad news of his resurrection, for they "did run to bring his disciples word ;" and yet the men were so far behind them in faith and feeling, as to regard their words of love and joy as an idle tale.

4. All antiquity agrees that there were female officers and teachers in the Primitive Church, the only dispute being about what their functions were, and by what title they were known. The fact is universally admitted that they were appointed to the office of deaconess, that is, there were female deacons. It would be improper to attempt extended extracts. I will therefore only refer to a few authorities. In Calmet's dictionary, under the word deaconess, it is said "They were in the Primitive Church, appointed to this office, with the imposition of hands." These persons appear to be the same as those whom Pliny, in his famous letter to Trajan, styles "*Ancillis quae ministrae dicebantur*," female attendants called assistants, ministers or servants. It appears then, that these were customary officers throughout the churches; and when the fury of persecution fell on Christians, these were among the first to suffer." See Robinson's Calmet.

Here we have not only the authority of Calmet, but that of Pliny also, who was a Roman Consul, and sometime governor of Bithynia where he checked the persecution against the Christians. His letter to Trojan the Emperor, above alluded to, was written with a design to check the persecution, in which he succeeded.

The same essential facts may be found copied into Watson's Dictionary. *Article Deacon.*

In Buck's Theological Dictionary, *Article Deaconess*, it is said "the apostolic constitutions, as they are called, mention the ordination of a deaconess, and the form of prayer used on that occasion," and refers to Lib. viii. Chap. 9. 20.

Dr. Adam Clarke says, "It is evident that they were ordained to their office by the imposition of the hands of the bishop ; and the form of the prayer used on the occasion is extant in the apostolic constitutions. In the tenth or eleventh century the order was suppressed in the Latin Church, but continued in the Greek Church till the end of the twelfth century. Clarke's Com. Rom. xvi. 1. Dr. Clarke refers to Broughton's Dictionary. Article Deaconess.

This discourse would be defective, should I not pay some attention to those scriptures which some suppose forbade females to exercise their gifts in public. There are, so far as I know, but two texts, that are, or can be relied upon as proof against the right of females to improve in public. They are as follows :

"Let your women keep silence in the churches : for it is not permitted unto them to speak ; but they are commanded to be under obedience, as also saith the law. And if they will learn any thing, let them ask their husbands at home : for it is a shame for woman to speak in the church." 1. Cor. xiv 34, 35.

"Let the women learn in silence with all subjection. But I suffer not a woman to teach, nor to usurp authority over the man, but to be in silence." 1 Tim. ii. 11, 12.

These two texts, I believe, are all the proof there is to offset the array of texts and arguments which have been adduced in proof of the right of females to preach the gospel. If I were to say, "I do not know what they mean," they could never disprove the fact that females did prophesy and pray in the church, and if explained at all, they must be so explained as to harmonize with that fact. Let us then examine the matter.

If these texts are to be understood as a general prohibition of the improvement of female gifts in public, it must be entire and absolute, and must cut females off from all vocal part in public worship. It will preclude them from singing and vocal prayer. The expression,

"Let your women keep silence in the churches," if it touches the case at all, forbids singing and vocal prayer. Can a woman sing and keep silence at the same time? Can she pray vocally, and keep silence at the same time? Such then is the true issue, and as we must meet the issue before the people, it is important that it be presented to them in its true light. Singing is as much a violation of the command to keep silence as praying or preaching. We must then put locks upon the lips of the sisterhood in time of prayer, and compel them to let their harps hang in silence while we, the lords of creation, chant Zion's songs, and leave the song itself dovoid of the softer melodies which flow from woman's soul.

Such a construction of these texts most clearly makes them conflict with other portions of divine truth. Glance for a moment at the weight of evidence on the other side. My text affirms, as a broad foundation on which to stand, "There is neither male nor female; for ye are all one in Christ Jesus." Miriam was a prophetess and led the host of women in Israel forth, and when the men sung of Jehovah's triumph, she responded loudly and gloriously in the face of all Israel. Deborah was a prophetess and was a judge of all Israel. Huldah was a prophetess, and dwelt in the College at Jerusalem, and prophesied in the name of the Lord, to king Josiah. "Thus saith the Lord God of Israel." Anna prophesied concerning Christ in the temple to all them that looked for redemption in Jerusalem. The prophet Joel foretold that daughters should prophesy under the New Dispensation; and God did pour out his Spirit on females and they spake with other tongues. Philip "had four daughters which did prophesy," sixty years after the birth of Christ. Paul the author of this supposed law of silence imposed upon females, tells us that Phebe was a deaconess or minister of the Church which was at Cenchrea; and commends several other females in the same chapter, who labored in the Lord. Paul also wrote to the church at Philippi, and told them to "help those women that labored in the gospel." And all antiquity agrees that women were set apart to some church office by the imposition of a bishop's hands.

Now, in the face of all this, are we to understand Paul as issuing a command, covering all countries and all ages, absolutely requiring all women to keep silence in the churches, and not to speak a word within the walls of the sanctuary? Those must believe it who can, but I cannot believe it with the light I now have, and must seek some explanation, which will, in my view, make a better harmony in the word of God.

Every writer should be so construed, if it be possible, as to make him agree with himself, and to do this, Paul must be so understood in these two texts, as to make the sense accord with what he has so plainly taught in other places, that females might and did exercise their gifts in public. Compare with 1 Cor. xi. 5, 6, 13, 14, 15.

"But every woman that prayeth or prophesieth with her head uncovered, dishonoreth her head ; for that is even all one as if she were shaven. For if the woman be not covered, let her also be shorn : but if it be a shame for a woman to be shorn or shaven, let her be covered. Judge in yourselves : is it comely that a woman pray unto God uncovered ? Doth not even nature itself teach you, that, if a man have long hair, it is a shame unto him ? But if a woman have long hair, it is a glory to her : for her hair is given her for a coverng."

Here the apostle most clearly gives directions how women are to pray and prophesy in public, and are we to understand him as first giving directions how females should pray and prophesy, and then in the same letter, absolutely forbid the thing he had given directions how to perform ? I cannot believe this, and must seek another exposition. It is clear that women did pray and prophesy in that church, and the apostle told them it must be done with their heads covered, that is wearing the customary veil. This was founded upon the customs of the times, to which it was necessary to conform in order to success, as to appear in public without a veil, in that community, subjected a female to suspicions of a want of virtue. What the apostle calls nature, was only the prejudice of education, which has now ceased to exist, or rather never existed among us. The Greek word, *phusis*, here translated *nature*, signifies not only nature, but "constitution, disposition, character, custom, habit, use." We have no such nature in this country, and as the rule grew out of the then existing customs and prejudices of soiciety, it is no longer binding, and females may appear with or without veils as may suit their taste or convenience. But the point is, that as Paul gives instructions for women to pray and prophesy with their heads covered, he cannot be understood as forbiding them to pray and prophesy under any and all circumstances. But what does the apostle mean when he says it is not permitted for women to speak ?

It is certain that he does not speak of female teachers or preachers, as such, for he comprehends the entire membership of the church. The twenty-third verse says, " If therefore the whole church be come together nto some place, and all speak with tongues," &c. This proves that the apostle is not treating of teachers as officers, as a distinct class, nor of the eligibility of persons to the office or teacher, as distinguished from the membership generally, but of the duties, rights and privileges of the membership in common, as members. If, therefore, the text precludes women from speaking in the church as a general rule, it precludes them, not merely as authorized teachers, but from the right of speaking as common or unofficial members of the church.

In view of the numerous and unanswerable proofs that God did employ females, under the Old and New Covenants, as public instrumentalities of spreading truth, all who hold the doctrine of the absolute equality of males and females, under all circumstances, and in all relations, will as a matter of course, regard these two texts as local and specific in their application, founded upon some peculiarity in the circumstances of the community at that time and in those places, and as having no general bearing on the question. It will be much easier for them to believe that there were circumstances, which were then understood, calling for such a rule, thus specific and local in its bearing, and constituting an exception to the general rule, that women had a right to, and did prophesy ; than to believe that the facts that they did teach, scattered, as they are, through a period of more than fifteen centuries, are proved by these two texts to be the exceptions to, and in violation of, a positive law of God, the foundation of which he has laid in nature. The simple admission of such numerous and wide spread exceptions to what is claimed to the law of God, having its foundation in nature, must come but little short of nullification For the benefit of those who hold as above, no further exposition is necessary. But as many conscientiously believe that the Scriptures teach that women are to be subordinate, especially to their husbands, it is proper to show that the texts will admit of an exposition which will hormonize their views with woman's right to preach the gospel. This I will now undertake.

The rule whatever it means, is based upon some law, which must have been known and understood by the Corinthian church. The clause reads thus :—" It is not permitted unto them to speak, but they are commanded to be under obedience, as also saith the law." It is worthy of remark that the words, " they are commanded" are not in the original text, but were added by the translators, to make plain what they supposed to be the sense. Without these words it reads, " Let your women keep silence in the churches, for it is not permitted unto them to speak, but to be under obedience as also saith the law." Supplying the ellipses in brackets, it reads, "It is not permitted unto them to speak [in the church] but to be under obedience as also saith the law."

From this aspect of the text it is clear, first that speaking is the antithesis of being under obedience, and that being under obedience, is the thing required by some law at the time known to the parties. "As also saith the law," is an appeal to the law, which proves that whatever the apostle commanded in this matter, it was only a reiteration of the sense of the law which already existed. To what law then does the apostle appeal? If we can decide this, it will determine the sense of the text.

I say then it cannot be any of the statute laws of Moses, for two reasons. First, no such law can be found, and secondly, if it existed, it must have been violated under divine sanction, by the existence of female teachers and rulers, as Miriam, Deborah and Huldah. If it was only some law of the Sanhedrim, or some law regulating Jewish Synagogues, it cannot be binding now, though Paul might have thought best to conform christian assemblies to Jewish Synagogues in some particulars at that time. But I do not say that it is any such law that is referred to in the text.

The universal opinion, so far as I know, is that the law referred to is, Gen. iii. 16 : "Thy desire shall be to thy husband, and he shall rule over thee." This is the reference made in all our reference Bibles. It is the opinion of Dr. Clarke, who held that women might speak in public. Dr. McKnight, who was an opposer of women's right to preach the gospel, supposes that the apostle refers to Genesis as the law in question. Scott is of the same opinion. Barnes, who is one of the most strenuous opposers of female improvements in public, holds the same view, and so far as I know, no person has ever expressed any other opinion. So far then as those are concerned who insist that the apostle forbids women to speak in the church, as a general rule, I may regard it as settled that when the apostle appeals to the law as teaching the doctrine of woman's obligation to be silent, he refers to the words addressed to the mother of us all, "Thy desire shall be to thy husband, and he shall rule over thee." As the apostle appeals to this, as expressing the same thing which he teaches, in it we must find the sense of the text in question. By this I am willing to abide, if those who have given this exposition will do the same.

Now, allowing that the above is the law referred to, two consequences must follow, fatal to the argument for female silence.

1. The law is binding only upon married women. As it is to their husbands that they are to be under obedience, the obedience can be required of none but such as have husbands. This must leave all unmarried females and widows free from the law of silence.

2. The law imposes silence on married women, only in obedience to the will of their husbands. If a woman has a husband who not only approves of her speaking in public, but who requests her so to do, her public improvement will be no violation of the law, but rather a compliance with its demand. The text already quoted from 1 Tim. ii. 11, 12, is in perfect harmony with the above exposition. It says, "Let the women learn in silence, with all submission." This explained by the same law, must mean submission to their husbands. But the apostle adds, "I suffer not a woman to teach or to usurp authority over the man." By "*the* man," a woman's husband must be meant, and keeping the same law before our eyes, she is forbidden to teach contrary to the wishes or command of her husband, by which she would seem to usurp authority over him, in violation of the law referred to, which says, "thy desire shall be to thy husband and he shall rule over thee."

This view is greatly strengthened by the fact that it was disorderly and contentious proceedings that the apostle was laboring to correct, and not a wrong proceeding, conducted with due solemnity and order. This will appear by reading the whole connection, as follows :

"How is it then, brethren ? when ye come together, every one of you hath a psalm, hath a doctrine, hath a tongue, hath a revelation, hath an interpretation. Let all things be done unto edifying. If any man speak in an unknown tongue, let it be by two, or at the most by three, and that by course ; and let one interpret. But if there be no interpreter, let him keep silence in the church ; and let him speak to himself, and to God. Let the prophets speak two or three, and let the other judge. If anything be revealed to another that sitteth by, let the first hold his peace. For ye may all prophesy one by one, that all may learn, and all may be comforted. And the spirits of the prophets are subject to the prophets. For God is not the author of confusion, but of peace, as in all churches of the saints. Let your women keep silence in the church ; for it is not permitted unto them to speak : but they are commanded to be under obedience, as also

saith the law. And if they will learn anything, let them ask their husbands at home; for it is a shame for women to speak in the church.'>
There was most obviously disorder and confusion, in consequence of all wishing to speak at the same time, and each wishing to advance different and conflicting views. It is also most clearly inferable that the women took part in these disorderly proceedings, and talked in opposition to their husbands, and questioned them and others on the disputed points, by which husbands and wives became opponents, increasing the confusion, and destroying the harmony of the church. The application of the law given to our mother Eve, specifically made by the apostle to this case, is proof positive that there must have been a violation of the law, by the insubordination of wives to their husbands in those disorderly meetings, as I have supposed above. If then the difficulty arose in part from conflicting movements of husbands and wives in the church, there was no way to cure the evil, by a specific direction, but to command the men or the women to keep silence, and the apostle did the latter, appealing to the law as a reason which says, "Thy desires shall be to thy husband, and he shall rule over thee."

Thus is it seen that the apostle's injunction was not given as a general rule, but as a remedy for a specific difficulty, and to construe it against the public efforts of competent and orderly female teachers, in the face of all the unanswerable proof that females did teach under divine sanction, is in my view, doing violence to the word of God.

This is still further supported by the doctrine of true expediency and utility. The females in the Corrinthian church, I presume were not divinely inspired, or church-appointed teachers, but common members, and perhaps recent converts from heathenism, ignorant and incompetent to teach. Such surely should keep silence, and ask their husbands at home. But suppose a woman to be ever so well qualified, intellectually and morally,—and a woman by study and prayer, may know as much of God, and divinity, and the plan of salvation, as a man,—if she has a husband, it would be a matter of very questionable expediency and utility, for her to undertake to preach the gospel, without the consent and in violation of the commands of her husband, even if there were no precept on the subject. But it has been seen that such females as have no husbands, of whom Paul says she " careth for the things of the Lord," and such as have husbands, who approve of their public efforts to persuade sinners to repent and be saved, are not estopped by the law upon which Paul bases his directions, that the women keep silence in the churches, even as understood by those who so contrue the apostle's words. Here I rest my argument, and will proceed to close this already too long discourse.

We are here assembled on a very interesting and solemn occasion, and it is proper to advert to the real object for which we have come together. There are in the world, and there may be among us, false views of the nature and object of ordination. I do not believe that any special or specific form of ordination is necessary to constitute a gospel minister. We are not here to make a minister. It is not to confer on this our sister, a right to preach the gospel. If she has not that right already, we have no power to communicate it to her. Nor have we met to qualify her for the work of the ministry If God and mental and moral culture have not already qualified her, we cannot, by anything we may do by way of ordaining or setting her apart. Nor can we, by imposition of our hands, confer on her any special grace for the work of the ministry, nor will our hands if imposed upon her head, serve as a special medium for the communication of the Holy Ghost, as conductors serve to convey electricity ; such ideas belong not to our theory, but are related to other systems and darker ages. All we are here to do, and all we expect to do, is, in due form, and by a solemn and impressive service, to subscribe our testimony to the fact, that in our belief, our sister in Christ, Antoinette L. Brown, is one of the ministers of the New Covenant, authorized, qualified, and called of God to preach the gospel of his Son Jesus Christ. This is all, but this even renders the occasion interesting and solemn. As she is recognized as the pastor of this flock, it is solemn and interesting to both pastor and flock, to have the relation formally recognized. But as a special charge is to be given to both, by others, I forbear to open the subject of their mutual responsibilities, and will conclude by invoking the blessing of the Father, and of the Son, and of the Holy Ghost upon both preacher and people. Amen.

ORDAINING WOMEN.

By Rev. B. T. ROBERTS, A. M.
Editor of "THE EARNEST CHRISTIAN,"
Author of FISHERS OF MEN,
WHY ANOTHER SECT, ETC.

"There is neither Jew nor Greek,
there is neither bond nor free,
there is neither male nor female:
for ye are all one in Christ Jesus."
—Galatians iii, 28.

ROCHESTER, N. Y.
EARNEST CHRISTIAN PUBLISHING HOUSE.
1891.

Entered according to act of Congress, in the year 1891,
BY B. T. ROBERTS,
in the office of the Librarian of Congress, at Washington.

CONTENTS.

CHAPTER I.—PREJUDICES. Truth. The Duke of Argyll. Daniel Webster. Law of Force. Aristotle. Slavery Defended. M. E. General Conference. Bishop Hopkins. Gospel Misunderstood. Lowell. Pages 10–13.

CHAPTER II.—WOMAN'S LEGAL CONDITION. Among the Romans. Spartans. In Africa—Stanley. In England—John Stuart Mill. The Germans. Not owning her own Children in this Nation. 14–21.

CHAPTER III.—WORDS. Bishop Berkeley. Primary Signification of Words. Importance of. Tertullian. Various Meanings of the Same Word. Archbishop Trench. 22–25.

CHAPTER IV.—ORDINATION. Views of Friends. Of Roman Catholics. Dr. Lightfoot. Priests. Sacrifices. John Wesley. Daniel Webster. Its True Signification. Rev. H. J. VanDyke, Sr., D. D. Ordination of Deacons—of Elders—of Apostles. McClintock and Strong. Women. Whitefield. 26–46.

CHAPTER V.—OBJECTIONS—OLD TESTAMENT. From Genesis. Matthew Henry. Dr. Adam Clarke. Christ. Primitive Law Re-enacted. Miriam. Deborah. 47–53.

CHAPTER VI.—OBJECTIONS—NEW TESTAMENT. Christ Not Quoted. The Twelve. Based on a Misunderstanding of Paul's Words. Rev. W. Gould. Answered. Dr. Adam Clarke. Keeping Silence in The Church not Literally Held. Explained. Madame Guyon. Women who Labored with Paul. Chrysostom. Whittier. 54–68.

CHAPTER VII.—OBJECTIONS—NATURAL. Physical. Aristotle. John Stuart Mill. Lowell. Women Soldiers. Artemisia. Amazons. Bryant. Stanley. Joan of Arc. 69–78.

CHAPTER VIII.—WOMEN APOSTLES. Order of Apostles Permanent. Junia an Apostle. Dean Alford. Dr. Adam Clarke. Luther. Chrysostom. Olshausen. 79-85

CHARTER IX.—WOMEN PROPHETS. First Prophecy. Henry Melville. Dr. Adam Clarke. Bishop Horne. Prophecy of Joel. Prophetess Anna. Primary Meaning of Prophesy. 86-92.

CHAPTER X.—DEACONS. Definition. Mosheim. New Testament Deacons Preachers. Women Deacons. Their Qualifications. Alford. Olshausen's Commentary. American Commentary. Jamieson, Fausett and Brown. Phebe. Pliny. 93-104.

CHAPTER XI.—DEACONESSES. Order of Deaconesses Same as Deacons. Mosheim. Practice of Modern Churches Inconsistent. The State. Maria Theresa. Tennyson. 105-110.

CHAPTER XII.—EVANGELIZING THE WORLD. Finney. Slow Progress of Christianity. Causes. Stephen. Melancthon. Frances Willard. 111-117.

CHAPTER XIII.—REQUIRED. Command of Christ. Necessity in Oriental Countries. Miss Fannie J. Sparkes. Refusal Unjust. Maria Mitchell. 118-124.

CHAPTER XIV.—FITNESS. Testimony of a Skeptic. Women of Jerusalem. Spirit of the Gospel. Clotilda. Bertha. Permanency of Wesley's Work due to his Mother. Miss Sewell. Women Practical. The Great Plague of 1348. Port Royal. Their Intellectual Ability. 125-138.

CHAPTER XV.—GOVERNING. Capacity for. Women took Part in Governing the Apostolic Church. Elizabeth. Catharine of Russia. Victoria. 139-149.

CHAPTER XVI.—HEATHEN TESTIMONY. Letter of Pliny. Comment upon it. 150-157.

CHAPTER XVII.—CONCLUSION. 158-159.

Index of Texts 160.

TO

My Beloved Wife,

WHO FOR FORTY-TWO YEARS

HAS FAITHFULLY STOOD BY ME IN THE GOSPEL MINISTRY,

Who has never shunned to be a partaker of the

AFFLICTIONS OF THE GOSPEL,

But has faced undismayed the fires of persecution,

WHO HAS BEEN TO ME A CONSTANT INSPIRATION

TO A FULLER UNDERSTANDING OF THE

Mysteries of the Kingdom,

These Pages are Affectionately Dedicated

BY THE AUTHOR.

PREFACE.

I have written this book from a strong conviction of duty. Christ commands us to let our light shine.

There is no reason why this subject should not be considered as calmly and candidly as any other. We should not refuse to examine it in the light of Scripture and of reason because of any apprehension of dreadful consequences if some women should be ordained. By the Friends, for over two hundred years, woman has been accorded the same rights as man, and yet she has lost none of her womanliness in consequence. Among no class of people are women more true, and modest, and domestic, and noble, and refined, and given to every good work than among them. Nowhere else can be found more beautiful, happy homes than in the Society of The Friends.

Nor need we have any fearful forebodings, if giving to women equal rights in the church should lead to giving her equal rights in the state. This experiment too has been tried.

United States senator Carey is reported as

saying: "In the State of Wyoming woman has had the ballot for twenty years. None of the objections which are made to this extension of the suffrage had been found in actual practice, in his State, to have a good basis. The result there has been more than satisfactory. It was not true that women in general took no interest in the question of suffrage. Those who were not originally advocates of it exercise their privileges when they once received them. There was fully as large a proportion of women who voted in his State to-day as of men. Anything that related at all to their interests was sure to bring out the full vote. He thought that the women gave more thought to the subject than the men, and were more conscientious in the exercise of their right. Their influence was exercised always on the side of good government and for the selection of the best men for office. Their influence in politics was of such a character as to make men more circumspect in the transaction of the duties of public office. He added that it was a particularly good element in all municipal elections. Women, as a class, can never be on the side of corruption, of the ignorant and the criminal elements which have such control in the municipal affairs of the leading cities of the United States."*

I have purposely avoided all appeals to sentiment and to ' the spirit of the age," and based my arguments mainly on the Word of God. Where texts have been interpreted contrary to the generally received meaning, reasons have been given, which, I trust, will be found satisfactory. I have endeavored to make everything plain.

I ask as a special favor of those who have decided not to agree with the position I have taken that they will read before they condemn. The subject is worthy of patient and prayerful investigation.

I have no misgivings as to the truth of what I have written, nor evil forebodings of the consequences that will result if the views herein advocated come to be generally received.

I only ask that truth may prevail, Christ be glorified, and His Kingdom be advanced on earth.

* T. Crawford in N. Y. *Tribune*, Feb. 22, 1891.

ORDAINING WOMEN.

CHAPTER I.

PREJUDICE.

"Errors, like straws, upon the surface flow ;
He who would search for pearls must dive below."
—*Dryden.*

"He that would seriously set upon the search of truth, ought in the first place to prepare his mind with a love of it, for he that loves it not will not take much pains to get it, nor be much concerned when he misses it." —*Locke.*

CHRIST lays great stress upon the truth. It has in it a saving quality. "*Sanctify them through thy truth.*"—John 17:17. It is not possible for us to be sanctified only as far as we open our hearts to receive the truth, and inwardly resolve to obey it. The Holy Spirit is the spirit of truth. Jno. 14:17.

"Let us," says the Duke of Argyl, "educate ourselves up to that high standard in the love of truth, under which we hate and disdain an intellectual fallacy as much as we hate and disdain a common lie."

Then, to the rights of women under the Gospel, as an important question, we should give our candid attention. If prejudiced, we should, as Daniel Webster said, "Conquer our prejudices." The feeling against woman's being accorded equal rights with man, is old and deeply rooted. Generally, among mankind, the law of force has been the prevailing law. The stronger have tyrannized over the weaker. Aristotle was one of the greatest of the old Greek philosophers. In his book on Politics and Economics he wrote: " By nature some beings command, and others obey, for the sake of mutual safety ; for a being endowed with discernment and forethought is, by nature, the superior and governor; whereas he who is merely able to execute by bodily labor is the inferior and a *natural slave;* and hence the interest *of master and slave is identical..*"*

"It is clear then, that some men *are free by nature, and others are slaves, and that in the case of the latter, the lot of slavery is both advantageous and just.*"†

Again, Aristotle wrote : " The art of war is, in some sense, a part of the art of acquisition ; for hunting is a part of it, which it is necessary for us to employ against wild beasts, and *against those of mankind who, being in-*

---
* Book .1 Ch. 2, p. 4.   † Book 2, Ch. 5, p. 13.

tended by nature for slavery, are unwilling to submit to it, and on this occasion, such a war is by nature just."*

Until recently, as long as there was any slavery to tolerate, human slavery was tolerated by the leading churches of this country. Reason and revelation were appealed to in defence of the practice of human slavery. No longer ago than 1836 the General Conference of the M. E. Church took the following action, as recorded on its journal :

"Resolved by the delegates of the Annual Conferences in General Conference assembled :

1. That they disapprove, in the most unqualified sense, the conduct of two members of the General Conference who are reported to have lectured in this city recently upon, and in favor of modern Abolitionism.

2. That they are decidedly opposed to modern Abolitionism, and wholly disclaim any right, wish, or intention to interfere in the civil and political relation between master and slave as it exists in the slave holding States of this Union."

Some time after slavery was abolished by war, the above resolutions were repealed, and another General Conference of the same Church

---
* Ch. 8, pp. 19, 20.

passed a resolution to the effect that it was a matter of congratulation that the Methodist Episcopal Church had always taken the lead of the sister churches in the anti-slavery movement.

About thirty years ago the Right Rev. John Henry Hopkins, D. D., LL. D., one of the learned men of his day, and the Protestant Episcopal Bishop of the diocese of Vermont, wrote and published a book in which he endeavored to prove that human slavery, as it then existed in these United States, was supported by "the authority of the Bible, the writings of the Fathers, the decrees of Councils, the concurrent judgment of Protestant divines, and the Constitution." The efforts to overthrow it he characterized as the "assaults of mistaken philanthropy, in union with infidelity, fanaticism, and political expediency."

If those who stood high as interpreters of Reason and Revelation, and who expressed the prevailing sentiment of their day, were so greatly mistaken on a subject which we now think so plain that it does not admit of dispute, that every man has a right to freedom, is it not possible that the current sentiment as to the position which WOMAN should be permitted to occupy in the *Church of Christ* may also be wrong?

Reader, will you admit this possibility? Will you sit as an impartial juror in the case, and carefully weigh the evidence we may present?

It has taken the world a long while to underderstand the Gospel of Jesus Christ; and even now it is but imperfectly understood.

We cannot ascertain the truth of an opinion by inquiries about its age. Let us decide that as the Church did, for ages, misinterpret the teachings of the Bible on the subject of slavery, so it may now fail to apprehend its teaching on the question of woman's rights.

Christian men and women should not wait until a righteous cause is popular before they give it their influence. Those who do, are simply following fashion, while they may think they are following the Lord.

> "These loud ancestral boasts of yours,
> How can they else than vex us?
> Where were your dinner orators
> When slavery grasped at Texas?
> Dumb on his knees was every one
> That now is bold as Cæsar;
> Merè pegs to hang an office on,
> Such stalwart men as these are."
> —*Lowell.*

It is not enough to say that the right will ultimately triumph; if we claim to be righteous we should help make the right triumph.

CHAPTER II.

WOMAN'S LEGAL CONDITION.

"There is who hopes (his neighbor's worth depressed),
Pre-eminence himself ; and covets hence,
For his own greatness that another fall."
—*Dante.*

IN most nations, except Jewish and Christian, the condition of woman has been, from time immemorial, one of slavery. She was sold in marriage. Rome has given laws to the world, yet the young Roman, says Gibbon, "according to the custom of antiquity bought his bride of her parents, and she fulfilled the *co-emption* by purchasing, with three pieces of copper, a just introduction to his house and household deities." Her servitude was decorated by the title of "adoption," and, by a legal fiction, she became the "daughter" of her husband and the "sister" of her own children. Parental power in its fullest extent belonged to the husband in relation to the wife, as well as to the children. " By his judgment or caprice her behavior was approved or censured, or chastised ; he exercised the

WOMAN'S LEGAL CONDITION. 15

jurisdiction of life and death; and it was allowed, that in the case of adultery or drunkenness, the sentence might be properly inflicted. She acquired and inherited for the sole profit of her lord; and so clearly was woman defined, not as a *person*, but as a *thing*, that, if the original title were deficient, she might be claimed, like other movables, by the *use* and possession of an entire year."*

The Spartan women were given the same physical training as men, and, as a consequence, they were more free in fact than the women of any other country of that age. "There can be little doubt," says Mill, "that Spartan experience suggested to Plato, among many other of his doctrines, that of the social and political equality of the sexes." Still, by law, in Sparta, as in the rest of Greece, the state of woman was that of subjection.

Stanley, writing of Central Africa, says: "Though a woman is as much a chattel in these lands as any article their lords may own, and is priced at from one to five head of cattle, she is held in honor and esteem, and she possesses rights which may not be overlooked with impunity. The dower stock may have been surrendered to the father, but if

---
* Gibbon's Rome 4, 345.

she be ill used she can easily contrive at some time to return to her parents, and before she be restored, the husband must repurchase her, and as cattle are valuable, he is likely to bridle his temper. Besides, there is the discomfort of the cold hearth, and the chilly arrangement of the household, which soon serve to subdue the tyrant."*

[Though Christianity has greatly ameliorated the condition of woman, it has not secured for her, even in the most enlightened nations, that equality which the Gospel inculcates.] A writer of only thirty years ago said: "The German women of the lower, and to some extent of the middle classes, are subjected to greater hardships than the women of any other nation of Europe. The farm laborer, the mechanic, and even the small farmer, makes his wife or mother his drudge, and compels her to perform the most menial and severe labors, while he sits or walks by her side unemployed, smoking his pipe. Within a few years, American citizens have witnessed, in Vienna, women acting as masons' tenders, carrying bricks and mortar up to the walls of lofty brick buildings in course of erection."†

---
* In Darkest Africa, vol. 2, p. 394.
† Woman, by L. P. Brackett, M. D., p. 55.

WOMAN'S LEGAL CONDITION. 17

John Stuart Mill, an English wiiter of highest authority, says :

"By the old laws of England, the husband was called the lord of the wife ; he was literally regarded as her sovereign, inasmuch that the murder of a man by his wife was called treason (petty as distinguished from high treason), and was more cruelly avenged than was usually the case with high treason, for the penalty was burning to death. Because these various enormities have fallen into disuse (for most of them were never formally abolished, or not until they had long ceased to be practiced) ; men suppose that all is now as it should be in regard to the marriage contract ; and we are continually told that civilization and Christianity have restored to the woman her just rights. Meanwhile the wife is the actual bondservant of her husband ; no less so, as far as legal obligation goes, than slaves commonly so called. She vows a life-long obedience to him at the altar, and is held to it all through her life by law. Casuists may say that the obligation of obedience stops short of participation in crime, but it certainly extends to everything else. She can do no act whatever but by his permission, at least tacit. She can acquire no property but for him ; the instant it becomes hers, even if by inheritance, it becomes *ipso facto* his. In this respect the wife's position under the common law of England is worse than that of slaves in the laws of many countries; by the Roman law, for example, a slave might have his *peculium*, which, to a certain extent, the law guaranteed to him for his exclusive use. The higher clas es in this country give an analogous advantage to their women, through special contracts setting aside the law, by conditions of pin-money, etc., etc.; since parental feeling being stronger with fathers than the class feeling of their own sex, a father generally prefers his own daughter to a son in-law who is a stranger to him. By means of settlements, the rich usually contrive to withdraw the whole or part of the inherited property of the wife from the absolute control of the husband; but they do not succeed in keeping it under her own control; the utmost they can do only prevents the husband from squandering it, at the same time debarring the rightful owner from its use. The property itself is out of the reach of both; and as to the income derived from it, the form of settlement most favorable to the wife (that called "to her separate use") only precludes the husband from receiving it instead of her; it must pass through her hands, but if he takes it from her by personal violence as soon as she receives it, he can neither be punished, nor compelled to restitution. This is the amount of the protection which, under the laws of this country, the most powerful nobleman can give to his own daughter as respects her husband. In the immense majority of cases there is no settlement, and the absorption of all rights, all property, as well as all freedom of action, is complete. The two are called "one person in law," for the purpose of inferring that whatever is hers is his, but the parallel inference is never drawn that whatever is his is hers; the maxim is not applied against the man, except to make him responsible to third parties for her acts, as a master is for the acts of his slaves, or of his cattle. I am far from pretending that wives are in general no better treated than slaves; but no slave is a slave to the same lengths, and in so full a sense of the word, as a wife is. Hardly any slave, except one immediately attached to the master's person, is a slave at all hours and all minutes; in general he has, like a soldier, his fixed task, and when it is done, or when he is off duty, he disposes, within certain limits, of his time, and has a family life into which the master rarely intrudes. 'Uncle

Tom' under his first master had his own life in his 'cabin,' almost as much as any man whose work takes him away from home, is able to have in his own family. But it cannot be so with the wife. * *

"What is her position in regard to the children in whom she and her master have a joint interest ? They are by law his children. He alone has any legal rights over them. Not one act can she do towards or in relation to them, except by delegation from him. Even after he is dead she is not their legal guardian, unless he by will has made her so. He could even send them away from her, and deprive her of the means of seeing or corresponding with them, until his power was in some degree restricted by Sergeant Talfourd's act.

"This is her legal state. And from this state she has no means of withdrawing herself. If she leaves her husband, she can take nothing with her, neither her children nor anything which is rightfully her own. If he chooses, he can compel her to return, by law, or by physical force ; or he may content himself with seizing for his own use anything which she may earn, or which may be given to her by her relations. It is only legal separation by a decree of a court of justice, which entitles her to live apart, without being forced back into the custody of an exasperated jailer—or which empowers her to apply any earnings to her own use, without fear that a man whom perhaps she has not seen for twenty years will pounce upon her some day and carry all off. This legal separation, until lately, the courts of justice would only give at an expense which made it inaccessible to any one out of the higher ranks. Even now it is only given in cases of desertion, or of the extreme of cruelty ; and yet complaints are made every day that it is granted too easily."

It is no wonder that our prejudices against the rights of woman, coming down to us from such sources, and infused into us from early childhood, should be so strong. But reason and grace serve to overcome prejudice.

In no other nation of the world is woman's legal condition as favorable as in this country, yet in thirty-six of our states the woman with a husband living is not the legal owner of her children. The husband has the legal control, and in some of the states he can will the child away from his wife before the child is born.

CHAPTER III.

WORDS.

"I am not so lost in lexicography as to forget that words are the daughters of earth, and that things are the sons of Heaven."
Samuel Johnson.

"WORDS," says Bishop Berkeley, "have ruined and overrun all the sciences.

"To view the deformity of error we need only undress it," that is, deprive it of its verbal disguises.

"Howbeit that was not first which is spiritual, but that which is natural; and afterward that which is spiritual."—1 Cor. 15:46.

This is true, not only of things, but of words which represent things. Πνεῦμα, *pneuma*, spirit, in its primary meaning signifies *wind, air, the air we breathe.*

Κῆρυξ, *kerux*, preacher, was a *herald*, who summoned the assembly and preserved order in it.

Ἀπόστολος, *apostolos*, apostle, was *one sent*, a messenger, envoy, ambassador.

Πρέσβυς, *presbus*, Πρεσβύτερος, *presbuteros*, elder,

older, in the comparative degree, was one older than the most—one of mature years.

Επισκοπος, *episkopos*, bishop, was an overseer, watcher, guardian.

Διάκονος, *diakonos*, deacon, a servant, waiting-man or woman. The word is of common gender.

So we might go through with all the ecclesiastical terms of the New Testament. They all had, primarily, a secular meaning. But when it is evident that a writer gives to a word a special, secondary meaning, we must not in his writings, take that word in any place in its primary meaning, *unless the connection absolutely requires that we should.* To do so, in order to support a theory, is highly improper. It can never be done in the interests of truth.

To make a word mean one thing in one passage, and then something else in essentially the same connection, for the purpose of making the writer support our views, violates the principles of right interpretation. Locke says: "In all discourses wherein one man pretends to instruct or convince another, he should use the same word constantly in the same sense. If this were done (which nobody can refuse without disingenuity), many of the controversies in dispute would be at an end."*

But where it is clear that a word is used in its primary signification we should so understand it. Thus the word ἐκκλησία, *ecclesia*, *church*, primarily, *assembly*, is found in the New Testament 115 times. It is properly translated church in all places except in Acts 19:32, 39, 41, where it evidently has its original meaning of Assembly.

"Fidelity in names," says Tertullian, "secures the safe appreciation of properties."

Words are arbitrary signs of ideas or of things. And often the same word represents things which have no relation to each other. The mother who brings up her children to obey her is sometimes obliged to use the *switch* upon the refractory child. The railroad man, by turning the *switch* wrong, wrecked the train. The fashionable woman when she buys a *switch* is careful to have it match her own hair.

The farmer cuts his wheat with a *cradle*. His wife rocks the baby in a *cradle*.

These illustrations show that in ascertaining the meaning of a word we must look at the connection in which it stands.

In our quotations we shall endeavor to give

* Of Human Understanding, p. 335.

to words the signification intended by those who used them.

Unless we give to words their true meaning we cannot arrive at the truth for which we search. "I shall urge upon you," says Archbishop Trench, "how well it will repay you to study the words which you are in the habit of using or of meeting, be they such as relate to highest spiritual things, or the common words of the shop and the market, and of all the familiar intercourse of life. It will indeed repay you far better than you can easily believe."

"The study of words," says Max Muller, "may be tedious to the school-boy, as breaking of stones is to the wayside laborer: but to the thoughtful eye of the geologist these stones are full of interest; he sees miracles on the high road and reads chronicles in every ditch. Language, too, has marvels of her own, which she unveils to the inquiring glance of the patient student. There are chronicles below her surface; there are sermons in every word."

CHAPTER IV.

ORDINATION.

"No blood, no altar now,
The sacrifice is o'er ;
No flame, no smoke ascends on high,
The Lamb is slain no more !
But richer blood has flowed from nobler veins,
To purge the soul from guilt, and cleanse the reddest stains."
—*Bonar.*

" Let all things be done decently, and in order."—*St. Paul.*

DIFFERENT denominations hold different views about ordination.

1. The Friends have no sacraments and no ordained preachers. Their great theologian, Robert Barclay, says:

"When they assemble together, to wait upon God, and to worship and adore him ; then such as the Spirit sets apart for the ministry, by its divine power and influence opening their mouths, and giving them to exhort, reprove and instruct with virtue and power : these are thus ordained of God and admitted into the ministry, and their brethren cannot but hear them, receive them, and also honor them for their work's sake."

He states as follows their position in reference to Baptism and the Lord's Supper:

"As there is one Lord and one faith, so there is one baptism ;

ORDINATION. 27

which is not the putting away the filth of the flesh, but the answer of a good conscience before God, by the resurrection of Jesus Christ. And this baptism is a pure and spiritual thing—to wit: the baptism of the Spirit and fire, by which we are buried with him, that being washed and purged from our sins, we may walk in newness of life; of which the baptism of John was a figure, which was commanded for a time, and not to continue forever."*

He takes a similar position in respect to the Lord's Supper:

"The communion of the body and blood of Christ is inward and spiritual, which is the participation of his flesh and blood, by which the inward man is daily nourished in the hearts of those in whom Christ dwells. Of which things the breaking of bread by Christ with his disciples was a figure, which even they who had received the substance used in the church for a time, for the sake of the weak; even as abstaining from things strangled, and from blood, the washing one another's feet, and the anointing of the sick with oil; all which are commanded with no less authority and solemnity than the former; yet seeing they are but shadows of better things, they cease in such as have obtained the substance."†

The main objection to this teaching is that it is contrary to the plain teaching of the New Testament. (1) All true ministers are called of the Holy Ghost. But before one becomes a minister of the Gospel in the fullest sense, his divine call must be acknowledged and duly ratified by the church. Thus, the successor to Judas was so appointed, as described in Acts 1:15-26. Thus Paul was divinely called and in a formal manner publicly ordained. Acts 26:16-18 and Acts 13:2, 3.

---
* Apology, p. 380. † Apology, p. 412.

(2.) *All* baptism *with* water is not John's baptism, as Robert Barclay teaches. Christian baptism is baptism *with* water. This is made perfectly clear. Paul, finding certain disciples at Ephesus, said unto them;

"Have ye received the Holy Ghost since ye believed? And they said unto him, We have not so much as heard whether there be any Holy Ghost.

"And he said unto them, Unto what, then, were ye baptized? And they said, Unto John's baptism.

"Then said Paul: John verily baptized with the baptism of repentance saying unto the people, that they should believe on him which should come after him, that is on Christ Jesus.

"When they heard this, they were baptized in the name of the Lord Jesus.

"And when Paul had laid his hands upon them, the Holy Ghost came on them; and they spake with tongues and prophesied."—Acts 19:2-6.

Here three acts, each distinct in itself, are specified:

1. The baptism of John.
2. Baptism in the name of the Lord Jesus— that is Christian baptism.

3. The coming upon them of the Holy Ghost in His miraculous power.

This shows that the baptism of the Holy Ghost did not do away with baptism by water.

The same is also taught with equal plainness in Acts 10:47. "Can any man forbid water, that these should not be baptized which have received the Holy Ghost as well as we?"

Here were people who had received the substance; they needs must now receive the sign. They had been accepted in the army of the Lord; they must now publicly come under his banner.

They belonged to Christ; they must now, before their fellow men, receive the mark of Christ upon them.

(3.) Equally unscriptural is the above position in regard to the Lord's Supper. In it the body of Christ must be partaken of in a spiritual manner. But there must also be the outward sign.

"For I have received of the Lord that which also I delivered unto you, That the Lord Jesus the same night in which he was betrayed took bread: And when he had given thanks, He broke it, and said, Take, eat: this is my body which is broken for you; this do in remembrance of me. For as oft as ye eat this bread, and drink this cup, ye do show the Lord's death till he come.—1 Cor. 11: 23-26.

(1.) It was not figurative, but *actual bread which they ate*. As oft as ye eat—not *this*, indefinitely—but THIS BREAD.

(2.) They were to do this openly—not as a sacrifice for sin—but as a *remembrance of Christ*.

(3.) It was not to be " used in the church for a time, for the sake of the weak," but for ALL TIME—as long as the world stands ; for in doing this, *ye do shew the Lord's death till he come*.

As to "abstaining from things strangled and from blood, all Christians abstain from them ; they still *wash one another's feet*, in the sense intended by our Lord ; and some still anoint the sick with oil.

Many more passages to the same effect as the above might be quoted ; but these are sufficient to show that the position taken by the Friends on the ministry and on the sacraments is contrary to the Scriptures.

2. THE ROMAN CATHOLICS. In striking contrast with the above views, is the teaching of the Church of Rome.

The Council of Trent, in the third canon of the twenty-third session, says :

ORDINATION.

"Whoever shall affirm that orders, or holy ordination are not a sacrament instituted by Christ the Lord, let him be accursed."

Again, in the fourth canon of the same session; "Whoever shall affirm that the Holy Spirit is not given by ordination, let him be accursed."

As to the power conferred by ordination the Roman Catechism says:

"The faithful then are to be made acquainted with the exalted dignity and excellence of this sacrament in its highest degree, which is the priesthood. Priests and bishops are, as it were, the interpreters and heralds of God, commissioned in his name to teach mankind the law of God, and the precepts of a Christian life. They are the representatives of God upon earth. Impossible therefore, to conceive a more exalted dignity, or functions more sacred. Justly, therefore, are they called not only 'angels' but gods, holding as they do the place and power, and authority of God on earth. But the priesthood, at all times an elevated office, transcends in the new law all others in dignity. The power of consecrating and offering the body and blood of our Lord, and of remitting sins, with which the priesthood of the new law is invested, is such as cannot be comprehended by the human mind, still less is it equalled by, or assimilated to, anything on earth."*

"In ordaining a priest, the bishop, and after him, the priests who are present, lay their hands on the candidate. The bishop then places a stole on his shoulder, and adjusts it. He next anoints his hands with sacred oil, reaches him a chalice containing wine, and a patena with bread, saying, 'RECEIVE POWER TO OFFER SACRIFICE TO GOD, AND TO CELEBRATE MASS AS WELL FOR THE LIVING AS FOR THE DEAD.' By these words and ceremonies he is constituted an interpreter and mediator between God and man, the principal function of the priesthood. Finally, placing his hands on the head of the person to be ordained, the bishop says, 'RECEIVE YE THE HOLY GHOST; WHOSE SINS YE SHALL FORGIVE, THEY ARE FORGIVEN THEM; AND WHOSE SINS YE SHALL RETAIN THEY ARE RETAINED. Thus investing him with that divine power

p. 283.

of forgiving and retaining sins, which was conferred by our Lord on his disciples. These are the principal and peculiar functions of the priesthood.*

These are wonderful pretensions! The apostles themselves claimed no such powers. They never pretended to transform bread and wine into *the body* and blood of our Lord Jesus Christ. There is no record of their claiming to forgive sin, in the place of God, or of pronouncing absolution from sin by his authority. They were to forgive those who sinned against them, but all Christians were to do the same. They laid down *authoritatively* the conditions on which God forgives sin.

Says Dr. Lightfoot: "The Holy Spirit directing them, they were to determine concerning the legal doctrine and practice, being completely instructed and enabled in both by the Holy Spirit descending upon them.

"As to the *persons*, they were endowed with a peculiar gift, so that, the same Spirit directing them, if they would retain and punish the sins of any, a power was delivered into their hands of *delivering* to *Satan*, of punishing with *diseases*, *plagues*, yea, death *itself*, which Peter did to *Ananias* and *Sapphira;* Paul to *Elymas*, *Hymeneus* and *Philetus*."

But the power which the twelve possessed

* Catechism, p. 295.

they never assumed to bestow upon others. The record does not show that Christ ever gave them any such power.

Simon Magus was the only one spoken of in the New Testament as ascribing to them such power. And he was most severely rebuked.— Acts 8 : 18–24.

As to the Romish priests transforming the bread and wine into *the actual body and blood of the Lord Jesus*, it is a blasphemous assumption. The apostles did not pretend to do any such thing. *For as often as ye eat this bread.* —1 Cor. 11–26.

Wherefore whosoever shall eat this bread, and drink this cup of the Lord, unworthily, shall be guilty of the body and blood of the Lord.—27th verse.

They eat unworthily who eat it to satisfy hunger and not to commemorate the sacrificial death of Christ. They do not discern *the Lord's body.*

But whether eaten worthily or unworthily, it is THE BREAD that is eaten.

On the unscriptural view that the Lord's Supper is of the nature of a sacrifice for sin is based the claim that Gospel ministers constitute a *priesthood*. This is an error of the greatest magnitude and fraught with the most direful consequences.

It is remarkable that, though the word *priest* is found in the New Testament one hundred and fifty-one times, *it is never once applied to a Christian minister.* Neither John, nor Peter, nor Paul, nor James is ever called *a priest.*

"What is the reason ?"

A *priest* is one who offers sacrifices for the sins of others. "For every high priest taken from among men is ordained for men in things pertaining to God, that he may offer both gifts and sacrifices for sins."—Heb. 5:1. See also Chap. 8:3.

But Christ has offered *himself* a sacrifice for our sins, ONCE FOR ALL. "And every priest standeth daily ministering and offering oftentimes the same sacrifices, which can never take away sins ; but this man after he had offered one sacrifice for sins forever, sat down on the right hand of God.—Heb. 10:12. Note well! that THE SACRIFICE FOR SINS IS FOREVER. It is *never to be repeated.*

"For such an high priest became us, who is holy, harmless, undefiled, separate from sinners, and made higher than the heavens ; who needeth not daily, as those high priests, to offer up sacrifice, first for his own sins, and then for

ORDINATION. 35

the people's; for this he did once, when he offered up himself.--Heb. 7:26, 27.

There is then a valid reason why the Christian religion has *no priests. It has no sacrifices for sins to offer.* The sacrifice for sin is complete. The Redeemer has appeared among men. *Man is redeemed.* For ministers to assume to be priests, in the priestly sense, is an open insult to Christ. It is a Heaven-daring usurpation.

[margin note: no priests.]

The *Christian priesthood* embraces *all* of God's people. It was to *all the saints* that St. Peter wrote: "Ye, also, as lively stones, are built up a spiritual house, an holy priesthood to offer up spiritual sacrifices, acceptable to God by Jesus Christ."—1 Pet. 2:5.

Also in the 9th verse: "But ye are a chosen generation, a royal priesthood." There is no dispute that all the saints are referred to in both these passages.

The *nature* of these sacrifices is clearly specified. They are—

1. *Our bodies.* "I beseech you, therefore, brethren, by the mercies of God that ye present your bodies a living sacrifice, holy, acceptable unto God, which is your reasonable service."—Rom. 12:1.

No priest is to offer this for another. Each

believer in Christ is to offer it for himself.

2. *Good Works.* "But to do good and to communicate, forget not; for with such sacrifices God is well pleased."—Heb. 13:16. See also Eph. 5:2.

This direction also is *to all* of God's people.

3. *Praise.* "By him, therefore, let us offer the sacrifice of praise to God continually, that is, the fruit of our lips giving thanks to his name.—Heb. 13:15.

This too is a *sacrifice* that all the saints are to offer. It is not to be done by priest or other proxy. No choir, however skilful, or how highly paid, can relieve us of this duty of offering praise to God.

These are *all* the sacrifices that Christians are directed, in the New Testament, to offer. And each and all of these they are to offer *for themselves.* Not one word is said about offering "the sacrifice of the Mass" as an atonement for our sins. All this is adding to the word of the Lord.

If Christian Ministers were called upon to slaughter cattle and sheep as sacrifices for sin, then it would be improper for women to be ministers. This is the reason why, in the Old Testament, no woman is called a priest. Some of them were *prophets* to instruct and reform the people, but no woman was a priest to offer sacrifices for sins.

In the primitive Christian Church, when the Ministers became proud and aspiring, and assumed priestly prerogatives, they assigned to woman a lower place in the Christian ministry; and finally, as they apostatized more fully, they dropped her from the ministry altogether.

Between these two extremes, of the Friends, who make absolutely nothing of ordination, and of the Romanists, who make an apotheosis, a deification of it, lies the truth.

By Protestants generally, ordination is looked upon as a solemn recognition by the church, of the authority to preach, of those whom God has called to this office, and who have made full proof of their ministry.

John Wesley, referring to ecclesiastics of the Church of England, to which he belonged, said that for forty years he had been in doubt over the question, "What obedience is due to Heathenish priests and mitred infidels?"

So it is quite evident that he did not regard ordination as bestowing a Christian, much less an angelic or godlike character.

Ordination is necessary to prevent improper persons from thrusting themselves into the ministry, and thus bringing the Gospel into contempt. Daniel Webster said; "Forms are as necessary as hoops on a barrel; they keep the whole from falling to pieces."

"The essential elements of the act of ordination," says Rev. H. J.Van Dyke, sr., D. D., "are *prayer, and the laying on of hands, with the avowed intention of setting apart the candidate to the work of the ministry, as one who, after due examination, is believed to be called of God to that office.*"[*]

For ordination there is the plain authority of the New Testament.

"*The Ordination of the Seven Deacons.*[†] This marked event in the history of the Church occurred in immediate sequence of the outpouring of the Holy Ghost at the Pentecost, and from the space allotted to it in the sacred record (Acts 6:2–6), as well as from the fact that all the apostles were present, it may now be considered, as it doubtless was during the whole apostolic period, a model ordination for the subsequent Church. Its characteristic features were: (1.) A demand for men of honest report, full of the Holy Ghost and wisdom; (2.) An election or choice by the church on that basis: (3.) Prayer by the apostles; (4.)

---
[*] Presbyterian Review for 1886, June No.
[†] McClintock & Strong's Cyclypedia, Art. Ordination

The laying on of hands, presumably, by several of the apostles, as representative of the whole body. In this act the apostles illustrated their ideas of the proper functions of the church in reference to its future ministers, and established a precedent, of perpetual authority. It was a precedent, moreover, in obvious harmony with the precept of our Lord, given in connection with his appointment of the seventy (Luke 10:2), "Pray ye, therefore, the Lord of the harvest, that he would send forth laborers into his harvest." The apostles evidently regarded this as the standing commission and perpetual duty of the church, in reference to the promotion of Christ's Kingdom in the earth. In it they saw that the Lord claimed the work of evangelizing the world as his own, and also the prerogative of calling and sending forth laborers, while at the same time, he charged the church with the responsibility of prayer and co-operation. This, too, was in harmony with the Saviour's promised gift of the Holy Ghost as the guide of the church when he should no longer be present as its visible head. The Spirit's influence was specially promised in answer to prayer, and it was only a praying church endowed with the Holy Ghost that could become the light of the world, and the agency of its salvation. So long as the church illustrated these characteristics, it gloriously fulfilled its mission. It grew rapidly by the addition of regenerated believers, many of whom, in proportion to the demands of its widening work, were called of God, and moved of the Holy Ghost to preach to others the same Gospel that had become to them the power of God unto salvation. The function of the church, therefore, as to ordination was, not to create or bestow the gift of the ministry, but simply to recognize and authenticate it when bestowed by the Head of the Church."

The ordination of elders. In the Apostolic Church, Bishops and Elders were the same. "And from Miletus he sent to Ephesus, and called the elders of the church." When they were come together he said to them; "Take heed, therefore, unto yourselves, and to all the flock over the which the Holy Ghost hath made you overseers, to feed the church of God, which he hath purchased with his own blood."—Acts 20:17, 28. The word here translated overseer is, in the original, *episcopos*, *bishop*. From this we learn—1. That those having the oversight of the Church were called *elders* or *bishops*. These two words were used interchangeably. 2. That preaching

ORDINATION. 41

was the chief business of these elders or bishops. They were made bishops by the Holy Ghost that they might FEED *the church of God.*

So, in the various lists that are given us in the New Testament, of the officers of the church, elders and bishops are never both found in the same list. These elders were ordained. "And when they had ordained them elders in every church, and had prayed with fasting, they commended them to the Lord, on whom they believed."—Acts 14:23.

"For this cause left I thee in Crete, that thou shouldest set in order the things that are wanting, and ordain elders in every city as I had appointed thee. If any be blameless, the husband of one wife, having faithful children not accused of riot or unruly. For a bishop must be blameless—Titus 1:5-7.

It is evident that those whom he calls elders in the fifth verse he calls bishops in the seventh.

We see also that the Apostolic churches were not independent, but the same men had official oversight of many churches.

Ordaining Apostles. "Now there were in the church that was at Antioch certain prophets and teachers; as Barnabas and Simeon that was called Niger, and Lucius of Cyrene, and

Manaen, which had been brought up with Herod the tetrarch and Saul.

"And as they ministered to the Lord and fasted, the Holy Ghost said, Separate me Barnabas and Saul for the work whereunto I have called them.

"And when they had fasted and prayed, and laid their hands on them they sent them away."—Acts 13:1-3.

"The events above narrated," say McClintock and Strong, "occurred some two years after the commission of Saul of Tarsus, following which 'straightway he preached Christ in the synagogues.'—Acts 9,20. Becoming associated with Barnabas, he also 'spake boldly in the name of the Lord Jesus' at Jerusalem. Both these men seem to have labored as evangelists whenever they had opportunity, and their ministry, having been given of God, was honored by his blessing. They were now called to higher responsibilities. 'They were to go forth under the sanction of the church, and not only to proclaim the truth, but also to baptize converts, to organize Christian congregations, and to ordain Christian ministers. It was therefore proper that, on this occasion, they should be regularly invested with the ecclesiastical commission. In the circumstantial record of this proceeding, in the Acts of the Apostles, we have a proof of the wisdom of the Author of Revelation. He foresaw that the rite of the laying on of hands would be sadly abused; that it would be represented as possessing something like a magic potency; and that it would at length be converted by a small class of ministers, into an ecclesiastical monopoly. He has therefore supplied us with an antidote against delusion by permitting us, in this simple narrative, to scan its exact import. And what was the virtue of the ordination here described? Did it furnish Paul and Barnabas with a title to the ministry? Not at all. God himself had already called them to the work, and they could receive no higher authorization. Did it necessarily add anything to the eloquence, or the prudence, or the knowledge, or the piety of the missionaries? No results of the kind could be produced by any such ceremony. What, then, was its meaning? The evangelist himself furnishes an answer. The Holy Ghost required that Barnabas and Saul should be *separated* to the work to which the Lord had called them, and the laying on of hands was the *mode* or *form* in which they were set apart or designated to the office. This rite to an Israelite, suggested grave and hallowed associations. When a Jewish father invoked a benediction on any of his family, he laid his hand upon the head of the child ; when a Jewish priest devoted an animal in sacrifice, he laid his hand upon the head of the victim ; and when a Jewish rabbi invested another with office, he laid his hand upon the head of the new functionary. The ordination of these brethren possessed all this significance. By the laying on of hands the ministers of Antioch implored a blessing upon Barnabas and Saul, and announced their separation or dedication to the work of the Gospel and intimated their investiture with ecclesiastical authority.' "*

There is nothing, then, in the nature of ordination which indicates that no woman should ever be ordained. If she is *called of God* to his work, and this is evident to the church, then may the church *separate* her to this work by ordination.

Ordination, while it does not, *in the rite itself*, convey any supernatural, or magical power, yet it should be the occasion of great and permanent blessing to the person ordained. But this depends, not upon the form, but upon the parties concerned. If those ordaining are proud, and worldly, and carnal, and formal,

---
* Killen, Ancient Church, p. 71, seq.

and the candidate is unconverted, ordination, in all probability, will only make him more proud, exacting and aspiring. But if those who ordain, are men *full of faith and of the Holy Ghost*, and the one ordained is spiritual, humble and fully consecrated to God, he may receive at his ordination such a baptism of the Spirit as shall give him new power all the rest of his days.

"God knows," says Whitfield, "how deep a concern entering into the ministry and preaching was to me. I have prayed a thousand times till the sweat has dropped from my face like rain, that God, of his infinite mercy, would not let me enter into the church, till he called me to and thrust me forth in his work. I said, Lord I cannot go. I shall be puffed up with pride, and fall into the condemnation of the devil. Lord, do not let me go yet. I pleaded to be at Oxford two or three years more. I intended to make one hundred and fifty sermons, and thought that I would set up with a good stock in trade. I remember praying, wrestling and striving with God. I said, I am undone. I am unfit to preach in thy great name. Send me not, Lord—send me not yet. I wrote to all my friends in town and country to pray against the bishop's solicitation, but they insisted I should go into orders before I was twenty-two. After all their solicitations these words came into my mind : 'Nothing shall pluck you out of my hands' ; they came warm to my heart. Then, and not till then, I said, Lord I *will* go; send me when thou wilt." He was ordained ; and he said: "When the bishop laid his hands upon my head, my heart was melted down, and I offered up my whole spirit and soul and body."

Complaint was made to the bishop that, by his first sermon he drove fifteen mad. The good man replied that he hoped their madness would last.

CHAPTER V.

OBJECTIONS—OLD TESTAMENT.

"God made all his creatures free ;
Life itself is liberty ;
God ordained no other bands
Than united hearts and hands."
—*James Montgomery.*

THE objections to the ordination of women may be classed under two heads—*Scriptural* and *natural.*

It is urged that the Bible represents the woman as inferior to the man, and subject to him; therefore she should not be permitted to occupy a position equal to his, either in church or in state. As proof of this, the fact that she was created last is presented.

But, if this proves anything, it proves her superiority. For the work of creation proceeded in regular gradation from the lower to the higher.

Matter is not eternal. Away back *in the beginning,* millions of millions of years before our earth was fitted up for the abode of man, *God created the heaven and the earth.*

On the first of our six days of creation, light appeared. On the second, the atmosphere was formed. On the third day, the waters of the earth were gathered together, the dry land appeared, and our vegetable world was brought into existence.

On the fourth day, light was concentrated around the sun, and it was made a luminous body, and the celestial luminaries were so arranged as to afford an accurate measurement of time, and to give distinction to the seasons.

On the fifth day, fish, fowls and reptiles were created.

On the sixth day, land animals were created —man last—the male first—the woman last of all.

Mathew Henry, in his comment on this verse, says: "That Adam was first formed, then Eve (1 Tim. 2-13), and she was made *of* the man and *for* the man (1 Cor. 11:8, 9), all which is urged there as reasons for the humility, modesty, silence and submissiveness of that sex in general, and particularly the subjection and reverence which wives owe to their own husbands. Yet man being made last of the creatures, as the best and most excellent of all, Eve's, being made *after* Adam, and *out of* him, puts an honor upon that sex, as the glory

OBJECTIONS—OLD TESTAMENT. 49

of the man.—1 Cor. 11:7. If man is the head, she is the crown ; a crown to her husband, the crown of the visible creation. The man was dust refined, but the woman was dust double refined, one remove further from the earth."

Woman was created, not as the *servant* of man, but as his *companion*, his *equal*. "And the Lord God said: *It is* not good that the man should be alone ; I will make him an help meet for him."—Gen. 2:18.

Dr. Adam Clarke, in his comment on this verse, says : "*I will make him a help meet for him; ezer kenegedo*, a help, a counterpart of himself, one formed from him, and a perfect resemblance of his person. If the word be rendered scrupulously literally, it signifies one *like*, or *as himself*, standing *opposite to* or *before him*. And this implies that the woman was to be a perfect resemblance of the man, possessing neither inferiority nor superiority, but being in all things *like* and *equal* to himself."

The *dominion* which God gave to man at the creation was a *joint* dominion. It was given to the woman equally as to the man.

"And God said: Let us make man in our image, after our likeness ; and let them have dominion over the fish of the sea, and over the fowl of the air, and over the cattle, and over all the earth, and over every creeping thing that creepeth upon the earth.

"So God created man in his own image, in the image of God created he him; male and female created he them."—Gen. 1: 26, 27.

Let THEM *have dominion.*

It is, then, evident that God created woman a *female man*—nothing more—nothing less. She had all the rights and prerogatives of the man. The dominion given to him was given equally to her.

Nothing was said of the subjection of woman before the fall. After that sad event, it was said to the woman, as a part of her punishment: "Thy desire shall be to thy husband and he shall rule over thee."—Gen. 3:16.

On this verse Dr. Adam Clarke says, "*And he shall rule over thee,* though at their creation both were formed with equal rights, and the woman had probably as much right to *rule* as the man; but subjection to the will of her husband is one part of her curse; and so very capricious is this *will* often, that a sorer punishment no human being can well have, to be at all in a state of liberty, and under the protection of wise and equal laws."

But it was promised that "The seed of the

OBJECTIONS—OLD TESTAMENT. 51

woman should bruise the serpent's head."—
Gen. 3:15. Christ was THE SEED OF THE WOMAN.
Woman gave to the world man's Redeemer.
If she was first in the fall, she was first in the
restoration. *Christ hath redeemed us from the
curse of the law, being made a curse for us.*—Gal.
3:13. The us includes *woman*.

The Pharisees asked Christ: "Is it lawful
for a man to put away his wife for every
cause?"

In his answer he did not appeal to existing
laws, or long established customs. He based
his answer on the *state of things that existed before
the fall*. "Have ye not read, that he which
made them at the beginning, made them male
and female?"—Mat. 19:4. Why this appeal
to *the beginning?* IT WAS TO RE-ENACT THE
LAW ENACTED THEN. *For this cause shall a man
leave father and mother, and shall cleave to his wife;
and they twain shall be one flesh.* Thus Christ *restored the primitive law*. He said nothing about
the *subjection of woman—not one word*.

"But," it is objected, "domestic society requires the wife to be subject to the husband."
This is a great mistake. If it did, Christ
would doubtless have given directions accordingly.

But it does not. The greatest domestic happiness always exists where husband and wife live together on terms of equality. Two men, having individual interests, united only by business ties, daily associate as partners for years, without either of them being in subjection to the other. They consider each other as equals; and treat each other as equals. Then, cannot a man and woman, united by conjugal love, the strongest tie that can unite two human beings, having *the same* interests, live together in the same manner?

Christ came to repair the ruin wrought by the fall. In Him, and in Him only, is Paradise *restored*.

The Gospel belongs to woman as much as to man.

But, it is again objected that under the Aaronic priesthood men only were priests.

This is true; but the priests were not the only or the chief religious teachers of the Jews. The prophets ranked in this respect above the priests.

But women prophesied. Miriam, was a prophetess—Ex. 15:20. And God in speaking of the deliverance of his people from Egypt, classes her with Moses and Aaron. "And I sent before thee Moses, Aaron and Miriam."—Micah 6:4. She was, then, one of the chosen leaders of his people sent by God. Does not this answer the question, Why did not God appoint a woman to be a leader, if it is ever right for a woman to lead? With Moses and Aaron God sent Miriam "before" His people—that is to lead them.

Deborah was a prophetess and a judge. She performed all the duties that men did who judged Israel, even, to leading their armies to successful battle—Judges 4:4. Huldah was a prophetess(2 Ki. 22:14); and so was Noadiah. Nah. 6:14.

Then we conclude that there is nothing in the creation of woman or in her condition under the law which proves that no woman should be ordained as a minister of the Gospel.

CHAPTER VI.

OBJECTIONS—NEW TESTAMENT.

"All mystery is defect, and cloudy words
Are feebleness, not strength; are loss, not gain;
Men win no victories with spectre swords;
The phantom barque plows the broad sea in vain."
—*Bonar.*

IN all that we have heard and read against the right of woman to be, in the fullest sense, a minister of the Gospel, we have never heard or read a single quotation from the words of Jesus against this right. This is significant. Christ applied the same rules of moral conduct to the woman as to the man. His treatment of the woman taken in adultery has scarcely a parallel. No woman ever came to him to be repulsed.

But, it is said, if women are to preach, why did he not choose a woman among the twelve?

We ask, in reply, if *gentiles* are to preach, why did he not choose a *gentile* among the twelve? Why were the twelve *Jews, every* one of them? The example is as binding in the one case as the other.

But, it is answered, Paul settles the question. "*There is neither Jew nor Greek, there is neither bond nor free, there is neither male nor female; for ye are all one in Christ Jesus.*" --Gal. 3:28. It is contrary to all sound principles of interpretation to say that this passage accords to a Greek the same rights in the Gospel that it does to a Jew, in *one sense,* and to a *woman* the same rights that it does to a *man* in *another,* and much more *restricted sense.*

If this gives to *men* of all nations the right to become ministers of the Gospel, it gives to *women* precisely the same right.

Make this the KEY TEXT upon this subject, and give to other passages such a construction as will make them agree with it, and all is harmony. The apparent conflict is at an end. The fetters are taken off from woman, and she is left free to serve Christ in any position she may be qualified and called to fill. Why should not this be done?

It is objected, in the strong, clear language of an able minister: "In what are male and female *one* in Christ Jesus? Certainly not in every respect. There is nothing in the context by which you can come to the conclusion that Paul is here laying down an abstract principle. applicable outside the limits of the subject under discussion. Now what is that subject? Is it not the one that runs through the entire epistle and especially through the chapter of which the verse in question forms a part? viz: That all men, Jews and Gentiles alike, are saved by faith, and not by the works of the law, according to the covenant of God made with Abraham. From first to last there is no other subject introduced or considered in this chapter. And therefore fairness of interpretation requires us to understand the teaching of the 28th verse to be simply this: In the matter of salvation all are one. The male is saved by faith. The female is saved by faith. The Jew is saved by faith and also the Greek. Likewise the bondman and the freeman. In this respect, all are one, being baptized into Jesus Christ, they become equally children of God, saved by faith alone. To carry this idea of *oneness* further is to bring into the text what is not there, and add to the inspired word."*

To this objection we reply:

1. If this verse referred *only to salvation by faith,* the *female* would not be specified. It would be a superfluity. As we have seen, woman is a *female man.*† *In the many offers*

---
* Rev. W. Gould. † See page 50.

of salvation made in the New Testament, woman is not *specially* mentioned. *Not once.* "He that believeth and is baptized shall be saved," includes woman as well as man. Every one so understood it. There was no dispute about it. So, in the first prayer meeting, it appears the women went ahead. "These all continued, with one accord, in prayer and supplication *with the women.*--Acts 1:14. Women believed in Christ. "And believers were the more added to the Lord multitudes, both of *men and women.*"—Acts 5:14. They were so active in his cause as to provoke persecution. "Saul, haling men and *women committed them to prison.*"—Acts 8:3. Though, in the Jewish church, the males only received the sign of the covenant, yet in the Christian church, women were, from the first, baptized. "*They* were baptized, both *men and women.*"—Acts 8:12. Yet there is no specific command to baptize *women,* nor any *separate* offer of salvation to them. So, if Gal. 3:28 referred to salvation alone, the female would not have been mentioned in it. The "Greek" and the "bond" might have been mentioned with propriety. For it took a miracle to convince Peter that a Greek, or Gentile, could be saved by Christ. But it would have stopped with them. All regarded women as included in the general provisions of the Gospel for the salvation of mankind.

So we must give this verse its full, natural, comprehensive, broad meaning. We must understand it to teach, as it actually does, the perfect equality of all, under the Gospel, in *rights* and *privileges*, without respect to *nationality*, or condition, or sex.

2. There are two correct modes of reasoning:

(1.) From particulars to deduce a general truth.

(2.) From a general, admitted truth, or axiom, make an application to particulars.

The apostle here adopts the first method. He shows that Abraham was justified by faith; that the Mosaic law was temporary, to last only till Christ came; that all who have faith in Christ become the children of God.

Then he makes two general statements—

1. That in Christ Jesus all *peculiar* privileges based on *nationality*, or *condition*, or *sex are abolished*. In the Gospel one nation has the *same* rights and privileges as *another*, the *bond* the same as the *free*, the *female* the same as the *male*.

2. That all, without distinction, who believe

in Christ, are the children of Abraham and heirs according to the promise.

With this agrees Dr. Adam Clarke in his comment on this verse. "*Neither male nor female.* With great reason the apostle introduces this. Between the privileges of *men* and *women* there was a great disparity among the Jews. A *man* might shave his head, and rend his clothes in the time of mourning; a *woman* was not permitted to do so. A *man* might impose the vow of *nasirate* upon his son; a woman could not do this on her daughter. A *man* might be shorn on account of the *nasirate* of his father; a woman could not. A *man* might betroth his daughter; a *woman* had no such power. A *man* might sell his daughter; a *woman* could not. In many cases they were treated more like *children* than *adults;* and to this day are not permitted to assemble with the men in the synagogues, but are put up in galleries, where they can scarcely see, nor can they be seen. Under the blessed spirit of Christianity they have equal *rights,* equal *privileges,* and equal blessings, and, let me add, they are equally *useful.*"

This is all we contend for. We are in full agreement with these words of the great commentator.

Again, it is urged that Paul in express words forbids women to become ministers of the Gospel. In proof of this, two passages are quoted:

"Let your women keep silence in the churches; for it is not permitted unto them to speak; but they are commanded to be under obedience, as also saith the law. And if they will learn anything let them ask their husbands at home; for it is a shame for women to speak in the church."—1 Cor. 14:34, 35.

"Let the woman learn in silence with all subjection. But I suffer not a woman to teach, nor to usurp authority over the man, but to be in silence."—1 Tim. 2:11, 12.

1. These are the only passages of the kind in the Bible. There are no others that seem to forbid woman to preach, or to perform all the other duties of a minister of the Gospel.

2. No denomination applies these passages *literally*. If they did, they would not allow:

(1.) Women to sing in church. For to sing is not to *keep silence*.

(2.) Nor to pray; for the same reason.

(3.) Nor to testify; for to testify is to *speak*.

(4.) Nor to teach in the Sabbath school or elsewhere; for the statement is general—*I suffer not a woman to teach.*

(5.) Nor to write religious books, or for

religious periodicals; for this is to *teach.*

Notice. *Preaching is not specified.* It is forbidden only as it is one method of *breaking the silence,* one mode of *teaching.* So far, then, all are agreed that these words of Paul are not to be taken *literally.* The most rigid Presbyterians allow women to sing in the church, and to teach in the Sabbath school.

Madame Guyon, and other holy women among the Roman Catholics, have written religious books, and so have taught.

3. It is evident that Paul did not intend to prohibit women from taking any part in religious services, or even from preaching. For, *in this same epistle,* he gives directions about their dress when in public congregations they take a part in the exercises,—pray and prophesy—that is, preach.

"But every woman that prayeth or prophesieth with her head uncovered dishonoreth her head; for that is even all one as if she were shaven."—1 Cor. 11:5.

This certainly assumes that she was to pray and prophesy in public.

Then Paul did not require all women to *keep silence* in the church, in an *absolute sense.* He did permit some women *to teach,* for unless they taught how could they *edify* their hearers? He would have them so dress as not to excite the suspicion that they were not modest women.

Priscilla was a woman. Apollos was an eloquent preacher of the Gospel. But Aquila and Priscilla expounded unto Apollos the way of God more perfectly.

Paul, in his epistles, sent his salutations to several women who *labored in the Lord.* "And I entreat thee also, true yoke-fellow, help those women which labored with me in the Gospel, with Clement, also, and with other my fellow laborers, whose names are in the book of life." —Phil. 4:3. The word here translated *labored with*, is συνηθλησαν, sunethlesan, from sun, together, and athleo, to strive, the word from which is derived our word *athletic.* It means to *strive along with one, on his side, to help vigorously.*

Clement was a celebrated minister, the same, it is supposed, who was afterwards bishop of Rome. These women gave Paul the same assistance that Clement did.

"Greet Priscilla and Aquila, my helpers in Christ Jesus; who have for my life laid down their own necks; unto whom not only I give thanks, but also all the churches of the Gentiles."

Helpers, συνεργους, sunergous, *fellow workers*. It seems that they not only labored *with the apostle*, but incurred such perils for his sake as secured for them the thanks of all the Gentile churches.

With others, he salutes Mary, Junia and Julia.

"Salute Tryphena and Tryphosa, who labor in the Lord. Salute the beloved Persis, which labored much in the Lord."—Rom. 16:12.

In his comments on this verse, Dr. Clarke says: "We learn from this, that Christian *women*, as well as *men*, labored in the ministry of the word.

"Many have spent much useless labor in endeavoring to prove that these women did not *preach*. That there were some *prophetesses* as well as *prophets* in the Christian church, we learn; and that a *woman* might *pray* or *prophesy*, provided she had her *head covered*, we know; and that whoever *prophesied* spoke unto others to *edification, exhortation*, and comfort, St. Paul declares.—1 Cor. 14:3. And that no preacher can do *more*, every person must acknowledge; because to *edify, exhort* and *comfort* are the prime ends of the Gospel ministry. If *women* thus *prophesied*, then women *preached*. There is, however, much more than this implied in the Christian ministry, of which men only, and men called of God, are capable."

In this last sentence we see the power of prejudice even over so great and good a man as Dr. Clarke. What this "much more" is, of which 'men only are capable," he fails to tell us, and we are at a loss to imagine.

St. Paul himself then makes it clear that the two verses quoted above, in which he appears to forbid, in general terms, women to *speak* in meeting, or to *teach*, either *in meeting or out*, are not to be construed literally.

4. Peter says that in all of Paul's epistles *are some things hard to be understood.*—2 Pet. 3:15. Why not class among these things *hard to be understood*, what he says about women keeping silence in the churches, and conform our practice to what we find, in other passages, that women actually did in the apostolic church? We can see nothing wrong in such a course. Some churches that do not allow women to pray or testify in their public meetings, and others that permit her to go thus far, but do not allow her equal rights in the church with a man, pay no attention whatever to the prohibition of women to adorn themselves in *gold, or pearls, or costly array.*"—1 Tim. 2:9.

Yet the whole tenor of Scripture is in harmony with the latter restriction!

5. But we think what he says about women keeping silence in the church may be satisfactorily explained.

The connection in 1 Cor. 14:34 shows that the Apostle is speaking of *disorder* and *confusion*, and not of the right of women to preach. "For God is not the author of confusion."—v. 33. The man is commanded to *be silent* under certain circumstances. *But if there be no interpreter let him keep silence in the church.* —v. 28.

Is the woman to be in subjection to proper authority? So is the man. *And the spirits of the prophets are subject to the prophets.*—v. 32.

Chrysostom, who lived in the fourth century, in his comment on 1 Cor. 14:34 throws light upon this subject.

"Having abated the disturbance both from the tongues, and from the prophesyings; and having made a law to prevent confusion, that they who prophesy should be silent when another begins; he next in course proceeds to the disorder which arose from the women, rooting out their unseasonable boldness of speech; and that very opportunely. For if to them that have the gifts it is not permitted to speak inconsiderately, nor when they will, and this though they be moved by the Spirit; much less to those women who prate idly and to no purpose. Therefore he represses their babbling and that with much authority, and taking the law along with him, thus he sews up their mouths; not simply exhorting here, or giving counsel, but he even laying his commands on them vehemently, by the recitation of an ancient law on that subject. For having said, "Let your women keep silence in the churches; and, it is not permitted unto them to speak but to be under obedience, he added, as also saith the law. And where does the law say this? (Thy desire shall be to thy husband and he shall rule over thee.")

Again, speaking of the behavior of women in the church, Chrysostom says: "There is apt to be great noise among them—much clamor, and talking, and nowhere so much as in this place. They may all be seen here talking more than in the market, or at the bath. For, as if they came hither for recreation, they are all engaged in conversing upon unprofitable subjects. Thus all is confusion."

The city of Corinth was the Paris of its day. The people were gay, giddy, devoted to pleasure. The Christian church in that city was composed of such of this people as had accepted Christ. The women admitted to the liberty of the Gospel, *abused* this liberty as the men also did. The larger part of this 14th chapter of 1 Corinthians is devoted to regulations for the men. When he speaks of women, it is, not in general terms, but *your women*,—the women that yield to the disorderly spirit that prevails among you. The prohibition (in the 34th verse) was local and temporary.

Timothy was laboring among churches composed chiefly of converts from heathenism. So when Paul says in his epistle to Timothy: "I suffer not a woman to teach, nor to usurp authority over the man, but to be in silence," the words are evidently used in the same meaning as the similar words in Corinthians: When a woman is properly authorized to teach she does not *usurp authority*. The authority duly given her she has a right to exercise in a proper manner and within the proper limits.

We conclude this chapter with a saying that all must admit. The restrictions which we have been considering stand just as much in the way of a woman's doing what the churches generally permit her to do—sing, or pray, or speak as they do in the way of her ordination.

We must either go back or we must go ahead.

We must either give her equal rights with men or we must reduce her to the servitude of by-gone ages. Either we must be governed by the Christian law of love and equity, or we must take a step back into barbarism and be governed by the law of brute force. Which shall it be?

The present position of the churches is not only wrong, but inconsistent. They concede to woman too much, if Paul's words restricting her are taken literally ; they concede too little, if these words are to be so understood as to harmonize with the rest of the Bible.

> "Now, shame upon ye, parish Popes!
> Was't thus with those your predecessors,
> Who sealed with racks and fire and ropes
> Their loving kindness to transgressors?"
>
> —*Whittier.*

If woman, in using her voice, in praising God, or declaring His truth, in your churches, is a transgressor, then silence her at whatever cost; if she is doing right then remove all shackles and give her the liberty of the Gospel.

CHAPTER VII.

OBJECTIONS—NATURAL.

*"In the still air the music lies unheard ;
In the rough marble beauty hides unseen ;
To wake the music and the beauty, needs
The master's touch, the sculptor's chisel keen."*
—*Bonar.*

IT IS objected that a woman in the pulpit is out of her place; that nature never designed her to be a minister of the Gospel.

With classical literature, the old heathen ideas about woman's true position have come down to us.

Aristotle said: "The relation of man to woman is that of the governor to his subject."

It is urged that woman is naturally unfitted for the duties of a minister of the Gospel ; that Nature by its inexorable laws stands in the way of her ordination ; that she is physically disqualified for the ministerial office

If this is so then there is not the slightest necessity for closing the pulpit against her. It requires no legislation to keep sheep from plunging into the river, or fish from invading the land.

"One thing we may be certain of," says John Stuart Mill, "that what is contrary to women's nature to do, they will never be made to do by simply giving their nature free play. The anxiety of mankind to interfere in behalf of nature, for fear lest nature should not succeed in effecting its purpose, is an altogether unnecessary solicitude. What women by nature cannot do it is quite superfluous to forbid them from doing. What they can do, but not so well as the men who are their competitors, competition suffices to exclude them from; since nobody asks for protective duties and bounties in favor of women; it is only asked that the present bounties and protective duties in favor of men should be recalled. If women have a greater natural inclination for some things than for others, there is no need of laws or social inculcation to make the majority of them do the former in preference to the latter.

Whatever women's services are most wanted for, the free play of competition will hold out the strongest inducements to them to undertake. And, as the words imply, they are most wanted for the thing for which they are most fit; by the apportionment of which to them the collective faculties of the two sexes can be applied on the whole with the greatest sum of valuable result."*

No special legislation, either by church or state, is needed to give to women their proper place. Leave them as free as the men are, and they will instinctively find their true place. If a woman's true position is that of wife, she will not hesitate to accept it if the right man makes the offer. But there are more women than men in the United States. Why may not some of these become ministers of the Gospel if God calls them to the position and they are duly qualified for it?

That some women possess the physical ability to preach is no longer a question; it is a demonstrated fact that they have this ability, for some women do preach, and do successfully the most exhaustive labors of a preacher—hold protracted meetings.

What does an ordained preacher do that is a greater draft upon the physical powers than preaching, and especially holding revival services? Some women have engaged in callings that tax the physical powers more than preaching and administering the sacraments.

They are successful physicians and lawyers.

* Subjection of Women, p. 48.

Lowell, one of our popular American poets, writes:

> "They talk about a woman's sphere
> As though it had a limit;
> There's not a spot in earth or heaven,
> There's not a task to mankind given
> Without a woman in it."

The vocation of a soldier would seem to be one for which women are specially unfitted by nature. Yet whenever they have undertaken it, they have met with, at least, the average success of the men.

Deborah won more honor than Barak in the battle which they fought under her direction.

In the battle fought by Xerxes against the Greeks, which decided the destiny of Europe, the only branch of his army that drove the enemy, was that commanded by Artemisia, queen of Halicarnassus. Herodotus, styled the father of history, speaks of an army of female warriors, called "Amazons," who were by no means deficient in the qualities of good soldiers. After they settled down, he says, they "retained their ancient mode of living, both going out on horseback to hunt with their husbands and without their husbands, and joining in war, and wearing the same dress as the men."* By their rules "no virgin was per-

---

† Herodotus' History, IV:117.

OBJECTIONS—NATURAL. 73

mitted to marry till she had killed an enemy."
The Athenians based their claims to precedence over the other tribes of Greece, among other things, on the fact that they "performed a valiant exploit against the Amazons, who once made an irruption into Attica from the river Thermidon."*

It was a Greek Amazon of more recent date that the poet, Bryant, represents as singing:

> "I buckle to my slender side
> The pistol and the scimitar,
> And in my maiden flower and pride
> Am come to share the tasks of war.
> And yonder stands my fiery steed,
> That paws the ground, and neighs to go,
> My charger of the Arab breed,—
> I took him from the routed foe."

Stanley speaks of the Amazons of the King of Uganda, and says: "What strikes us most is the effect of discipline."†

During the Hundred Years' war between France and England there came a time when it seemed as if France must perish from among the nations. The English had possession of most of the large cities. The French King, Charles VI. had died, and the Parliament of Paris had recognized Henry VI. of England as "King of England and France." The rightful

---
* Herodotus' History, IX:27.
† Through the Dark Continent, V. 1, p. 400.

heir to the French throne was regarded as an indolent and frivolous prince. What remained of the French army was disheartened and demoralized. Orleans, the chief city still in possession of the French, was closely besieged by a powerful army.

At this juncture a peasant girl of sixteen announced that she was called of God to deliver the kingdom. She was unlettered, modest, industrious, and deeply pious. Her neighbors believed and respected her. To one of the French Knights who went to see her, as she was trying to find some one to take her to the King, she said: "Assuredly, I would far rather be spinning beside my poor mother; for this other is not my condition; but I must go and do the work because my Lord wills that I should do it."

"Who is your Lord?" demanded the knight.

"The Lord God," replied the maid.

"By my faith," said the knight, "I will take you to the King, God helping."

She was furnished with a coat of mail, a lance, a sword, and a horse—in short with the complete equipment of a man-at-arms.

She rode on horseback four hundred and fifty miles, with a suitable escort, in eleven days, through a country, occupied here and there by the English, and everywhere a theatre of war.

The King received her, though some of his officers were greatly displeased at seeing more confidence placed in a peasant girl than in experienced warriors.

She was examined by the Chancellor of France, the archbishop of Rheims, five bishops, the King's counsellors, and several learned doctors. The examination lasted a fortnight. Addressing one of them, a learned doctor, she said:

"I know not A. nor B.; but in our Lord's Book there is more than in your books; I come on behalf of the King of Heaven to cause the siege of Orleans to be raised, and to take the King to Rheims that he may be crowned and anointed there."

The doctors decided in Joan's favor.

They reported that, "After a grave inquiry there had been discovered in her nought but goodness, humility, devotion, honesty, simplicity. Before Orleans she professes to be going to show her sign; so she must be taken to Orleans; for to give her up without any appearance of evil on her part would be to fight against the Holy Spirit, and to become unworthy of aid from God."

She was then examined by three of the greatest ladies of the Kingdom as to her life as a woman. They found in her "nothing but truth, virtue and modesty." "She spoke to them," says the chronicle, "with such sweetness and grace that she drew tears from their eyes."

She excused herself to them for the dress she wore, though the sternest doctors had not reproached her for it. "It is more decent," said the archbishop of Embrun "to do such things in man's dress, since they must be done along with men."

She went to Orleans at the head of a small but enthusiastic band of troops.

The population received her with "joy as great as if they had seen God come down among them." "They felt," says the journal of the siege, "all of them recomforted and, as it were, disbesieged by the divine virtue which they had been told existed in this simple maid."

The English were defiant. To her summons to depart and return to their own country they replied with coarse insults. A fierce battle was fought. Joan placed a scaling ladder against a rampart and was the first to mount. She was wounded between the neck and shoulder. She felt faint, but prayed, and pulled out the arrow with her own hand. A dressing of oil was applied to the wound, and she retired and was continually in prayer.

The French were becoming tired and discouraged, and showed signs of retreating. She resumed her arms, mounted her horse, waved her banner, and rushed forward to the battle. The French took courage, the English were struck with consternation and fled. The next day they retreated and the siege of Orleans was raised.

In many other movements Joan was successful. At length the King, Charles VII., of France was crowned at Rheims.

"Anger is cruel and wrath is outrageous, but who can stand before envy ?"

Many in authority who should have been her friends, secretly plotted against her, so that her counsels were disregarded, and at last she was betrayed into the hands of the English, who burned her alive at the stake. She met fate with the same heroic devotion that had characterized her life. Two of the Judges who had condemned her to that cruel death, as she ceased to live cried out: "Would that my soul were where I believe the soul of that woman is."

And the Secretary of the King of England,

on returning from the execution, said: "We are all lost: we have burned a saint."

It is true this is an extraordinary case.

But who shall say that, in these days, when the world has so nearly led the church into captivity that God would not, if his Spirit could have free course, raise up matrons and maidens to drive back the hosts of hell, and lead on the army of believers to glorious victories?

On whatever shoulders God is pleased to place the epaulettes man should not dare pull them off.

All these examples certainly prove that some women may possess the physical strength and endurance, and the courage to discharge all the duties of an ordained minister of the Gospel.

CHAPTER VIII.

WOMEN APOSTLES.

"How ready is the man to go
Whom God hath never sent!
How timorous, diffident and slow
His chosen instrument."
—*Charles Wesley.*

"*Thus have ye made the commandment of God of none effect by your tradition.*"—*Jesus.*

IT IS assumed that there were but twelve apostles, and that the apostolical office expired with them. Nothing can be plainer than that the New Testament teaches the contrary. "And God hath set some in the church, first apostles, secondarily prophets, thirdly teachers, after that miracles, then gifts of healings, helps, governments, diversities of tongues."— 1 Cor. 12:28.

This language implies, not a temporary provision, but a permanent arrangement.

While the twelve are spoken of in the Gospel, by way of pre-eminence, as *the apostles*, yet other apostles are mentioned in the New Testament.

Thus Matthias, who was chosen to succeed Judas, is called an apostle (Acts 1:26); so are Paul and Barnabas (Acts 14:14); and so is Epaphroditus (Phil 2:25), *messenger* in our version, but *apostle* in the original; the brethren to whom Paul refers in 2 Cor. 8:23; and Andronicus and Junia, Rom. 16:7. All these in the original are called apostles.

So strong are the prejudices of even our most candid commentators that they resort to every expedient known to criticism in order so to explain this striking text (Rom. 16:7) that it will not prove that a woman was an apostle. It seems impossible to them that a woman was an apostle in the apostolic church: and they therefore feel obliged to explain away the plain declaration of Paul that Junia was an apostle.

1. They raise the question whether Junia was a woman.

Adam Clarke says: "*Junia* may probably be the name of a woman."

Dean Alford, who is usually so fair, says: "Ιουνιὰ, may be fem. from Ιουνια (Junia), in which case she is probably the wife of Andronicus,— or masc, from Ιουνιάς (Junianus contr. Junias)."

It is very significant that neither Dean Alford nor Dr. Clarke gives any reason for the doubt they suggest whether Junia was a woman. They generally abound in reasons for their opinions.

But that *Junia* was a woman there is not the slightest reason to doubt.

(1.) We have four different editions of the Greek Testament, including the text from which the Revised version was made, and they all have Ιουνιαν, Junia.

(2.) If in any of the manuscripts this word was written with the circumflex accent, showing that it might be a contraction, some of the sharp-eyed critics would have noticed it.

(3.) Chrysostom asserts positively that *Junia* was a *woman*.

2. Dr. Clarke expresses a doubt whether Junia was an apostle. He says: "*of note among the apostles.*" Whether this intimates that they were *noted apostles* or only highly respected *by the apostles*, is not absolutely clear; but the latter appears to me the most probable.

"They were not only well known to St. Paul, but also to the rest of the apostles."

Considering the prejudices of the age in which he lived, this doubt is a great concession.

But that Junia *was an apostle* will be evident to all who will carefully weigh the following reasons:

1. Dean Alford says: "Two renderings are given: (1.) '*of note among the apostles!*' so that *they themselves are counted among* the apostles; thus the Greek ff. In support of this view he refers to Chrysostom, Calvin, Est, Wolf, Tholuck, Kolln, Olshausen and others.

"Or (2.) '*noted among the apostles,*' *i. e. well known* and spoken of by the apostles. Thus Beza Grotius, Koppe, Reiche, Meyer, Fritz DeW. But, as Thol. remarks, had this latter been the meaning, we should have expected some expression like διὰ πασῶν τῶν εκκλησιων. 2 Cor. 8:18, *throughout all the churches.*

"I may besides remark, that for Paul to speak of any persons as *celebrated among the apostles*, in sense (2), would imply that he had more frequent intercourse with the other apostles than we know that he had; and would besides be improbable on any supposition. The whole question seems to have sprung up in modern times from the idea that οἱ ἀπόστολοι must mean *the Twelve only.* If the wider sense found in Acts 14:4, 14. 2 Cor. 8:23. 1. Thess. 2:6 (compare i:1) be taken, there need be no doubt concerning the meaning."

Dean Alford, then, has no doubt that Junia was an apostle.

Luther, in his German Bible, translates this clause as follows: "welche sind beruhmte Apostele." *who are renowned apostles.*

Chrysostom also makes the meaning clear beyond the shadow of a doubt. He was a man of great learning; the Greek was his native language; he was born A. D. 347, at Antioch. In his comments on this verse he says:

"*Who are of note among the apostles.* And indeed to be apostles at all is a great thing. But to be even amongst these of note, just consider what a great encomium this is! But they were of note owing to their works, to their achievements. Oh! how great is the devotion of this woman, that she should be counted worthy of the appellation of apostle! But even here he does not stop, but adds another encomium besides, and says, who were also in Christ before me."

Thus Chrysostom plainly declares, 1. That Junia was a woman. 2. That she was an apostle.

Olshausen, in his comment on Rom. 16:7, says: "Junia appears to have been the wife of Andronicus.

"The title of apostle is of course to be taken

here in the wider sense of the word." By "wider" he means not confined to the Twelve.

It is without dispute that the apostles are the highest order of the ministry. God has placed them in the highest rank.

Nowhere is it said in the New Testament that this order of the ministry became extinct with the first generation of Christians. God *has set* them in His church. No matter what arrangements men make, God raises up *apostles* from time to time. LUTHER was an *apostle*, sent by God to lead on the great Reformation.

JOHN WESLEY was an apostle.

ELIZABETH FRY was an apostle, sent by God to offer salvation to the hardest criminals; and to set in motion reformatory influences that will never cease to operate.

WILLIAM TAYLOR is as truly an apostle as St. Paul was.

Since, then, we find that, at the very beginning of the Christian church, a woman was an apostle, we should not, on account of her sex, exclude woman from any position in the church to which God may call her, and for which she possesses, in the judgment of those whose duty it is to decide in such matters, as ample qualifications as are re-

WOMEN APOSTLES.

quired of men who aspire to the same position.
It is high time that the tyranny of sex was overthrown. And the Church of Jesus Christ should lead the way in treating all human beings with absolute impartiality.

Paul says he was ordained both a preacher and an apostle.—1 Tim. 2:7; and so we may conclude that Junia was ordained.

God only can make apostles But if he sends a woman out to do the work of an apostle, and she does it faithfully, why should we hesitate to give the Scriptural name to the office, to fill which she is called and qualified of God?

> "What could I other than I did?
> Could I a singing bird forbid?
> Deny the wind stirred leaf? Rebuke
> The music of the forest brook?"
> —*Whittier.*

God gives lights that they may shine; and the church should cease its efforts to put out these lights, or to so wall them in as to limit to a small number those whom they may enlighten.

CHAPTER IX.

WOMEN PROPHETS.

> "Thyself and thy belongings
> Are not thine own so proper, as to waste
> Thyself upon thy virtues, they on thee.
> Heaven doth with us as we with torches do,
> Not light them for themselves ; for if our virtues
> Did not go forth of us, 'twere all alike
> As if we had them not."
> —*Shakespeare.*

THAT women are to take a prominent part in evangelizing the world was as clearly foretold in the prophecies of old as was the Gospel itself. The first great prophecy declares that the seed of the woman "shall bruise the serpent's head."—Gen. 3:15. As Henry Melville says, "This is a wonderful passage, spreading itself over the whole of time, and giving outlines of the history of this world from the beginning to the final consummation." It was by " the seed of the woman," Christ, that our redemption was purchased.

Not only this, but it was predicted that woman was to have a distinguished part in making the glad tidings of salvation known. "The Lord gave the word, great was the company of those that published it."—Ps. 68:11.

As these words stand, in our common version, there does not appear in them anything out of the common order. It is quite otherwise in the original.

In his comment on this verse, Dr. Adam Clarke says: "*Of the female preachers there was a great host.* Such is the literal translation of this passage ; the reader may make of it what he pleases."

We make of it a prediction that in the days spoken of in this psalm, when "Ethiopia shall stretch out her hands unto God," women were to preach the Gospel.

In the Revised version a similar meaning to Dr. Clarke's translation is given—

"The Lord giveth the word ;
The women that publish the tidings are a great host."

Bishop Horne regards this Psalm as one relating to the Messiah. He says: "It seems evidently to have been composed on that festive and joyful occasion, the removal of the ark to Mount Sion. Under this figure, David, foreseeing the exaltation of Messiah, speaks of him whom he describes as arising and vanquishing his enemies, as causing the faithful to rejoice, and showing mercy to the afflicted; as bringing his church out of bondage, supporting her in the world by the Word and the Spirit, purging away her corruptions, and subduing her adversaries."

In harmony with this, is the prophecy of Joel as quoted by St. Peter.

"And it shall come to pass in the last days, saith God, I will pour out of my Spirit upon all flesh; and your sons and your daughters shall prophesy, and your young men shall see visions, and your old men shall dream dreams; and on my servants and on my handmaidens I will pour out in those days of my Spirit and they shall prophesy."—Acts 2:18.

1. All the preaching here foretold is included in the word "prophesy."

2. No distinction whatever is made between the "sons and daughters," between the "servants and handmaidens." Whatever is affirmed of the one is affirmed of the other. No higher ministry is given to the sons than is given to the daughters. If one may be ordained so may the other.

This prediction was not exhausted on the day of Pentecost. It was to continue to be fulfilled throughout the entire Christian dispensation. This is implied in the words, *in the last days.* If on the day of Pentecost they were in "the last days," then certainly we are now in "the last days." Then are we to look for the same outpouring of the Spirit on the women as on the men. Then have they the same divine right to declare, under the influence of the Holy Spirit, the wonderful power and great willingness of Christ to save.

Under the Old Dispensation, as we have seen, women were prophets.

At the coming of Christ, Anna was a prophetess.—Luke 2:36.

But these were the exceptions. Under the Gospel, the *rule* is that upon women, equally as upon men, the prophetic influence is to be poured out, and they are to prophesy. No distinction of sex is to be observed in the power and liberty given by God to speak for Him.

It must be kept in mind that the primary meaning of prophesy is to speak for another, to speak under the direct influence of the Spirit of God.

The first place in the Bible where the word prophet occurs is where God says of Abraham: *For he is a prophet, and he shall pray for thee.*—Gen. 20:7. Here is no allusion to the foretelling of future events. Dr. Adam Clarke says: "The proper ideal meaning of the original word is, *pray, entreat, make supplication.* Thus it is said that the *Spirit of God* came upon Saul and *he prophesied.*"— 1 Sam. 10:10. But there is no intimation that he foretold future events.

But as God specially makes known His will to those who live in intimate communion with Him by prayer and faith, some of these men were inspired to foretell future events. Hence a prophet is generally considered to be one who foretells. But in the Bible sense, a prophet is one who speaks the truth of God, inspired by His Spirit, whether this truth relates to things present or to come. A large part of the writings of the prophets recorded in the Old Testament are exhortations.

St. Paul declares: *But he that prophesieth speaketh unto men to edification and exhortation and comfort.*—1 Cor. 14:3. In his comment on this verse, Dr. Clarke quotes Whitby: "The person who has the gift of *teaching* is much more useful to the church than he who has only the gift of *tongues*, because he speaks to the profit of men—viz: to their edification, by the Scriptures which he expounds; to their *exhortation* by what he teaches; and to their comfort by his revelation."

Again, *Greater is he that prophesieth.* Says

Dr. Clarke: "A useful, zealous preacher, though unskilled in learned languages, is much *greater* in the sight of God, and in the eye of sound common sense, than he who has the gift of those learned tongues; except he interpret; and we seldom find *great scholars good preachers.* This should humble the scholar who is too apt to be proud of his attainments, and despise his less learned, but more useful brother. This judgment of St. Paul is too little regarded."

We come then to these

CONCLUSIONS.

1. That prophets are an established order of ministers in the Church of Christ. It was foretold in the Old Testament, and declared in the New Testament, that they should be.

2. That they rank next to the Apostles. *And God hath set some in the church, first apostles, secondarily prophets.*—1 Cor. 12:28. See also Eph. 4:11, 12. This last passage declares that God gives them *for the work of the ministry, for the edifying of the body of Christ;* that is for the sanctification of believers and the conversion of sinners.

3. That in the New Testament sense, *prophets* are those called of God, and inspired by His Spirit to preach the Gospel.

4. That in the prophetic office not the slightest distinction is made between women and men.

5. The inference is unavoidable that if men who give satisfactory evidence to the church that they are called of God to *prophesy*, that is, to *preach* should be ordained, then women who give equally satisfactory evidence that they are called of God to preach should be ordained. We see not how this conclusion can be avoided.

If it is evident that God has called a woman to his great work, and eminently adorned her with gifts and graces for its performance, then should the church speed her on her mission by solemnly indorsing it before the world, in setting her apart for the work to which God has called her. Whether done by man or woman, it is a work worthy of all recognition,

"To guide the people in the way of truth
By saving doctrine, and from error lead,
To know, and knowing, worship God aright."

CHAPTER X.

DEACONS.

> "Not unto manhood's heart alone
> The holy influence steals ;
> Warm with a rapture not its own,
> The heart of WOMAN feels.
> As she who by Samaria's well
> The Saviour's errand sought—
> As those who with the fervent Paul
> And meek Aquila wrought.
> —*Whittier.*

IT IS generally assumed that the seven, whose appointment as assistants of the Apostles is described in Acts 6:1-6, were deacons. Probably they were. We will not question it. But the fact deserves notice that they are never called deacons. It should also be borne in mind that the only record we have of their acts is of their performing the work of a preacher of the Gospel. "And Stephen, full of faith and power, did great wonders and miracles among the people."—Acts 6:8.

"And they were not able to resist the wisdom and the spirit by which he spake."

It is said that Philip, the evangelist, was one of the seven."—Acts 21:8. So that while "the seven" were to look after the charitable distributions of the church it nowhere appears that their work was confined to this. They were assistants of the Apostles, and as such they preached.

Nothing can be clearer than that the New Testament deacons were preachers.

"Who then is Paul, and who is Apollos, but ministers,") in the original deacons,) "by whom ye believed."—1 Cor. 3:5.

"Who also hath made us able ministers (deacons), of the New Testament."—2 Cor. 3:6.

"Whereof I was made a minister (deacon)." Eph. 3:7.

"To all the saints in Christ Jesus which are at Philippi, with the bishops and deacons."—Phil. 1:1. Here the Apostle mentions but two classes or orders of ministers, one of which is the *deacons*.

"Whereof I, Paul, am made a minister (deacon).—Col. 1:23.

"Timotheus, our brother and *minister (deacon)* of God."—1 Thess. 3:2.

In short, there is not a *single passage* in which the word *deacon* is used to designate an *officer of the church*, where there is any indication that this deacon *was not a preacher.* But in the passages quoted above, and in other passages, there can be no doubt but that the person styled a *deacon* was a preacher. Then the conclusion must be that the New Testament deacons were preachers. They were all preachers.

Mosheim, in writing of the church in the first century, says: "Both presbyters and deacons preached and administered the sacrament of baptism, and the former the Lord's Supper."*

There are some passages in which the word is taken in its primary signification of *servant,* such as Mat. 23:11, John 2:5, 9, but in these passages the meaning is clear. They afford no more reason for asserting that the deacons of the church were servants, or any particular deacon was a *servant,* in the sense in which the word *servant* is commonly understood, than the use of the word *ecclesia* in Acts 19:39, proves that the same word in Rev. 2:1, shows that the "church of Ephesus" was not a church at all, but a riotous assembly.

When any words are given an ecclesiastical meaning in the New Testament they must always be understood as having that meaning when used in treating of church officers, and the connection warrants it. The word διακονος,

---
* V. 2, p. 330.

deacon, where used in the New Testament as referring to an officer of the church, when translated at all, in both our common and revised versions is uniformly translated *minister*, except in one solitary instance. *That is where it refers to a woman.* "I commend unto you Phebe, our sister, which is a servant (in the original διακονος, *deacon*) of the church which is at Cenchrea.— Rom, 16:1.

Here you see the power of prejudice in even learned and pious men. Paul, when called a *deacon*, our translators call a *minister;* but Phebe, when called a *deacon* they make a *servant.* That there might be no dispute about her sex Paul calls her, *our sister.*

That there might be no doubt about her ecclesiastical position he calls her *deacon* or *minister of the church at Cenchrea.* Nothing can be more clear; nothing can be more definite.

The churches of that day had no *servants,* in the ordinary sense of the word servant. The churches were poor. Their meetings were held in private houses. They had no church edifices.

Here, then, we have a record in the New Testament of one woman who was a *minister.*

The apostle states the qualifications which the women deacons must possess.

"Even so *must their* wives *be* grave, not slan-

DEACONS. 97

derers, sober, faithful in all things."—1 Tim. 3:11. We had read this passage hundreds of times without suspecting its meaning. Lately, in reading it in the original, its meaning struck us as if by revelation. The word translated *wives* should be *women*. *Their* before wives is not found in the original. So that what the apostle here writes, is not about the *wives of deacons*, but about *women deacons*.

Chrysostom says of this, the eleventh, verse: "Some have thought that this was said of women generally, but it is not so, for why should he introduce anything about women to interfere with his subject? He is speaking of those who hold the rank of Deaconesses.

"This must be understood, therefore, to relate to deaconesses. For that order is necessary and useful and honorable in the church. Observe how he requires the same virtue from the Deacons as from the Bishops, for though they were not of equal rank, they must equally be blameless; equally pure."

Dr. *Adam Clarke*, in his comment on this verse, says:

"I believe the apostle does not mean here the wives either of the *bishops* or *deacons* in particular, but the Christian *women* in general. The original is simply γυναικας ωσαυτως σεμνας—*gun-*

aikas osautos semnas. Let the women likewise be grave. Whatever is spoken here becomes women in general; but if the apostle had those termed *deaconesses* in his eye, which is quite possible, the words are peculiarly suitable to *them.* That there was such an *order* in the apostolic and primitive church, and that they were appointed to their office by the *imposition of hands*, has already been noticed on Rom. 16:1. Possibly, therefore, the apostle may have had this *order of deaconesses* in view, to whom it was as necessary to give counsels and cautions as to the *deacons* themselves; and to prescribe their qualifications, lest improper persons should insinuate themselves into that office."

Considering the time when Dr. Clarke wrote, this was saying a great deal.

Dean Alford, one of the most learned of modern commentators, is still more explicit. In his Greek Testament, on this passage he says: "(The) women in like manner. Who are these? Are they (1) women who were to serve as deacons,—deaconesses?— or (2) wives of the deacons?—or (3) wives of the deacons and overseers?—or (4) women in general? I conceive we may dismiss (4) at once, for Chrysostom's reason.

'For why should he wish to insert anything

DEACONS.

about women foreign to the subject of which he was speaking'?

(3.) Upheld by Calv. Est. Calev. and Mack, may for the same reason, seeing that he re-returns to διακονοι, *diakonoi ;* again in verse 12, be characterized as extremely improbable. (2) has found many supporters among modern commentators; Ludi, Beza. Beng., (who strangely adds, 'pendet ab *habentes*, ver. 9,) Rosenm. Heinr, Comyb., al., and E. V. But it has against it (*a*) the omission of all expressed reference to the deacons, such as might be given by αυτων, *auton their*, or by τάς *tas, they ;* (*b*) the expression of ωσαυτως, (osautos, likewise,) by which the διακονοι (deacons) themselves were introduced, and seems to mark a new ecclesiastical class; (*c*) the introduction of the injunction respecting the deacons, εστωσαν μιας γυναικος ανδρες (husbands of one wife) as a new particular, which would hardly be if their wives had been mentioned before; (*d*) the circumstances connected with the mention of Phebe as διακονος (deacon) of the church at Cenchrea on Rom. 16:1, that unless these are deaconesses, there would be among these injunctions no mention of an important class of persons employed as officers of the church.

We come thus to consider (1) that these

γυναικες are *deaconesses*, ministrae, *ministers*, as Pliny calls them in his letter to Trajan. In this view the ancients are, as far as I know, unanimous, Of the moderns, it is held by Grot. Marb. Micb. DeW., Wiesinger, Ellicott. It is alleged against it—(*a*) that thus the return to the διακονοι, (deacons), ver. 12, would be harsh, or as Conyb. "on that view, the verse is most unnaturally interpolated in the midst of the discussion concerning the deacons."

But the ready answer to this is found in Chry's. view of ver 12, that under διακονοι, and their household duties he comprehends in fact both sexes under one; ταῦτα καί περί γυναικῶν διακόνων ἁρμόττει εἰρῆσθαι—("it is fitting that these things should be said about women deacons;") (*b*) that the existence of deaconesses as an order in the ministry is not after all so clear. To this it might be answered, that even were they nowhere else mentioned, the present passage stands on its own grounds; and if it seemed from the context that such persons were indicated here, we should reason from this to the fact of their existence, not from the absence of other mention to their non-indication here.

'I decide, therefore, (1) that these women are 'deaconesses; (must be), grave, not slanderers," corresponds to Μη διλογους (not double-tongued) in the males, being the vice to which the female sex is addicted; * * διαβολος (" diabolos") in this sense (reff) is peculiar in N. T. to these epistles; "sober" corresponding to Μη οινω πολλω προσερχοντας—(not given to much wine) "faithful in all things corresponds to Μη αισχροκεδεις, (not greedy of gain;) trusting in the distribution of the alms committed to them, and in all other ministrations.

12. General directions repecting those in the diaconate (of both sexes, the female being included in the male, see Chrys., cited above with regard to their domestic condition and duties, as above (verses 4, 5), respecting the episcopate."

We have given this learned note in full that none might think they are reading only a garbled extract. The careful English reader will have no difficulty in understanding it with the translations we have given.

Notice 1. That though he gives the strongest authorities to be found against his opinion, yet he himself is not in doubt as to the true meaning of the verse in question.—1 Tim. 3:11.

2. "I decide." What does he decide? That the apostle refers in this verse, not to women in general, nor to the wives of deacons, but to "women deacons, deaconesses." This is the

conclusion of Dean Alford of the church of England, one of the most learned and honored of English prelates. With this view the most learned of modern commentators agree. Olshausen's Commentary, edited by Prof. Kendrick, says on 1 Tim. 3:11: "It will scarcely admit of a doubt that γυναικες (gunaikes) here is to be understood as deaconesses. The apostle having specified the moral qualifications of a deacon, is led by the homogeneousness of the office to connect with those such as are proper to deaconesses.

The American Commentary, edited by Alvah Hovey, D. D. LL. D., has the following on this verse: "Women in like manner—that is women filling the deacon's office, deaconesses." After giving contrary opinions, he says: "Decisive reasons, however, seem here to require its reference to the deaconesses, who may, indeed, often have been the wives of deacons, but who are here mentioned as the female members of the diaconate."

Jamieson, Faussett and Brown, in their comment on this verse, say:
"THEIR WIVES," rather "the women," *i. e.*, "the deaconesses." For there is no reason that special rules should be laid down as to the wives of the deacons, and not also as to the wives

DEACONS.   103

of the Bishops or overseers. Moreover, if the wives of the deacons were meant, there seems no reason for the omission of "their" (not in the Greek.) Also the Greek for "even so," (the same as for "likewise," v. 8, and "in like manner," ch. 2:9,) denotes a transition to another class of persons.

"Further, there were doubtless deaconesses, at Ephesus, such as Phœbe was at Cenchrea (Rom. 16-1, "servant," Greek, "deaconess"), yet no mention is made of them in this epistle if not here; whereas, supposing them to be meant here, ch. 3, embraces in due proportion all the persons in the service of the church. Naturally, after specifying the qualifications of the deacons, Paul passes to those of the kindred office, the deaconess. "Grave" occurs in the case of both.

"Not slanderers" here, answers to "not double-tongued" in the deacons; so "not false accusers." (Titus 2:3.)

"Sober" here answers to "not given to much wine" in the case of the deacons, (v. 8). Thus it appears he requires the same qualifications in female deacons as in deacons, only with such modifications as the difference of sex suggested. Pliny, in his celebrated letters to Trajan, calls them "female ministers." FAITH-

FUL IN ALL THINGS—of life as well as faith. Trustworthy in respect to the alms committed to them, and their other functions, answering to "not greedy of filthy lucre," v. 8, in the case of the deacons."

Thus we see, 1. That the officers of the New Testament church called *deacons* were preachers of the Gospel. They did other things, but these were incidental to the preaching. They were a regularly constituted and acknowledged order of the ministry. Paul addresses one of his epistles, "to all the saints in Christ Jesus which are at Philippi, with the bishops and deacons." The deacons were not laymen, but one order of the ministry.

2. That in the New Testament church some of the deacons were women.

3. That provision was made for women to be deacons in the church of Christ for all time to come, for the qualifications that they must possess are given, as well as the qualifications of the men who are deacons, and these qualifications are essentially the same.

Then the New Testament gives to the Church ample authority to ordain women for the work of the ministry.

CHAPTER XI.

DEACONESSES.

> "The breach though small at first, soon opening wide,
> In rushes folly with a full-moon tide,
> Then welcome errors of whatever size,
> To justify it by a thousand lies.
> As creeping ivy clings to wood or stone,
> And hides the ruin that it feeds upon ;
> So sophistry cleaves close to and protects
> Sin's rotten trunk, concealing its defects."
> —*Cowper.*

THE deacons of the New Testament, as we have seen, were preachers. They were assistants of the apostles. They aided them in spreading a knowledge of the Gospel; for they were to *hold the mystery of the faith in a pure conscience.*—1 Tim 3:9. They attended to the distribution of the charities of the church, and assisted in administering the sacraments.

There is not, in the New Testament, the slightest intimation that the work of the deaconesses was, *in any respect, different from that of the deacons.*

The office was one—the functions the same.

A postmistress discharges all the duties, and enjoys all of the privileges of a postmaster.

A Queen, who succeeds to the throne in her own right, possesses all the prerogatives of a King. Elizabeth of England was no less a sovereign than her father, Henry VIII, whom she succeeded.

So a deaccness, in the New Testament sense of the term, is simply a woman who possesses the functions and discharges the duties of a deacon.

Mosheim, in speaking of the Church of the first century, says : "The church had ever belonging to it, even from its very first rise, a class of ministers, composed of persons of either sex and who were termed deacons and deaconesses. Their office was to distribute the alms to the necessitous ; to carry the orders or messages of the elders wherever necessary ; and to perform various other duties, some of which related merely to the solemn assemblies that were held at stated intervals, whilst others were of a general nature."*

This opinion that the deacons and deaconesses were essentially the same, and were "a class of ministers," is doubtless correct. Their duties in the "solemn assemblies" were, in the

---
* Commentaries, v. 1, p. 176.

absence of an elder, to conduct the services and preach the word.

"Learned men," says the same historian, "have been led to conclude, and apparently with much reason, that those who had given unequivocal proof of their faith and probity in the capacity of deacons, were, after a while, elected into the order of presbyters."*

The practice of some of our modern churches of placing *deacons* where they belong, as *an order in the ministry*, eligible to promotion, and classing *deaconesses* among *lay-workers*, without any possibility of ever rising to the higher ministries of the church, has neither reason nor Scripture for its support. It is giving a stone to those who call for bread. It is conferring a shadow and withholding the substance; it is bestowing a name and keeping back that which is implied in the name. In short it is a stupendous sham, of which any body of men claiming common honesty should be ashamed. It is an insult to womankind, and should be resented by them as such. Every woman should refuse to accept the name unless there is given with it all that is implied in the name.

* Commentaries, v. 1, p. 176.

It is a wonderful presumption upon the ignorance or servility of its members, for a great church to say in its book of discipline: "The duty of a Travelling Deacon is: 1. To administer Baptism and to solemnize Matrimony. 2. To assist the Elder in administering the Lord's Supper. 3. To do all the duties of a Traveling Preacher."

"The duties of the deaconesses are to minister to the poor, visit the sick, pray with the dying, care for the orphan, seek the wandering, comfort the sorrowing, save the sinning, and, relinquishing wholly all other pursuits, devote themselves, in a general way, to such forms of Christian labor as may be suited to their abilities."

All these things may be good and important. That is not the question. But why make the duties of Deacons and Deaconesses so widely different? Why clothe the men deacons with ministerial dignity, and send them into the pulpit to preach, and into the altar to help administer the sacraments; and refuse these prerogatives to the *women deacons*, but send them to the garrets and cellars to hunt up the depraved, the destitute and the dying? Why give to the deacons the dignity and to the deaconesses the drudgery? What reason or Scripture is there

DEACONESSES. 103

for such partiality? The State does not make such odious distinctions. When Maria Theresa fell heir to the throne of Austria and Hungary, though the laws of Hungary recognized males only as successors to the Kingly power, she presented herself before her nobles with her babe in her arms, and the nobles, with one voice, shouted, "Hungarians, behold your *King!*" Not a monarch of her day had a more loyal following, or a more vigorous and glorious reign. Though a Queen she had all the prerogatives of a King.

What would be thought of a Board of Education that, in its proposals for Teachers should say:

"It shall be the duty of the School Master to instruct their pupils, maintain order and discharge the duties of a School Teacher.

"It shall be the duty of the School Mistress to look up poor children, provide for them, bind up the wounds of those that get hurt, and devote her whole time to labors among necessitous children."

All this might be necessary and useful, but the number of qualified female teachers who would apply for the position would be small.

No. The disgraceful business of insulting womanhood, by giving to woman an office with an honorable name, and then divesting that office of the functions that belong to it when filled by a man, is confined to professed churches of Jesus Christ. Women ought to put an end to it by refusing to submit to such a glaring imposition.

To relieve the suffering is a Christ-like work. In it all Christians and especially Christian ministers should bear a part. If the church depute it to some of its more devoted female members, we will not complain, but the church should not dignify these almoners of its bounty with a ministerial title, and yet forbid them to exercise the functions belonging to that order of the ministry, which bears the same title.

"And the parson made it his text that
week and he said likewise,
That a lie which is half a truth is ever
the blackest of lies,
That a lie which is all a lie may be met
and fought with outright,
But a lie which is part a truth is a
harder matter to fight."
—*Tennyson.*

That a Christian church may have women deacons is true ; but this truth loses its essence by refusing to give to this office the functions that belong to it when filled by men.

CHAPTER XII.

EVANGELIZING THE WORLD.

> "Lo! in the clouds of heaven appears
> God's well-beloved Son;
> He brings a train of brighter years,
> His Kingdom is begun.
> He comes a guilty world to bless
> With mercy, truth and righteousness."
> —*Bryant.*

THE progress of the Gospel is slow. A large part of the human race have never heard of Christ. The darkness of idolatry rests upon a great majority of the families of the Earth. The number of heathen and Mohammedans is vastly greater than the number of even nominal Christians.

In the most favored Christian lands, how few *real* Christians are found! How small the numbers who even profess to be born of God! and of these how small the proportion who give Scriptural evidence of this supernatural change! "We know that whosoever is born of God sinneth not; but he that is begotten of

God keepeth himself, and that wicked one toucheth him not "—1 Jno. 5:18.

" How monstrous," says Finney, "and how melancholy the fact, that the great mass of professing Christians to this day recognize the 7th and not the 8th chapter of Romans as their own experience! According to this, the new birth or regeneration does not break the power of the propensities over the will. The truth is, and must not be disguised, that they have not any just idea of regeneration. They mistake conviction for regeneration. They are so enlightened as to perceive and affirm their obligation to deny the flesh, and often resolve to do it, but in fact do it not. They only struggle with the flesh, but are continually worsted and brought into bondage: and this they call a regenerate state. O, sad! How many thousands of souls have been blinded by this delusion and gone down to hell!"

What is the cause of this comparative failure of Christianity? The Gospel is designed by God for all nations. It is adapted to them. It is intended for every individual. It gives a happiness that nothing else can afford. Every nation that embraces Christianity is elevated by it. Prosperity attends its progress. In its triumphal march it scatters blessings with a lavish hand. Wherever it goes, it establishes schools and churches, it builds homes and hospitals, it brings peace and comfort. Yet this outward prosperity is but "the dust of that diamond which constitutes her crowning gift—the shed blossoms of that tree of life of which the office of Christ is to dispense the immortal fruit." Even opposers of the Gospel admit the beneficent effects of the Gospel. "So conspicuous have been the triumphs of the cross in many of the most hopeless parts of the heathen world, that even the magicians of worldly philosophy begin to acknowledge that this is the finger of God, and to despair of ever being able to do the same with their enchantments."

Why then is not the Gospel carried to the ends of the earth? Why is it not preached to every creature? It is not for lack of means. Money is poured out freely for enterprises bearing the Christian name, but serving chiefly as monuments of pride. The amount expended to build and run a fashionable church would build and run a dozen equally commodious, and better adapted to the spread of Christianity. But the Gospel does not depend on edifices; it can use money, but it is not dependent upon it. The apostles went out without purse or scrip. The early evangelists had no salaries. One can be converted in a tent more easily than in a cathedral, as cathedrals are controlled. A multitude assembled under God's great canopy is as accessible to divine truth as if they were standing in Westminster Abbey. It was their out-door work which made Wesley and Whitfield the great apostles of their day.

Nor is it for lack of influence that the Gospel does not make more rapid progress in Christian and in heathen lands. Our great statesmen, and soldiers, and men of science openly avow their belief of the Gospel. Said Henry Clay: "I believe in the truth of Christianity, though I am not certain of having experienced that change of heart which divines call the new birth. But I trust in God, and Jesus, and I hope for immortality. I have tried the world and found its emptiness. It cannot fill and satisfy the human mind."

Says Stephens, a celebrated literary man of England: "In the long annals of skeptical philosophy no single name is to be found to which the gratitude of mankind has been yielded or is justly due." The benefactors of mankind are Christians. The Gospel is no longer an experiment. Its beneficent effects are seen and acknowledged. This of itself opens the way for the heralds of the cross.

In addition to all these human influences in its favor, the Gospel, wherever it is faithfully proclaimed, carries with it a divine energy that nothing but the free will of man can withstand. It is the "power of God unto salvation to every one that believeth." The promise, "Lo, I am with you alway, even unto the end of the world," still holds good. Where Christ is, there His power is exerted, silently it may be, but nevertheless powerfully for the good of all present. No other advocate has such assistance as he who, possessed of the Holy Spirit, advocates the Gospel. He may be wanting in human learning. Men may oppose him and persecute him, and put him to death, but they are not "able to withstand the wisdom and the Spirit by which he speaks." There is a convincing power in his plain, simple words to which it is difficult to reply.

Melancthon said: "That Luther's words were born, not on his lips, but in his soul."

Why, then, we repeat, does not Christianity root out all false religions? and why does it not have a more marked effect upon the lives of those who acknowledge its truth? There must be a cause.

The reason is, *that the vast majority of those*

who embrace the Gospel are not permitted to labor according to their ability, for the spread of the Gospel.

It is said that about two-thirds of all the members of all the Protestant churches ot this country are women. Yet in these churches a woman, no matter what may be her qualification, and devotion, and zeal, is not permitted to occupy the same position as a man. The superior must, sometimes, give place to the inferior. The bungler must give directions, the adept must obey. The incompetent coward must command, if no competent man is found, while the competent woman is relegated to the rear. A Deborah may arise, but the churches, by their laws, prohibit her from coming to the front. And these laws must be enforced though all others are disregarded.

In some of the churches a woman is forbidden to speak or pray in even a social meeting if men are present! In none of these, except among the Friends. is woman given the same position, or the same opportunity for advancement as the man. She is, of set purpose kept back, while cunning contrivances are adopted to make her think that she is accorded all the liberty she wants. She suffers in consequence, but the cause of God suffers most.

What a loss the world would have sustained if John Wesley had been suppressed in infancy! The work which Frances Willard is doing in the cause of temperance, and of moral reform, gives us some idea of what woman is capable of doing when left free to exercise the gifts and graces which God has given her. It is impossible to estimate the extent to which humanity has suffered by the unreasonable and unscriptural restrictions which have been put upon women in the churches of Jesus Christ. Had they been given, since the days of the first Apostles, the same rights as men, this would be quite another world. Not only would the Gospel have been more generally diffused among mankind, but its influence, where its truth is acknowledged, would have been inconceivably greater. Our so-called Christian nations would have been more in harmony with the teachings of Christ, in their laws, their institutions and their practices.

CHAPTER XIII

REQUIRED.

*" In God's own might
We gird us for the coming fight,
And, strong in Him, whose cause is ours,
In conflict with unholy powers,
We grasp the weapons He has given,
The Light, and Truth, and Love of Heaven.*
—*Whittier.*

"WHY *ordain* women as long as the right to preach is quite generally conceded to them? Why should they not be satisfied with the privileges they now enjoy?"

Reader, will you consider candidly our answers to these questions?

The last, great Command of Christ requires that they who make converts should be invested with authority to administer the sacrament of baptism. "Go ye, therefore, and teach all nations, baptizing them in the name of the Father, and of the Son, and of the Holy Ghost; teaching them to observe all things whatsoever I have commanded you, and, lo, I am with you alway, even unto the end of the world. Amen."—Mat. 28:19, 20.

Notice the close connection of *teach* and *baptize* in this important text: *Go ye, therefore, and make disciples of all the nations, baptizing them.*—R.V. This certainly implies that those who make disciples for Christ,—get sinners converted, should, as a rule, baptize them. The same persons who are commanded to make disciples are commanded to baptize them. Till they have done this, their work is not complete. The one is a part of their mission as well as the other. They who catch the fish may string the fish.

These revivalists may be "proved first," (1 Tim. 3:10,) but if found worthy and reliable, they should be clothed with authority to administer the sacraments to those whom they get converted.

If a woman, then, is permitted to hold revivals,—to do the work of an evangelist,—she should, when properly tried, if found duly qualified, be ordained. The churches must either stop her work or allow her to complete her work. Woman must either be permitted to baptize, or she must not be permitted to make converts.

By the present arrangement, the Churches

separate what God has joined together.

"Must, then, every one who gets a sinner converted, baptize him?"

We do not affirm this. But if he keeps on getting sinners converted, and is evidently called of God to make this the business of life, then the Church, when it is satisfied of this, should authorize him to administer the sacraments. Whoever makes full proof of a call to the ministry should, in due time, be invested with the full functions of the ministry.

In oriental countries, where women are kept in great seclusion, it is necessary that women should be authorized to administer baptism to their female converts. That this right is not conceded is one reason why the progress of the Gospel is comparatively so slow in those lands

Miss Fannie J. Sparkes, a well-known, able missionary to India, sends us the following incident:

"I was in camp at Bahere, in the Bareilly district, with Rev. and Mrs. J. H. Gill. We went one evening to the house of a poor, low caste man in a near village where three men and one woman were to be baptized. A number of the neighbors came in; all sat on the ground in the little enclosed yard in front of the house, the men on one side and the women on the other. The baptismal service began, and when the usual questions were asked, simplified so as to be easily understood by the candidates, the men responded readily, but the woman remained silent. Mr. Gill tried to persuade her to respond, but in vain ; and finally said to me, ' You ask her the questions.' I did so, and immediately received ready, satisfactory replies.

The three men were then baptized ; the woman was kneeling in the midst of a little group of women near Mrs. Gill and myself. As Mr. Gill was about to place his hand upon her head, with a quick, nervous movement she drew her chaddah over her face, and put her head upon the ground in a position quite out of the reach of his hand, and could not be induced to consent to the baptism that evening. We got her to promise to visit us at our tents the next morning, which she did, and after some persuasion, she again consented to be baptized. The questions were put and answered as before ; the little woman was growing painfully nervous and began to give her chaddah little twitches, as the minister was again about to place his hand upon her head. Seeing that she was likely to repeat the action of the previous evening, I placed my hand upon her head. She recognized the touch and remained perfectly quiet until the ceremony was finished."

To this woman, as to every one of the millions of women of India, the touch of the hand of any man except that of her husband means pollution. It is the necessary result of the education of centuries. Do you say it is a prejudice? If so, it is one to be admired; and one which the Church of Christ should respect. It is impossible for a nation to become a Christian nation until its women become Christians. The women of India must be reached mainly by women. Then there should be women missionaries, clothed with authority to administer all the ordinances, as well as to offer all the consolations of the Christian religion.

But Christianity is intended for all lands. It is adapted to all nations. The churches of America should adopt such regulations as will enable them to meet the wants of the people of Asia.

Again, it is unjust to invite a woman to become a worker in the Church, and then, whatever may be her qualifications, her abilities and her success, forever exclude her by arbitrary enactments from its higher ministries.

Honorable worldlings do not act so unjustly. Is a woman permitted to teach a primary class in our schools ? Then may she, when qualified, teach Latin and Greek and Algebra, become Principal and even school Superintendent. The highest scholastic honors are not withheld from her simply because she is a woman. Dartmouth and Columbia, two of our renowned Colleges, conferred, each of them, the title of LL. D. on Maria Mitchell, one of the greatest astronomers of the age.

When the captain and owner of a Mississippi river boat suddenly died, his wife assumed command, and when the civil authorities, after a rigid examination, found that she possessed the necessary qualifications, they promptly licensed her as a Captain. Her sex did not debar her from promotion in a calling for which men are specially adapted. Nor was the precedent considered dangerous. The gallant sailors did not fear that they would be superseded by women as commanders of ships.

Is a woman permitted to conduct a trial in a Justice's Court ? She may also be admitted to practice in the higher courts. There is, in the aggregate, quite a number of women lawyers in the several states. Yet the men of the world do not appear to have any apprehension lest they should be crowded out of the legal profession.

Woman owes her elevation to Christianity. She shows her appreciation by rallying around the cross of Christ.

Justice, then, demands that all barriers placed by men in the way of the elevation of woman to any office in the gift of the church be removed.

"Even if we could do without them," writes John Stuart Mill, "would it be consistent with justice to refuse to them their fair share of honor and distinction, or to deny to them the equal moral right of all human beings to choose their occupation (short of injury to others) according to their own preferences, at their own risk? Nor is the injustice confined to them; it is shared by those who are in a position to benefit by their services. To ordain that any kind of persons shall not be physicians, or shall not be advocates, or shall not be members of parliament, is to injure not them only, but all who employ physicians or advocates, or elect members of parliament, and who are deprived of the stimulating effect of greater competition on the exertions of the competitors, as well as restricted to a narrower range of individual choice."

CHAPTER XIV.

FITNESS.

> " 'Tis hers to pluck the amaranthine flower
> Of Faith, and round the Sufferer's temples bind
> Wreaths that endure affliction's heaviest shower,
> And do not shrink from sorrow's keenest wind.
> —*Wordsworth.*

NATURALLY, woman is, to say the least, equally qualified with men for the ministry of the Gospel.

A celebrated skeptic bears the following testimony to the character of woman:

"I tell you women are more prudent than men. I tell you, as a rule, women are more truthful than men. I tell you that women are more faithful than men—ten times as faithful as men. I never saw a man pursue his wife into the very ditch and dust of degradation and take her in his arms. I never saw a man stand at the shore where she had been morally wrecked, waiting for the waves to bring back even her corpse to his arms; but I have seen woman do it. I have seen woman with her white arms lift man from the mire of degradation, and hold him to her bosom as though he were an angel."

Dr. Lardner says of the women of Jerusalem in the days of Christ: "The number of women who believed in Jesus as the Christ, and professed faith in Him was not inconsiderable. Many of these there were, who had so good understanding, and so much virtue, as to overcome the common and prevailing prejudice. Without any bias or passion or worldly interests, and contrary to the judgments and menaces of men in power, they judged rightly in a controverted point, of as much importance as was ever debated on earth."*

A Greek writer of the second century said: "It is wonderful what women these Christians have."

1. Women comprehend and drink in the Spirit of the Gospel more readily than men.

Christ very plainly told the Twelve that he would rise again the third day. But they did not seem to understand it. But the women appeared to understand it ; and, at early dawn, on the third morning "came Mary Magdalene and the other Mary to see the sepulchre." They were on the lookout, and to them Christ

---
* Works, v. ix. p. 437.

first showed himself after his resurrection. It was a woman that he commissioned to go to his disciples and foretell them of his ascension. Woman entered readily into the spirit of his words. It was in the apostolic church that woman began to teach the teachers of the Christian religion. Fettered as she has been, Christianity owes much to her for the progress it has already made.

Clovis, King of the Franks, was a great warrior, and a pagan. His people, too, were idolaters. He married Clotilde, a Burgundian princess, a Christian, absorbed in works of piety and charity. Through her influence he became a Christian. To Remi, a godly bishop whom his wife had sent for, in about the year A. D. 496, to baptize him, he said: "I will listen to thee, most holy father, willingly; but there is a difficulty. The people that follow me will not give up their gods." The King called the people together. They were better disposed than he thought they were. The influence of his wife had been more powerful than he supposed. The great multitude cried out: "We abjure the mortal gods; we are ready to follow the immortal God whom Remi preacheth." So France became a Christian nation.

About the year A. D. 568, Ethelbert, King

of Kent in England, married Bertha, the only daughter of Caribert, King of Paris, one of the descendants of Clovis. Ethelbert and his Saxons were fierce warriors, and staunch idolaters. But his wife, devout, irreproachable in conduct, exerted her influence to the utmost, for the conversion of her husband, and the Anglo-Saxons with their King embraced Christianity.

If woman has done so much, under the restrictions placed upon her in the days of barbarism, under the reign of force, and which have been perpetuated to our day, what might she not have done had all restrictions on account of sex been removed, and she been free to exert her abilities to the utmost in the cause of Christ?

Fenelon was one of the most godly, learned and useful ministers that has ever taught in the Roman Catholic church. But he was free to acknowledge that he received spiritual instruction from Madame Guion. His writings on religious experience are read with deep interest by Protestants to this day.

The work begun by John Wesley was carried on mainly by uneducated preachers. But for his employment of these lay-preachers, there is no reason to believe that the work of Wesley would have had any greater permanence than did that of Whitefield. But for the adoption of this powerful agency Wesley was indebted to his mother.

Mr. Wesley was a strong churchman, and could not tolerate any violation of what he considered the order of the Church. Thomas Maxfield was the first layman among his followers who attempted to preach.

"It was," says Dr. Adam Clarke, "in Mr. Wesley's absence that Mr. Maxfield began to preach. Being informed of this new and extraordinary thing, he hastened back to London to put a stop to it. Before he took any decisive step, he spoke to his mother on the subject, and informed her of his intention. She said, (I have had the account from Mr. Wesley himself):

'My son, I charge you before God, beware what you do ; for Thomas Maxfield is as much called to preach the Gospel as you were.' This was one of the last things that a person of such high church principles might be expected to accede to."*

But in this, as in many other things, Mr. Wesley followed the advice of his mother. The survival of Methodism is largely, and I think wholly, due to this. If the work had

* The Wesley Family, p. 412.

been carried on only by the labors of clergymen of the Church of England, it never would have attained to the proportions it did; and it would have been absorbed by the Church.

If, then, women are quicker than men to comprehend the mystery of godliness, if they have keener spiritual perceptions, and deeper intuitions, they should not be, by arbitrary enactments, excluded on account of their sex, from any position that can make their influence more widely felt. Every one should be placed in the position where she can do most good.

2. *Woman has a special aptitude for teaching.*

This is acknowledged by the general selection of women to teach in our public schools. They succeed as teachers.

In the work of the ministry, so far as they have been permitted to attempt it, women have acquitted themselves as creditably as men.

Where they have labored, prejudices have been removed.

His biographer says that Adam Clarke had "considerable prejudice against this kind of ministry." But he went to a circuit on which *Miss Mary Sewel* had preached.

"Meeting her, he questioned her concerning

her call. She modestly answered, by referring him to the places where she had preached, and wished him to inquire whether any good had been done. He did so, and heard of numbers who had been awakened under her ministry, and with several of them he conversed, and found their experience in Divine things Scriptural and solid. He thought, then, This is God's work, and if he chooses to convert men by employing such means, who am I that I should criticise the ways of God?"

After hearing her preach he wrote: "I have this morning heard Miss Sewel preach; she has a good talent for exhortation, and her words spring from a heart that evidently feels deep concern for the souls of the people; and consequently her hearers are interested and affected. I have formerly been no friend to female preaching, but my sentiments are a little altered. If God give to a holy woman a gift for exhortation and reproof, I see no reason why it should not be used. This woman's preaching has done much good; and fruits of it may be found copiously in different places in the circuit. I can therefore adopt the saying of a shrewd man, who, having heard her preach, and being asked his opinion of the lawfulness of it, answered, 'An *ass* reproved Balaam, and a cock reproved Peter, and why may not a *woman* reprove sin ?'

"Such women should be patterns of all piety, of unblamable conversation, correct and useful in their *families*, and furnished to every good work. This certainly is the character of Miss Sewel, and may she ever maintain it."

Hearing another woman preacher, Mrs. Proudfoot, he wrote: "She spoke several pertinent things, which tended both to conviction and consolation ; and seems to possess genuine piety. If the Lord choose to work in this way, shall my eye be evil because he is good ? God forbid ! Rather let me extol the God who, by contemptible instruments and the foolishness of preaching, saves those who believe in Jesus. Thou, Lord, choosest to confound the wisdom of the world by *foolishness,* and its *strength* by *weakness*, that no soul may glory in thy presence, and the excellency of the power may be seen to belong to thee alone. Had not this been the case, surely I had never been raised up to call sinners to repentance."

This testimony is the more valuable, coming from a reluctant witness, who confesses that he was prejudiced.

To the objection that such cases are exceptions, we reply in the words of John Stuart Mill:

"It is not sufficient to maintain that women on the average are less gifted than men on the average, with certain of the higher mental faculties, or that a smaller number of women than of men are fit for occupations and functions of the highest intellectual character. It is necessary to maintain that no women at all are fit for them, and that the most eminent women are inferior in mental faculties to the most mediocre of the men on whom those functions at present devolve. For if the performance of the function is decided either by competition, or by any mode of choice which secures regard to the public interest, there needs be no apprehension that any important employments will fall into the hands of women inferior to the average men, or to the average of their male competitors. The only result would be that there would be fewer women than men in such employments; a result certain to happen in any case, if only from the preference always likely to be felt by the majority of women for the one vocation in which there is nobody to compete with them. Now, the most determined depreciator of women will not venture to deny, that when we add the experience of recent times to that of ages past, women, and not a few, merely, but many women, have proved themselves capable of everything, perhaps without a single exception, which is done by men, and of doing it successfully and creditably. The utmost that can be said is, that there are many things which none of them have succeeded in doing as well as they have been done by some men—many in which they have not reached the very highest rank. But there are extremely few, dependent on mental faculties, in which they have not attained the rank next the highest. Is not this enough, and much more than enough, to make it a tyranny to them, and a detriment to society, that they should not be allowed to compete with men for the exercise of these functions? Is it not a mere truism to say, that such functions are often filled by men far less fit for them than numbers of women, and who would be beaten by women in any fair field of competition?"

3. The practical turn of woman's mind specially fits her for the work of the Gospel ministry.

Women generally are not given to abstractions. They make the most of the realities about them. Cases occur where the father of a family, overwhelmed with misfortune, dies in despair; the mother, though unused to the management of affairs, gathers up the fragments, gradually retrieves their fortunes, and raises her family in respectability and honor.

In the year 1348 a fearful plague, which started in China, visited Europe. In London, one hundred thousand people died. Italy lost half its inhabitants. It is estimated that in Europe twenty-five million people perished. The survivors were panic-stricken. Men tried to stop the plague by murdering the Jews. In Mayence alone, twelve thousand of this persecuted race were sacrificed in the vain hope of stopping the ravages of this terrible plague.

Then they tried a painful, humiliating penance. They formed companies, called Flagellants, and marched from town to town in processsion, robed in sombre garments, with red crosses on their breasts, their faces bent down, and bearing in their hands triple scourges having points of iron, with which, at stated times, they lacerated their bodies till the blood ran down to the ground.

The women, more sensible, formed bands to nurse and tend the sick. The miseries they could not prevent they sought to alleviate.

This disposition of woman to look at the present, and make the best of existing circumstances, would be of great benefit to the cause of Christianity if all restrictions on account of sex were removed, and she were left free to do good according to her inclination and ability.

4. Women are not wanting in the courage and fortitude essential to the minister of the Gospel. The bold Peter denied Christ, but the New Testament gives us no account of any woman who opened her mouth against him in the face of danger. The annals of the church, in the days of persecution, tell us of many a noble, tender, gentle woman who met death in its most terrific form rather than deny Christ.

At Port Royal, in the days of Louis XIV., were assembled some women of noble birth and great talents, who had consecrated themselves wholly to God, and who made it their one business to serve and please Him in all things. Though devout Catholics, the doctrine of holiness which they taught rendered them obnoxious to worldly ecclesiastics and a corrupt court. The Archbishop of Paris made them a visit to persuade them to renounce their faith. Not succeeding, he said angrily as he left:

"They are pure as angels and proud as demons."

Persecution was kindled against them. To a friend who came to see her, Mother Angelica said:

"Madame, when there is no God I shall lose courage; but so long as God is God, I shall hope in Him."

Jacqueline Pascal wrote: "What have we to fear? Banishment and dispersion for the nuns, seizure of temporalities, imprisonment and death, if you will; but is not that our glory, and should it not be our joy? Let us renounce the Gospel or follow the maxims of the Gospel, and deem ourselves happy to suffer somewhat for righteousness' sake. I know that it is not for daughters to defend the truth, though one might say, unfortunately, that since the bishops have the courage of daughters, the daughters must have the courage of bishops: but, if it is not for us to defend the truth, it is for us to die for the truth, and suffer everything rather than abandon it."

Of woman's mental ability to meet all the requirements of the Christian ministry, but little more need be said. It is not long, since colleges were closed against women, because they were not thought capable of acquiring a complete and thorough education. But experience has demonstrated that there are women capable of standing side by side with men in the highest departments of scholarship.

The higher mathematics are generally considered the severest test of intellectual strength. Yet several women have excelled as mathematicians. Caroline Herschel, who died in 1848, aged 98 years, was one of the great astronomers of the world. She was elected a member of the Royal Society, which conferred on her their gold medal for completing the catalogue of nebulae and stars observed by her brother. One of her astronomical works was published at the expense of the Royal Society.

In the colleges to which young women are admitted, they at least come up to the average standing of young men.

If, then, woman has the spiritual discernment, the aptitude for teaching, the prudence and courage necessary to qualify her for the work of the ministry in all its departments, why not ordain her ? Why deprive the church and the world, in any degree, of the services they need, and which she is able and willing to render ?

CHAPTER XV.

GOVERNING.

> "Mightier far
> Than strength of nerve, or sinew, or the sway
> Of magic potent over sun and star,
> Is love, though oft to agony distrest,
> And though his favorite seat be feeble woman's breast."
> —*Wordsworth.*

"IF women are ordained, it will open the way for them to take a prominent part in the Government of the Church."

And why should they not? "Because Paul says: 'I suffer not a woman to usurp authority over the man.'"—1 Tim. 2:12.

But to exercise authority with which one is *lawfully invested*, is not to *usurp* authority. Queen Victoria exercises authority over men; but she is not a usurper.

Dean Alford translates this passage, *nor to lord it over.*

In the original, the word is αυθεντειν, authentein, *to be a despot.* Neither must *men be lords over God's heritage.*—1 Pet. 5:3.

Women took a prominent part in the government of the apostolic church.

The apostles, inspired as they were, did not assume to govern the Church. They recognized the authority to govern as belonging *to the church itself—to the men, and women* of whom it was composed.

The first Christian church met in Jerusalem, in an upper room. *The women* are specially mentioned as being present.—Acts 1:14. Peter stood up in the midst of the disciples, and addressed them: "Men and brethren." These words, like the word "disciples," are generic terms, and include both men and women. He told them that, out of the men who had companied with them from the beginning, "must one be ordained to be a witness with us of his resurrection."—Acts 1:22. *And they appointed two.* The word "they" here refers to the whole body of the disciples, of whom "there were together about one hundred and twenty." Thus the members of the Church, and not the apostles, made the selection.

Again, when the twelve needed assistants to minister to the necessities of dependent believers, they did not themselves make the selection. They called together *the multitude of the disciples.* That this *multitude* included women, there can be no question. To them the apostles said: "Wherefore, brethren, look ye out among you seven men of honest report, full of the Holy Ghost and wisdom, whom we may appoint over this business."— Acts 6:3. "*And this saying pleased the whole multitude.*" They chose seven: "Whom they set before the apostles; and when they had prayed, they laid their hands on them."—Acts 6:6. The *whole* does not mean *a part*—much less the smaller part. He who asserts that women had no place in this transaction must furnish proof for the assertion. But none can be had. The *whole multitude* of the disciples comprehends women.

There is no Scripture which forbids the ordination of woman on the ground that, being ordained, she will have a part in the government of the church.

The *elders* were rulers, in both the Jewish and the Christian church. "Let the elders that rule well be counted worthy of double honor, especially they who labor in the word and doctrine."—1 Tim. 5:17. The word "elder," in the original, as in the English, is in the comparative degree. It is found sixty-seven times in the New Testament. In sixty-three passages it evidently means a church officer. It is used in the following passages only, in its primary signification of *one older* than another. "Now his *elder* son was in the field."—Luke 15:22. "And your *old men* shall dream dreams.—Acts 2:17. "Likewise ye younger submit yourselves unto the *elder*.—1 Pet. 5:5.

Concerning one passage is there a doubt. "Rebuke not an elder but entreat him as a father."—1 Tim. 5:1. If, as the translators of both our common, and of the Revised, versions, appear to think, the word *elder* here denotes an officer of the church, then we contend the same meaning should be given it in the second verse, which is a part of the same sentence. Then it would read: "The women elders as mothers," instead of "the elder women."

No writer who aims at clearness would use, in the same connection, and in the same sentence, the word King in one sense, and the word Queen in another.

If the word elder is to be taken here, where it refers to men, as it is used generally in the New Testament, to denote an officer of the church, then must it have the same meaning in the same sentence where it refers to women.

We must not change the meaning of words, as is done when πρεσβυτερος, presbuteros, is translated "elder" in one clause of this verse, and the same word, in the feminine form, is translated "elder women" in another clause of the same sentence. This appears to be done in order to adjust this text to the theory, that women must not have the same part as men in the governing of the church.

That woman possesses the administrative ability to exercise properly all the governing power usually vested in ordained preachers of the Gospel, is fully demonstrated by experience. That some women can govern well, we know, because some women have governed well. It is not a matter of theory. It is a demonstrated fact. Occasionally a woman has been placed at the head of the government of a country. In all such cases her administration will compare favorably with that of the men who preceded and followed her. Queen Elizabeth's reign was not eclipsed by that of any monarch of her day. The historian Hume says of Elizabeth :

"Few sovereigns of England succeeded to the throne in more difficult circumstances, and none ever conducted the government with such uniform success and felicity.

"Her vigor, her constancy, her magnanimity, her penetration, vigilance, address, are allowed to merit the highest praises, and appear not to have been surpassed by any person that ever filled a throne.

"Though unacquainted with the practice of toleration, the true secret for managing religious factions, she preserved her people by her superior prudence, from those confusions in which theological controversy had involved all the neighboring nations; and though her enemies were the most powerful princes of Europe, the most active, the most enterprising, the least scrupulous, she was able by her vigor to make deep impressions on their states; her own greatness, meanwhile, remained untouched and unimpaired.

"The wise ministers and brave warriors who flourished under her reign, share the praise of her success; but instead of lessening the applause due to her, they make great addition to it. They owed, all of them, their advancement to her choice; they were supported by her constancy; and, with all their abilities, they were never able to acquire any undue ascendant over her. In her family, in her court, in her kingdom, she remained equally mistress."[*]

Catharine II. of Russia was one of the ablest monarchs of her day. She was a German

---
[*] History 4, 342, 3.

princess by b'rth. Elizabeth, Empress of Russia, chose her to become the wife of her nephew Peter, heir to her throne. On seeing her betrothed, the princess was so disappointed that she became sick, and was confined to her bed for weeks. However, she resigned herself to her fate; and was married at the age of seventeen. She applied herself to study, and mastered the Russian language, became familiar with the customs of the people, and won their affections.

Elizabeth died January 5, 1762, and Peter III. ascended the throne of Russia. He banished his wife to a separate abode, and abandoned himself to drunkenness and debauchery. At the instigation of his mistress he formed the design of divorcing his wife, and raising his mistress to the throne. Encouraged by the nobles, the Archbishop proclaimed Catharine Empress of Russia, while Peter was lying drunk at his chateau twenty-four miles from St. Petersburg. This bold undertaking met with the hearty approval of the people and the army. Her reign was a long one and did much to raise Russia to its high position among the nations. She died Nov. 10, 1796.

"Few sovereigns," says Allison, "will occupy a more conspicuous place in the page of history, or have left in their conduct on the throne, a more exalted reputation. Prudent in council, and intrepid in conduct, cautious in forming resolutions, but vigorous in carrying them into execution; ambitious, but of great and splendid objects only; passionately fond of glory, without the alloy, at least in public affairs, of sordid or vulgar inclinations; discerning in the choice of her counsellors, and swayed in matters of state only by lofty intellects; munificent in public, liberal in private, firm in resolution, she dignified a despot's throne by the magnanimity and patriotism of a more virtuous age."*

"Victoria, Queen of England, and Empress of India, furnishes a still better illustration of the capacity of woman to govern. For, she has not only proved herself one of the first rulers of the age; but she has given the world an illustrious example of noble womanhood in the several relations of daughter, wife and mother.

When a modest, shrinking girl of eighteen, she was awakened early one morning, long before day, by a visit from the Archbishop of Canterbury and several nobles, who came to salute her as Queen of England. She dropped

---
* History of Europe, Vol. 1, p. 425.

upon her knees and begged the archbishop to pray for her.

On the 20th of June, 1837, as she stood in an assembly composed of the highest nobility, veteran officers and statesmen of the Kingdom, she heard it officially proclaimed that "The high and mighty Princess, Alexandrina Victoria is the only lawful and rightful liege lady, and, by the grace of God, Queen of the United Kingdom of Great Britain and Ireland, Defender of the Faith." Overcome with emotion, she threw her arms around her mother's neck and burst into tears. The august assemblage was deeply moved. The young Queen soon won the hearts of her people.

No country of the world has been better governed than Great Britain has, during her long and peaceful reign. She has manifested the deepest interest in the highest welfare of her people, has selected wise and just, and patriotic men to administer the affairs of the government, and has pursued an equitable policy towards other nations. In the general upheaval among the thrones of Europe some years ago, hers remained secure, protected by the loving loyalty of her people. In her high position, her domestic example has been a great blessing to the world at large, while her beneficent reign has secured for her people unparallelled prosperity.

"We know," says Mill, "how small a number of reigning queens history presents, in comparison with that of Kings. Of this smaller number, a far larger proportion have shown talents for rule; though many of them have occupied the throne in difficult periods. It is remarkable, too, that they have, in a great number of instances, been distinguished by merits the most opposite to the imaginary and conventional character of women; they have been as much remarked for the firmness and vigor of their rule, as for its intelligence. When, to queens and empresses, we add regents, and viceroys of provinces, the list of women who have been eminent rulers of mankind swells to a great length."

"But," it is retorted, "women reign so successfully by placing in important offices men of eminent ability."

The objection only proves the fitness of women to govern. The highest quality of a talent to rule, is the ability to select the most competent persons to fill the various subordinate offices. Napoleon not only knew how to plan a campaign, but he knew whom to select for officers to fight the battles. If woman possesses an instinctive insight into character, in a greater degree than man, then she is naturally, to that degree, in that respect, better fitted to fill positions of responsibility.

If she can, as she has done, successfully fill the thrones of Russia and Austria and Great Britain, then may she, with safety, be left free to fill any position in the church to which she may be called.

The church has no right to forbid the free exercise of abilities to do good which God has given. To do so is ursurpation and tyranny.

Men had better busy themselves in building up the temple of God, instead of employing their time in pushing from the scaffold their sisters, who are both able and willing to work with them side by side.

All restrictions to positions in the church based on race have been abolished; it is time then that those based on sex were also abolished.

CHAPTER XVI.

HEATHEN TESTIMONY.

"O, small shall seem all sacrifice
And pain and loss,
When God shall wipe the weeping eyes,
For suffering give the victor's prize,
The crown for cross!"
—*Whittier.*

PLINY, the younger, was born in Italy in A. D. 62. He was praetor under the Emperor Domitian, and Consul under Trajan. He was sent by the latter into Pontus and Bithynia as governor.

About the year 107, Pliny wrote the following letter to the Emperor Trajan. We give the translation of Dr. Nathaniel Lardner:

"Pliny to the Emperor Trajan wisheth health and happiness.

"It is my constant custom, sir, to refer myself to you in all matters concerning which I have any doubt, for who can better direct me where I hesitate, or instruct me where I am ignorant? I have never been present at any trials of Christians; so that I know not well what is the subject-matter of punishment, or of inquiry, or what strictness ought to be used in either. Nor have I been a little perplexed to determine whether any difference ought to be made upon account of age, or whether the young and tender, and the full-grown and robust, ought to be treated all alike : whether repentance should entitle to pardon, or whether all who have once been Christians ought to be punished, though they are now no longer so ; whether the name itself although no crimes be detected, or crimes only belonging to the name ought to be punished. Concerning all these things I am in doubt.

"In the meantime I have taken this course with all who have been brought before me, and have been accused as Christians. I have put the question to them, whether they were Christians. Upon their confessing to me that they were, I repeated the question a second and a third time, threatening also to punish them with death. Such as still persisted, I ordered away to be punished ; for it was no doubt with me, whatever might be the nature of their opinion, that contumacy, and inflexible obstinacy, ought to be punished. There were others of the same infatuation, whom, because they are Roman citizens, I have noted down to be sent to the city.

"In a short time, the crime spreading itself, even whilst under persecution, as is usual in such cases, divers sorts of people came in my way. An information was presented to me without mentioning the author, containing the names of many persons, who upon examination denied that they were Christians, or had ever been so; who repeated after me an invocation of the gods, and with wine and frankincense made supplication to your image, which for that purpose I have caused to be brought and set before them, together with the statues of the deities. Moreover, they reviled the name of Christ. None of which things, as is said, they who are really Christians can by any means be compelled to do. These, therefore, I thought proper to discharge.

"Others were named by an informer, who at first confessed themselves Christians, and afterwards denied it. The rest said they had been Christians, but had left them; some three years ago, and some longer, and one, or more, above twenty years. They all worshiped your image, and the statues of the gods; these also reviled Christ. They affirmed that the whole of their fault, or error, lay in this, that they were wont to meet together on a stated day before it was light, and sing among themselves alternately, a hymn to Christ, as a God, and bind themselves by an oath, not to the commission of any wickedness, but not to be guilty of theft, or robbery, or adultery, never to falsify their word, nor to deny a pledge committed to them, when called upon to return it. When these things were performed, it was their custom to separate, and then to come together again to a meal, which they ate in common, without any disorder; but this they had forborne, since the publication of my edict, by which, according to your commands, I prohibited assemblies.

"After receiving this account I judged it the more necessary to examine, and that by torture, two maid-servants, which were called ministers. But I have discovered nothing, beside a bad and excessive superstition.

"Suspending, therefore, all judicial proceedings, I have recourse to you for advice; for it has appeared unto me a matter highly deserving consideration, especially upon account of the great number of persons who are in danger of suffering. For many of all ages, and every rank, of both sexes likewise, are accused, and will be accused. Nor has the contagion of this superstition seized cities only, but the lesser towns, also, and the open country. Nevertheless, it seems to me that it may be restrained and corrected. It is certain that the temples, which were almost forsaken, begin to be more frequented. And the sacred solemnities, after a long intermission, are revived. Victims likewise are everywhere bought up, whereas for some time there were few purchasers. Whence it is easy to imagine what numbers of men might be reclaimed, if pardon were granted to those who shall repent."

So writes Pliny. We are now to observe the Emperor's rescript.

"Trajan to Pliny wisheth health and happiness.

"You have taken the right method, my Pliny, in your proceedings with those who have been brought before you as Christians; for it is impossible to establish any one rule that shall hold universally. They are not to be sought for. If any are brought before you, and are convicted, they ought to be punished. However, he that denies his being a Christian, and makes it evident in fact, that is, by supplicating to our gods, though he be suspected to have been so formerly, let him be pardoned upon repentance. But in no case of any crime whatever, may a bill of information be received without being signed by him who presents it;

for that would be a dangerous precedent, and unworthy of my government."

There are many things in this letter of Pliny of great importance.

1. It shows the great influence that Christianity was already exerting upon the minds of the people. The temples of the gods *were almost forsaken.* Christianity spread so rapidly that it was called *a contagion.* It affected alike cities and towns and the open country.

2. It is a striking testimony to the purity of the character of these Christians. Though their enemies, to justify their treatment of them, accused them of gross crimes, a strict investigation resulted in finding that their lives were blameless and their adherence to the doctrines and morals of the Gospel firm and unwavering. They bound themselves by an oath, *not to the commission of any wickedness, but not to be guilty of theft, or robbery, or adultery, never to falsify their word, nor to deny a pledge committed to them, when called upon to return it.*

3. It shows that they held to the doctrine of the Divinity of Christ. They sang hymns *to Christ* as a God.

4. But the point to which I wish to call particular attention is the fact that the *Ministers*

of this church were women. This is seen—1. In Pliny's express statement, "which were called ministers." That women are meant is perfectly clear in the Latin word, ministrae, which is in the feminine gender. That this word is not used to designate their condition is plain; for that is expressed by the word *ancillis*—maid servants. 2. He would *naturally* examine the officers of the church.

Here is a governor possessed of arbitrary power. A hated, despised society is charged with secretly holding pernicious doctrines, and practicing abominable rites.

The governor is determined to go to the root of the matter, and ascertain the truth in the case. He examines witnesses in the usual way, and finds out nothing to their disadvantage. He now determines to adopt the last resort known to ancient despots, and to examine by torture. But who shall he examine? Who would he naturally select as being in possession of all the secrets of the society?

Evidently those who occupy the *highest position* in the society, who understand all its mysteries, and are acquainted with all its doings—its officers or teachers. So, too, when Pliny says that these two women *were called ministers,* he uses the term minister in the sense in which the Christians understood it—in the ecclesiastical sense. He does not himself call them "ministers;" if he did, it might be claimed that he uses the word in its secular sense, "a female attendant or assistant," though in the classics it is sometimes used to denote a "ministress at religious worship." But Pliny says, "they are called ministers," that is, by the Christians.

Nothing is said in this letter about bishops, or elders or deacons, or any other church officers.

It is not to be supposed that a man of Pliny's ability and learning, and discrimination would give his Emperor a carefully prepared description of a Christian church and make no mention of its officers or teachers. And he certainly does not unless these women were officers or teachers, or, as they *were called, ministers*.

Women, it seems, could be ministers of the church at this early age, while it was poor and persecuted, but afterwards, when it became rich and popular, they were set aside.

CHAPTER XVII.

CONCLUSION.

"What are we, what our race,
How good for nothing and base,
Without fair woman to aid us ?
What could we do, where should we go,
How should we wander in night and wo,
But for woman to lead us !"
Cristoval DeCastillejo,
A. D. 1590.

IN the preceding pages the following propositions have been clearly proved.

1. Man and woman were created equal, each possessing the same rights and privileges as the other.

2. At the fall, woman, because she was first in the transgression, was, as a punishment, made subject to her husband.

3. Christ re-enacted the primitive law and restored the original relation of equality of the sexes.

4. The objections to the equality of man and woman in the Christian Church, based upon the Bible, rest upon a wrong translation of some passages and a misinterpretation of others.

The objections drawn from woman's nature are fully overthrown by undisputed facts.

5. In the New Testament church, woman, as well as man, filled the office of Apostle, Prophet, Deacon or preacher, and Pastor. There is not the slightest evidence that the functions of any of these offices, when filled by a woman, were different from what they were when filled by a man.

6. Woman took a part in governing the Apostolic church.

We come, then, to this final CONCLUSION: THE GOSPEL OF JESUS CHRIST, IN THE PROVISIONS WHICH IT MAKES, AND IN THE AGENCIES WHICH IT EMPLOYS, FOR THE SALVATION OF MANKIND, KNOWS NO DISTINCTION OF RACE, CONDITION, OR SEX, THEREFORE NO PERSON EVIDENTLY CALLED OF GOD TO THE GOSPEL MINISTRY, AND DULY QUALIFIED FOR IT, SHOULD BE REFUSED ORDINATION ON ACCOUNT OF RACE, CONDITION, OR SEX.

INDEX OF TEXTS.

	PAGE		PAGE		PAGE
Gen. 1, 26–27,	50	" 10, 47, . .	29	" 8, 23, . .	80
" 2, 18, . .	49	" 13. 1–3, . .	42	Gal. 3, 13, . .	51
" 3, 16, . .	50	" 13, 2–3 .	27	" 3, 28, . .	55
" 3, 15 . .	51	" 14 4–14, . .	82	" 3, 28, . . .	57
" 3, 15, . .	86	" 14, 14. . .	80	Eph, 3, 7, . .	94
" 20, 7, . .	89	" 14.23, . .	41	" 4, 11–12, . .	91
Ex. 15, 20 . .	52	" 19. 2–6, . .	28	" 5, 2, . .	36
Judges 4. 4, .	53	" 19, 39, . .	95	P.il. 1, 1; . . .	94
1 Sam. 10, 10, . .	90	" 19 32–39–41,	21	" 2, 25, . .	80
2 Kings 22, 14, .	53	" 20, 17–48, . .	40	" 4, 3, . .	62
Ps. 68, 11, . .	87	" 21. 8, . . .	94	Col. 1 23, . .	94
Micah 6. 4, . .	12	" 26, 16–18, . .	27	1 Thess. 2, 6, . .	82
Nahum 6.14, . .	53	Romans 12. 1, .	35	" 3. 2, . .	94
Matt. 19, 4, . .	51	" 16, 3–4, .	63	1 Tim. 2, 13, . .	48
" 23, 11. . .	95	" 16, 12, . .	63	" 2, 11–12. .	60
" 28.19–20, .	119	" 16, 7, . .	80	" 2. 12, .	139
Luke 2. 36, . . .	89	" 16. 7, . . .	83	" 2. 9, . .	64
" 10, 2, . .	39	" 16, 1, .	96	" 2.7. . .	85
" 15. 22, . . .	142	1 Cor 3, 5, . .	94	" 3, 11, .	97, 101
John 2, 5–9, .	95	" 11, 23–26, .	30	" 3. 11, .	102
" 14, 17, . .	9	" 11, 26, . .	23	" 3, 9, .	105
" 17, 17, . .	9	" 11, 27, . .	33	" 3, 10, . .	119
Acts 1. 15–26, .	27	" 11, 8–9, . .	48	" 5, 17, . .	141
" 1, 14, . .	57	" 11, 7, . .	49	" 5, 1, .	142
" 1, 14, .	140	" 11. 5, . .	61	Titus 1, 5–7, . .	41
" 1, 22, . .	140	" 12, 28, . .	79	" 2. 3, . .	103
" 1, 26, . .	80	" 12. 28, . .	91	Heb. 5, 1, . .	31
" 2, 17, . .	142	" 14, 3, . .	63	" 7, 26–27, .	35
" 2, 18, . .	83	" 14, 3, .	90	" 8. 3, . .	31
" 5, 14, . .	57	" 14. 34, . .	65	" 10, 12, .	31
" 6. 1–6, . .	93	" 14. 33, . .	65	" 13, 16' . .	36
" 6 2–6, . .	38	" 14. 28, . .	65	" 13, 15, . .	36
" 6. 3, . .	141	" 14, 32, . .	65	1 Pet. 2, 5, . .	35
" 6. 6, . .	141	" 14, 34, . .	65	" 2, 9, . .	85
" 6. 8, . .	93	" 14, 34–35, .	60	" 5. 3, . .	139
" 8, 3, . .	57	" 15, 46, . .	22	" 5, 5, . .	142
" 8, 12. . .	57	2 Cor. 3, 6, . .	94	2 Pet. 3, 15, . .	64
" 8, 18–24, . .	33	" 8, 23, . .	82	1 John 5, 18, . .	112
" 9, 20, . .	42	" 8, 18, .	82	Rev. 2, 1, . . .	65

FEMALE MINISTRY;

OR,

Woman's Right to Preach the Gospel.

By MRS. BOOTH.

"And your sons and your daughters shall prophesy."—*Joel.*

London:
MORGAN & CHASE, 38, LUDGATE HILL.

PRICE ONE PENNY.

Quantities can be had at considerable reduction from Mr. BOOTH, Gore Road, Victoria Park Road, London, N.E.

PREFACE.

The principal arguments contained in the following pages were published in a pamphlet entitled Female Teaching, which, I have reason to know, has been rendered very useful.

In this edition all the controversial portions have been expunged, some new matter added, and the whole produced in a cheaper form, and thus, I trust, rendered better adapted for general circulation.

Our only object in this issue is the elicitation of the truth. We hold that error can in the end be profitable to no cause, and least of all to the cause of Christ. If therefore we were not fully satisfied as to the correctness of the views herein set forth, we should fear to subject them to the light; and if we did not deem them of vast importance to the interests of Christ's kingdom, we should prefer to hold them in silence. Believing however that they will bear the strictest investigation, and that their importance cannot easily be over-estimated, we feel bound to propagate them to the utmost of our ability.

In this paper we shall endeavour to meet the most common objections to female ministry, and to present, as far as our space will permit, a thorough examination of the texts generally produced in support of these objections. May the great Head of the Church grant the light of His Holy Spirit to both writer and reader.

FEMALE MINISTRY;

OR

WOMAN'S RIGHT TO PREACH THE GOSPEL.

The first and most common objection urged against the public exercises of women, is that they are unnatural and unfeminine. Many labour under a very great but common mistake, viz. that of confounding nature with custom. Use, or custom, makes things appear to us natural, which, in reality, are very unnatural; while, on the other hand, novelty and rarity make very natural things appear strange and contrary to nature. So universally has this power of custom been felt and admitted, that it has given birth to the proverb, "Use is second nature." Making allowance for the novelty of the thing, we cannot discover anything either unnatural or immodest in a Christian woman, becomingly attired, appearing on a platform or in a pulpit. By *nature* she seems fitted to grace either. God has given to woman a graceful form and attitude, winning manners, persuasive speech, and, above all, a finely-toned emotional nature, all of which appear to us eminent *natural* qualifications for public speaking. We admit that want of mental culture, the trammels of custom, the force of prejudice, and one-sided interpretations of Scripture, have hitherto almost excluded her from this sphere; but, before such a sphere is pronounced to be unnatural, it must be proved either that woman has not the *ability* to teach or to preach, or that the possession and exercise of this ability unnaturalizes her in other respects; that so soon as she presumes to step on the platform or into the pulpit, she loses the delicacy and grace of the female character. Whereas, we have numerous instances of her retaining all that is most esteemed in her sex, and faithfully discharging the duties peculiar to her own sphere, and at the same time taking her place with many of our most useful speakers and writers. Why should woman be confined exclusively to the kitchen and the distaff, any more than man to the field and workshop? Did not God, and has not nature, assigned to man *his* sphere of labour, "to till the ground, and to dress it"? And, if exemption is claimed from this kind of toil for a portion of the male sex, on the ground of their possessing ability for intellectual and moral pursuits, we must be allowed to claim the same privilege for woman; nor can we see the exception more unnatural in the one case than the other, or why God in this solitary instance has endowed a being with powers which He never intended her to employ.

There seems to be a great deal of unnecessary fear of women occupying any position which involves publicity, lest she should be rendered unfeminine by the indulgence of ambition or vanity; but why should woman any more than man be charged with ambition when impelled to use her talents for the good of her race. Moreover, as a labourer in the GOSPEL her position is much higher than in any other public capacity; she is at once shielded from all coarse and unrefined influences and associations; her very vocation tending to exalt and refine all the tenderest and most womanly instincts of her nature. As a matter of fact it is well known to those who have had opportunities of observing the private character and deportment of women engaged in preaching the gospel, that they have been amongst the most amiable, self-sacrificing, and unobtrusive of their sex.

"We well know," says the late Mr. Gurney, a minister of the Society of Friends, "that there are no women among us more generally distinguished for modesty, gentleness, order, and right submission to their brethren, than those who have been called by their Divine Master into the exercise of the Christian ministry."

Who would dare to charge the sainted Madame Guyon, Lady Maxwell, the talented mother of the Wesleys, Mrs. Fletcher, Mrs. Elizabeth Fry, Mrs. Smith, Mrs. Whiteman, or Miss Marsh with being unwomanly or ambitious. Some of these ladies we know have adorned by their private virtues the highest ranks of society, and won alike from friends and enemies the highest eulogiums as to the devotedness, purity, and sweetness of their lives. Yet these were all more or less public women, every one of them expounding and exhorting from the Scriptures to mixed companies of men and women. Ambitious doubtless they were; but theirs was an ambition akin to His, who, for the "joy that was set before Him, endured the cross, despising the shame;" and to his, who counted all things but dung and dross, and was willing to be regarded as the off-scouring of all things that he might win souls to Jesus and bring glory to God. Would that all the Lord's people had more of this ambition.

Well, but, say our objecting friends, how is it that these whose names you mention, and many others, should venture to preach when female ministry is *forbidden in the word of God?* This is by far the most serious objection which we have to consider—and if capable of substantiation, should receive our immediate and cheerful acquiescence; but we think that we shall be able to show, by a fair and consistent interpretation, that the very opposite view is the truth. That not only is the public ministry of woman unforbidden, but absolutely enjoined by both precept and example in the word of God.

And, first, we will select the most prominent and explicit passages of the New Testament referring to the subject, beginning with 1 Corinthians xi. 1-15 : "Every man praying or prophesying, having his head covered, dishonoureth his head. But every woman that prayeth or prophesieth with her head uncovered, dishonoureth her head: for that is all one as if she were shaven," etc. "The character," says a talented writer, "of the prophesying here referred to by the apostle is defined 1 Corinthians xiv. 3, 4, and 31st verses. The reader will see that it was directed to the 'edification, exhortation, and comfort of believers;' and the result anticipated was the conviction of unbelievers and unlearned persons. Such were the public services of women which the apostle allowed, and such was the ministry of females predicted by the prophet Joel, and described as a leading feature of the gospel dispensation. Women who speak in assemblies for worship, under the influence of the Holy Spirit, assume thereby no personal authority over others; they simply deliver the messages of the gospel, which imply obedience, subjection, and responsibility, rather than authority and power." Dr. A. Clarke, on this verse, says, "Whatever may be the meaning of praying and prophesying in respect to the man, they have precisely the same meaning in respect to the woman! So that some women at least, as well as some men, might speak to others to edification, exhortation, and comfort. And this kind of prophesying or teaching was predicted by Joel ii. 28, and referred to by Peter (Acts ii. 17). And, had there not been such gifts bestowed on woman, the prophecy could not have had its fulfilment. The only difference marked by the apostle was, the man had his head uncovered, because he was the representative of Christ: the woman had hers covered, because she was placed by the order of God in subjection to the man; and because it was the custom both among Greeks and Romans, and among the Jews an express *law*, that no woman should be seen abroad without a veil. This was and is a custom through all the East, and none but public prostitutes go without veils; if a woman should appear in public without a veil, she would *dishonour her head—her husband*. And she must appear like to those women who have their hair shaven off as the punishment of adultery." See also Doddridge, Whitby, and Cobbin.

We think that the view above given is the only fair and common-sense interpretation of this passage. If Paul does not here recognise the *fact* that women did actually pray and prophesy in the primitive Churches, his language has no meaning at all; and if he does not recognise their *right* to do so by dictating the proprieties of their appearance while so engaged, we leave to objectors the task of educing any sense whatever from his language. If, according to the logic of Dr. Barnes, the apostle here, in arguing against an improper and indecorous mode of performance, forbids the performance itself, the prohibition extends to the *men* as well as to the women; for Paul as expressly reprehends a man praying with *his* head covered as he does a woman with *hers* uncovered. With as much force might the doctor assert that in reproving the same Church for their improper celebration of the Lord's Supper (1 Cor. xi. 20, 21), Paul prohibits all Christians, in every age, celebrating it at all. "The question with the Corinthians was not whether or not the women should pray or prophesy at all, that question had been settled on the day of Pentecost; but whether, as a matter of convenience, they might do so without their veils." The apostle kindly and clearly explains that by the law of nature and of society it would be improper to uncover her head while engaged in acts of public worship. We think that the reflections cast on these women by Dr. Barnes and other commentators are quite gratuitous and uncalled for. Here is no intimation that they ever had uncovered their heads while so engaged; the fairest presumption is that they had not, nor ever would till they knew the apostle's mind on the subject. We have precisely the same evidence that the men prayed and preached with their hats on, as that women removed their veils, and wore their hair dishevelled, which is simply none at all. We cannot but regard it as a signal evidence of the power of prejudice, that a man of Dr. Barnes's general clearness and acumen should condescend to treat this passage in the manner he does. The doctor evidently feels the untenableness of his position; and endeavours, by muddling two passages of distinct and different bearing, to annihilate the argument fairly deducible from the first. We would like to ask the doctor on what authority he makes such an exception as the following: "But this cannot be interpreted as meaning that it is improper for females to speak or to pray in meetings of their own sex." Indeed! but according to the most reliable statistics we possess, two-thirds of the whole Church is, and always has been, composed of their own sex, If, then, no rule of the New Testament is more positive than this, viz. that women are to keep *silence* in the Churches, on whose authority does the doctor license them to speak to by far the larger portion of the Church.

A barrister writing us on the above passage, says, " Paul

here takes for granted that women were in the habit of praying and prophesying; he expresses no surprise nor utters a syllable of censure, he was only anxious that they should not provoke unnecessary obloquy by laying aside their customary head-dress or departing from the dress which was indicative of modesty in the country in which they lived. This passage seems to prove beyond the possibility of dispute that in the *early* times women were permitted to speak to the "edification and comfort" of Christians, and that the Lord graciously endowed them with grace and gifts for this service. What He did then may He not be doing now? It seems truly astonishing that Bible students, with the second chapter of the Acts before them, should not see that an imperative decree has gone forth from God, the execution of which women cannot escape; whether they like or not, they '*shall*' prophesy throughout the whole course of this dispensation; and they have been doing so, though they and their blessed labours are not much noticed."

Well, but say our objecting friends, hear what Paul says in another place:—"Let your women keep silence in the Churches, for it is not permitted unto them to speak; but they are commanded to be under obedience, as also saith the law. And if they will learn* anything, let them ask their husbands at home; for it is a shame for women to speak in the Church" (1 Cor. xiv. 34, 35). Now let it be borne in mind this is the same apostle, writing to the same Church, as in the above instance. Will any one maintain that Paul here refers to the same kind of speaking as before? If so, we insist on his supplying us with some rule of interpretation which will harmonize this unparalleled contradiction and absurdity. Taking the simple and common-sense view of the two passages, viz. that one refers to the devotional and religious exercises in the Church, and the other to inconvenient asking of questions, and imprudent or ignorant talking, there is no contradiction or discrepancy, no straining or twisting of either. If, on the other hand, we assume that the apostle refers in both instances to the same thing, we make him in one page give the most explicit directions **how a thing** shall be performed, which in a page or two **further on,** and writing to the *same* Church, he expressly forbids **being performed** at all. We admit that "it *is* a shame for women to speak in the Church," in the sense here intended by the

* "*Learning* anything by asking their husbands at home," cannot mean *preaching.* That is not learning, but *teaching* "the way of God." It cannot mean being inspired by the Holy Ghost to foretell future events. No woman having either taught or prophesied, would have to ask her husband at home before she knew what she had done, or understood what she had said. Such women would be only fit to "learn in silence with all subjection." The reference is evidently to subjects under debate.

apostle; but before the argument based on these words can be deemed of any worth, objectors must prove that the "speaking" here is synonymous with that, concerning the manner of which the apostle legislates in 1 Corinthians xi. Dr. A. Clarke, on this passage, says, "according to the prediction of Joel, the Spirit of God was to be poured out on the women as well as the men, that *they* might prophesy, *that is teach*. And that they did prophesy or teach is evident from what the apostle says (1 Cor. xi.), where he lays down rules to regulate this part of their conduct while ministering in the Church. All that the apostle opposes here is their *questioning, finding fault, disputing, etc.*, in the Christian Church, as the Jewish men were permitted to do in their synagogues (see Luke ii. 46); together with attempts to usurp authority over men by setting up their judgment in opposition to them; for the apostle has reference to acts of disobedience and arrogance, of which no woman would be guilty who was under the influence of the Spirit of God."

The Rev. J. H. Robinson, writing on this passage, remarks: "The silence imposed here must be explained by the verb, to speak (λαλεῖν), used afterwards. Whatever that verb means in this verse, I admit and believe the women were forbidden to do in *the Church*. But what does it mean? It is used nearly three hundred times in the New Testament, and scarcely any verb is used with so great a variety of adjuncts. In *Schleusner's Lexicon*, its meaning is traced under *seventeen* distinct heads, and he occupies *two* full pages of the book in explaining it. Among other meanings he gives *respondeo, rationem reddo, præcipio, jubeo*; I answer, I return a reason, I give rule or precept, I order, decree." In *Robinson's Lexicon* (Bloomfield's edition), two pages nearly are occupied with the explanation of this word; and he gives instances of its meaning, "as modified by the *context*, where the sense lies, not so much in λαλεῖν (*lalein*) as in the adjuncts." THE PASSAGE UNDER CONSIDERATION IS ONE OF THOSE TO WHICH HE REFERS AS BEING SO "MODIFIED BY THE CONTEXT." *Greenfield* gives, with others, the following meanings of the word: "to prattle—*be loquacious as a child;* to speak in answer—*to answer*, as in John xix. 10; harangue, plead, Acts ix. 29.; xxi. To direct, command, Acts iii. 22." In *Liddel and Scott's Lexicon*, the following meanings are given: "*to chatter, babble;* of birds, *to twitter, chirp;* strictly, *to make an inarticulate sound*, opposed to articulate speech; but also generally, *to talk, say.*"

"It is clear then that λαλεῖν may mean something different from mere speaking, and that to use this word in a prohibition does not imply that absolute silence or abstinence from speaking is enjoined; but, on the contrary, that the prohibition applies to an improper kind of speaking, which is to be understood, not from the word itself, but, as Mr. Robinson says, from 'the context.' Now, 'the context' shows that it was not *silence* which was imposed upon women in the Church, but only a refraining from such speaking as was inconsistent with the words, 'they are commanded to be under obedience,' or, more literally, 'to be obedient:' that is, they were to refrain from such questionings, dogmatical assertions, and disputatious, as would bring them into collision with the men—as would ruffle their tempers, and occasion an unamiable volubility of speech. This kind of speaking, and this alone, as it appears to me, was forbidden by the apostle in the passage before us. This kind of speaking was the only supposable antagonist to, and violation of 'obedience.' Absolute silence was not essential to that 'obedience.' My studies in 'Biblical criticism,' etc., have not informed me that a woman must cease to speak before she can obey; and I am therefore led to the irresistible conclusion, that it is not *all* speaking in the Church which the apostle forbids, and which he pronounces to be shameful; but, on the contrary, a pertinacious, inquisitive, domineering, dogmatical kind of speaking, which, while it is unbecoming in a *man*, is shameful and odious in a woman, and especially when that woman is in the Church, and is speaking on the deep things of religion."

Parkhurst, in his lexicon, tells us that the Greek word "'lalein,' which our translation renders speak, is *not* the word used in Greek to signify to speak with premeditation and prudence, but is the word used to signify to speak imprudently and without consideration, and is that applied to one who lets his tongue run but does not speak to the purpose, but says nothing." Now unless Parkhurst is utterly wrong in his Greek, which it is apprehended no one will venture to affirm, Paul's fulmination is not launched against speech with premeditation and prudence, but against speech devoid of these qualities. It would be well if all speakers of the male as well as the female sex were obedient to this rule.

We think that with the light cast on this text by the four eminent Greek scholars above quoted, there can be no doubt in any unprejudiced mind as to the true meaning of "lalein" in this connection. And we find from Church history that the primitive Christians thus understood it, for that women did actually speak and preach amongst them we have indisputable proof. God had promised in the last days to pour out His Spirit upon all flesh, and that the *daughters* as well as the sons of mankind should prophesy.

And Peter says most emphatically, respecting the outpouring of the Spirit on the day of Pentecost, "This *is that* which is spoken of by the prophet Joel," etc. (Acts ii. 16, 18.)

Words more explicit, and an application of Prophecy more direct than this does not occur within the range of the New Testament.

Commentators say, "If women have the gift of prophecy, they must not use that gift in public." But God says, by His prophet Joel, they *shall* use it just in the same sense as the sons use it. When the dictation of men so flatly opposes the express declaration of the "sure word of prophecy," we make no apology for its utter and indignant rejection.

Presbuteros, a talented writer of the Protestant Electoral Union, in his reply to a priest of Rome,* says:—

"Habituated for ages, as men had been, to the diabolical teaching and delusions practised upon them by the papal 'priesthood,' it was difficult for them, when they did get possession of the Scriptures, to discern therein the plain fact, that among the primitive Christians preaching was not confined to men, but women also, gifted with power by the Holy Spirit, preached the gospel; and hence the slowness with which, even at the present time, this truth has been admitted by those giving heed to the word of God, and especially those setting themselves up as a 'priesthood' or a 'clergy.' As shown in page 66, God had, according to His promise, on the day of Pentecost poured out his Holy Spirit upon believers—men and women, old and young—that they should *prophesy*, and they *did* so. The prophesying spoken of was not the foretelling of events, but the *preaching* to the world at large the glad tidings of salvation by Jesus Christ. For this purpose it pleased God to make use of *women* as well as men. It is plainly the duty of every Christian to insist upon the fulfilment of the will of God, and the abrogation of every single thing inconsistent therewith. I would draw attention to the fact that Phœbe, a Christian woman whom we find in our version of the Scripture (Rom. xvi. 1) spoken of only as any common servant attached to a congregation, was nothing less than one of those gifted by the Holy Spirit for *publishing the glad tidings*, or *preaching the gospel*. The manner in which the apostle (whose only care was the propagation of evangelical truth) speaks of her, shows that she was what he in Greek styled her, a deacon (diaconon) or preacher of the word. Our translators speak of *her* (because she was a *woman*) only as 'a *servant* of the Church which is at Cenchrea.' The men 'deacons' they styled ministers, but a woman on the same level as themselves would be an anomaly, and therefore she was to be only the *servant* of men *ministers*, who, in the *popish sense*, constituted *the Church !*"

* We strongly commend this pamphlet to the perusal of our readers. It contains much valuable information as to the origin of much of the popish nonsense of our times. Published by the Protestant Electoral Union 14, Tavistock Street, Covent Garden. Price 6d.

The apostle says of her—"I commend unto you Phebe our sister, who is a minister (diaconon) of the Church which is at Cenchrea: that ye receive her in the Lord, as becometh saints, and that ye assist her in *whatsoever business* she hath need of you." To the common sense of disinterested minds it will be evident that the apostle could not have requested more for any one of the most zealous of men preachers than he did for Phebe! They were to assist "her in *whatsoever business* she" might require their aid. Hence we discern that she had no such trifling position in the primitive Church as at the present time episcopal dignitaries attach to deacons and deaconesses! Observe, the same Greek word is used to designate her that was applied to all the apostles and to Jesus Himself. For example: "Now I say that Jesus Christ was a minister (diaconon) of the circumcision" (Rom. xv. 8). "Who then is Paul, and who is Apollos, but ministers (diaconoi) by whom ye believed" (1 Cor. iii. 5). "Our sufficiency is of God; who also hath made us able ministers (diaconous) of the new testament" (2 Cor. iii. 6). "In all things approving ourselves as the ministers (diaconoi) of God" (vi. 4). The idea of a woman deacon in the "*three orders!*"—it was intolerable, therefore let her be a "servant." Theodoret however says, "The fame of Phebe was spoken of throughout the world. She was known not only to the Greeks and Romans, but also to the Barbarians," which implies that she had travelled much, and propagated the gospel in foreign countries. See Doddridge, Cobbin, and Wesley, on this passage.

"Salute Andronicus and Junia, my kinsmen and my fellow-prisoners, who are of note among the apostles; who also were in Christ before me" (Rom. xvi. 7). By the word "kinsmen" one would take Junia to have been a man; but Chrysostom and Theophylact, who were both Greeks, and consequently knew their mother tongue better than our translators, say *Junia was a woman*. Kinsmen should therefore have been rendered kinsfolk; but with our translators it was out of all character to have a *woman* of note amongst the apostles, and a fellow-prisoner with Paul for the gospel: *therefore let them be* kinsmen!

Justin Martyr, who lived till about A.D. 150, says, in his dialogue with Trypho, the Jew, "that both men and women were seen among them who had the extraordinary gifts of the Spirit of God, according as the prophet Joel had foretold, by which he endeavoured to convince the Jews that the latter days were come."

Dodwell, in his dissertations on Irenæus says, "that the gift of the spirit of prophecy was given to others besides the apostles; and, that not only in the first and second, but in the third century—even to the time of Constantine—all sorts and ranks of men had these gifts; yea, and *women* too."

Eusebius speaks of Potomania Ammias, a prophetess, in Philadelphia, and others, "who were equally distinguished for their love and zeal in the cause of Christ."

"The scriptural idea," says Mrs. Palmer, "of the terms preach and prophesy, stands so inseparably connected as one and the same thing, that we should find it difficult to get aside from the fact that women did preach, or, in other words, prophesy, in the early ages of Christianity, and have continued to do so down to the present time to just the degree that the spirit of the Christian dispensation has been recognised. And it is also a significant fact, that to the degree denominations, who have once favoured the practice, lose the freshness of their zeal, and as a consequence, their primitive simplicity, and, as ancient Israel, yield to a desire to be like surrounding communities, in a corresponding ratio are the labours of females discountenanced."

If any one still insists on a literal application of this text, we beg to ask how he disposes of the preceding part of the chapter where it occurs. Surely, if one verse be so authoritative and binding, the whole chapter is equally so; and therefore, those who insist on a literal application of the words of Paul, under all circumstances and through all time, will be careful to observe the apostle's order of worship in their own congregations. But, we ask, where is the minister who lets his whole Church prophesy one by one, and himself sits still and listens while they are speaking, so that all things may be done decently and in order? But Paul as expressly lays down this order as he does the rule for women, and he adds, "The things that I write unto you are the commandments of the Lord" (ver. 37). Why then do not ministers abide by these directions? We anticipate their reply— "Because these directions were given to the Corinthians as temporary arrangements; and, though they were the commandments of the Lord to them at that time, they do not apply to all Christians in all times." Indeed; but unfortunately for their argument, the prohibition of women speaking, even if it meant what they wish, was given amongst those very directions, and to the Corinthians *only*: for it reads, "Let *your* women keep silence," etc.; and, for aught this passage teaches to the contrary, Christian women of all other Churches might do what these women were forbidden to do; until, therefore, learned divines make a personal application of the rest of the chapter, they must excuse us declining to do so of the 24th verse; and we challenge them to show any breach of the Divine law in one case more than the other.

Another passage frequently cited as prohibitory of female labour in the Church, is 1 Timothy ii. 12, 13. Though we have never met with the slightest proof that this text has any reference to the public exercises of women; nevertheless, as it is often quoted, we will give it a fair and thorough examination. "It is primarily an injunction," says the Rev. J. H. Robinson. "respecting her personal behaviour at home. It stands in connection with precepts respecting her apparel and her domestic position; especially her relation to her husband. No one will suppose that the apostle forbids a woman to 'teach' absolutely and universally. Even objectors would allow her to teach her own sex in private; they would let her teach her servants and children, and, perhaps, her husband too. If he were ignorant of the Saviour, might she not teach him the way to Christ? If she were acquainted with languages, arts or sciences, which he did not know, might she not teach him these things? Certainly she might! The 'teaching,' therefore which is forbidden by the apostle, is not every kind of teaching any more than, in the previous instance, his prohibition of speaking applied to every kind of speaking in the Church; but it is such teaching as is domineering, and as involves the usurpation of authority over the man. This is the only teaching forbidden by St. Paul in the passage under consideration."

"If this passage be not a prohibition of every kind of teaching, we can only ascertain what kind of teaching is forbidden by the modifying expressions with which *didaskein* stands associated: and, for anything these modifying expressions affirm to the contrary, her teaching may be public, reiterated, urgent, and may comprehend a variety of subjects, provided it be not dictatorial, domineering, nor vociferous; for then, and then only, would it be incompatible with her obedience."

The Rev. Dr. Taft says, "This passage should be rendered 'I suffer not a woman to teach *by* usurping authority over the man.' This rendering removes all the difficulties and contradictions involved in the ordinary reading, and evidently gives the meaning of the apostle." "If the nature of society," says the same writer, "its good and prosperity, in which women are jointly and equally concerned with men; if in many cases their fitness and capacity for instructors, being admitted to be equal to the other sex, be not reasons sufficient to convince the candid reader of woman's right to preach and teach because of two texts in Paul's epistles, let him consult the paraphrase of Locke, where he has proved to a demonstration that the apostle, in these texts, never intended to prohibit women from praying and preaching in the Church provided they were dressed as became women professing godliness, and were qualified for the sacred office."

"It will be found," says another writer, "by an examination of this text with its connections, that the teaching here alluded to stands in necessary connection with usurping authority, as though the apostle had said, the gospel does not alter the relation of women in view of priority, for Adam was first formed, then Eve."

"This prohibition," says the before-named barrister, "refers exclusively to the private life and domestic character of woman, and simply means that an ignorant or unruly woman is not to force her opinions on the man whether he will or no. It has no reference whatever to good women living in obedience to God and their husbands, or to women sent out to preach the gospel by the call of the Holy Spirit."

If the context is allowed to fix the meaning of *didaskein* in this text, as it would in any other, there can be no doubt in any honest mind that the above is the only consistent interpretation; and if it be, then this prohibition has no bearing whatever on the religious exercises of women led and taught of the Spirit of God: and we cannot forbear asking on whose skirts the mischief resulting from the false application of this text will be found? Thank God the day is dawning with respect to this subject. Women are studying and investigating for themselves. They are claiming to be recognised as responsible beings, answerable to GOD for their convictions of duty; and, urged by the Divine Spirit, they are overstepping those unscriptural barriers which the Church has so long reared against its performance.

Whether the Church will allow women to speak in her assemblies can only be a question of time; common sense, public opinion, and the blessed results of female agency will force her to give us an honest and impartial rendering of the solitary text on which she grounds her prohibitions. Then, when the true light shines and God's words take the place of man's traditions, the Doctor of Divinity who shall teach that Paul commands woman to be silent when God's Spirit urges her to speak, will be regarded much the same as we should now regard an astronomer who should teach that the sun is the earth's satellite.

Another argument urged against female preaching is, that it is unnecessary; that there is plenty of scope for her efforts in private, in visiting the sick and poor and working for the temporalities of the Church. Doubtless woman ought to be thankful for any sphere for benefiting her race and glorifying God. But we cannot be blind to the supreme selfishness of making her so welcome to the hidden toil and self-sacrifice, the hewing of wood and the drawing of water, the watching and waiting, the reproach and persecution attaching to her Master's service, without allowing her a tittle of the honour which He has attached to the ministration of His gospel. Here, again, man's theory and God's order are at variance. God says, "Them that honour me I will honour." Our Lord links the joy with the suffering, the glory with the shame, the exaltation with the humiliation, the crown with the cross, the finding of life with the losing of it. Nor did He manifest any such horror at female publicity in His cause as many of His professed people appear to entertain in these days. We have no intimation of His reproving the Samaritan woman for her public proclamation of Him to her countrymen; nor of His rebuking the women who followed Him amidst a taunting mob on His way to the cross. And yet, surely, *privacy* was *their* proper sphere. On one occasion He *did* say, with reference to a woman, " Verily, I say unto you, wheresoever this gospel shall be preached in the whole world, there shall also this, that this woman hath done, be told for a memorial of her" (Matt. xxvi. 12 ; see also Luke vii. 37-50).

As to the obligation devolving on woman to labour for her Master, I presume there will be no controversy. The particular sphere in which each individual shall do this must be dictated by the teachings of the Holy Spirit and the gifts with which God has endowed her. If she have the necessary gifts, and feels herself called by the Spirit to preach, there is not a single word in the whole book of God to restrain her, but many, very many to urge and encourage her. God says she SHALL do so, and Paul prescribes the manner in which she shall do it, and Phebe, Junia, Philip's four daughters, and many other women actually did preach and speak in the primitive Churches. If this had not been the case, there would have been less freedom under the new than under the old dispensation. A greater paucity of gifts and agencies under the Spirit than under the law. Fewer labourers when more work to be done. Instead of the destruction of caste and division between the priesthood and the people, and the setting up of a spiritual kingdom in which all true believers were "kings and priests unto God," the division would have been more stringent and the disabilities of the common people greater. Whereas we are told again and again in effect, that in "Christ Jesus there is neither bond nor free, male nor female, but ye are all one in Christ Jesus."

We commend a few passages bearing on the ministrations of woman under the old dispensation to the careful consideration of our readers. "And Deborah, a prophetess, the wife of Lapidoth, she judged Israel at that time," etc. (Jud. iv. 4-10). There are two particulars in this passage worthy of note. First, the authority of Deborah as a prophetess, or revealer of God's will to Israel, was acknowledged and submitted to as implicitly as in the cases of the male judges who succeeded her. Secondly, she is made the military head of ten thousand men, Barak refusing to go to battle without her.

Again, in 2 Kings xxii. 12-20, we have an account of the king sending the high-priest, the scribe, etc., to Huldah, the prophetess, the wife of Shallum, who dwelt at Jerusalem, in the college; to inquire at her mouth the will of God in reference to the book of the law which had deen founb in the house of the Lord. The authority and dignity of Huldah's message to the king does not betray anything of that trembling diffidence or abject servility which some persons seem to think should characterize the religious exercises of woman. She answers him as the prophetess of the Lord, having the signet of the King of kings attached to her utterances.

"The Lord gave the word, and great was the company of those that published it" (Ps. lxviii. 11). In the original Hebrew it is, "Great was the company of women publishers, or women evangelists." Grotius explains this passage, "The Lord shall give the word, that is plentiful matter of speaking; so that he would call those which follow the great army of preaching women, victories, or female conquerors." How comes it that the feminine word is actually excluded in this text? That it is there as plainly as any other word no Hebrew scholar will deny. It is too much to assume that as our translators could not *alter* it, as they did "Diaconon" when applied to Phebe, they preferred to leave it out altogether rather than give a prophecy so unpalatable to their prejudice. But the Lord gives the word and He will choose whom He pleases to publish it; notwithstanding the condemnation of translators and divines.

"For I brought thee up out of the land of Egypt, and redeemed thee out of the house of servants; and I sent before thee Moses, Aaron, and Miriam" (Mic. vi. 4).

God here classes Miriam with Moses and Aaron, and declares that *He* sent her before His people. We fear that had some of our friends been men of Israel at that time, they would have disputed such a leadership.

In the light of such passages as these, who will dare to dispute the fact that God did under the old dispensation endue his handmaidens with the gifts and calling of prophets answering to our present idea of preachers. Strange indeed would it be if under the *fulness of* the gospel dispensation, there were nothing analogous to this, but "positive and explicit rules," to prevent any approximation thereto. We are thankful to find, however, abundant evidence that the "spirit of prophecy which is the testimony of Jesus," was poured out on the female as fully as on the male disciple, and "His daughters and His handmaidens" prophesied. We commend the following texts from the New Testament to the careful consideration of our readers.

"And she (Anna) was a widow of about fourscore and four years, which departed not from the temple, but served God with fastings and prayers night and day. And she coming in that instant, gave thanks likewise unto the Lord, and spake of Him to all them that looked for redemption in Jerusalem " (Luke ii. 37, 38). Can any one explain wherein this exercise of Anna's differed from that of Simeon, recorded just before? It was in the same public place, the temple. It was during the same service. It was equally public, for she "*spake* of Him to all who looked for redemption in Jerusalem" (see Watson on this passage).

Jesus said to the two Marys, "All hail! And they came and held Him by the feet, and worshipped Him. Then said Jesus unto them, Be not *afraid*: go, tell my brethren that they go before me into Galilee" (Matt. xxviii. 9, 10). There are two or three points in this beautiful narrative to which we wish to call the attention of our readers.

First, it was the *first* announcement of the glorious news to a lost world and a company of forsaking disciples. Second, it was as *public* as the nature of the case demanded; and intended ultimately to be published to the ends of the earth. Third, Mary was expressly commissioned to reveal the fact to the apostles; and thus she literally became their teacher on that memorable occasion. Oh, glorious privilege, to be allowed to herald the glad tidings of a Saviour risen! How could it be that our Lord chose a *woman* to this honour? Well, one reason might be that the male disciples were all missing at the time. They all forsook Him and fled. But woman was there, as she had ever been, ready to minister to her risen, as to her dying, Lord—

> "Not she with traitorous lips her Saviour stung,
> Not she denied Him with unholy tongue;
> She, whilst apostles shrunk, could danger brave;
> Last at the cross, and earliest at the grave."

But surely, if the dignity of our Lord or His message were likely to be imperilled by commiting this sacred trust to a woman, He who was guarded by legions of angels could have commanded another messenger; but, as if intent on doing her honour and rewarding her unwavering fidelity, He reveals Himself *first* to her; and, as an evidence that He had taken out of the way the curse under which she had so long groaned, nailing it to His cross, He makes her who had been first in the transgression, first also in the glorious knowledge of complete redemption.

"Acts i. 14, and ii. 1, 4. We are in the first of these passages expressly told that the women were assembled with the disciples on the day of Pentecost; and in the second, that the cloven tongues sat upon them *each*, and the Holy Ghost filled them *all*, and they spake as the Spirit gave them utterance. It is nothing to the point to argue that the gift of tongues was a miraculous gift, seeing that the Spirit was the primary bestowment. The tongues were only emblematical of the office which the Spirit was henceforth to sustain to His people. The Spirit was given alike to the female as to the male disciple, and this is cited by Peter (16, 18), as the peculiar speciality of the latter dispensation. What a remarkable device of the devil that he has so long succeeded in hiding this characteristic of the latter day glory! *He* knows, whether the Church does or not, how eminently detrimental to the interests of his kingdom have been the religious labours of woman; and while her Seed has mortally bruised his head, he ceases not to bruise her heel; but the time of her deliverance draweth nigh."

"PHILIP THE EVANGELIST HAD FOUR DAUGHTERS, VIRGINS, WHICH DID PROPHESY." FROM EUSEBIUS, THE ANCIENT ECCLESIASTICAL HISTORIAN, WE LEARN THAT PHILIP'S DAUGHTERS LIVED TO A GOOD OLD AGE, ALWAYS ABOUNDING IN THE WORK OF THE LORD. "MIGHTY LUMINARIES," HE WRITES, "HAVE FALLEN ASLEEP IN ASIA. PHILIP, AND TWO OF HIS VIRGIN DAUGHTERS, SLEEP AT HIERAPOLIS; THE OTHER, AND THE BELOVED DISCIPLE, JOHN, REST AT EPHESUS."

"And I entreat thee also, true yokefellow, help those women which laboured with me in the gospel, with Clement also, and with other my fellow-labourers" (Phil. iv. 3).

This is a recognition of *female labourers*, not *concerning* the gospel but *in* the gospel, whom Paul classes with Clement, and other his fellow-labourers. Precisely the same terms are applied to Timotheus, whom Paul styles a "minister of God, and his fellow-labourer in the gospel of Christ" (1 Thess. iii. 2).

Again, "Greet Priscilla and Aquila, my helpers in Christ Jesus; who have for my life laid down their own necks; unto whom not only I give thanks, but all the Churches of the Gentiles" (Rom. xvi. 3, 4).

THE WORD RENDERED HELPERS MEANS A FELLOW-LABOURER, ASSOCIATE, COADJUTOR,* WORKING TOGETHER, AN ASSISTANT, A JOINT LABOURER, A COLLEAGUE.† IN THE NEW TESTAMENT SPOKEN ONLY OF A CO-WORKER, HELPER IN A CHRISTIAN WORK, THAT IS OF CHRISTIAN TEACHERS.‡ HOW CAN THESE TERMS, WITH ANY SHOW OF CONSISTENCY, BE MADE TO APPLY MERELY TO THE EXERCISE OF HOSPITALITY TOWARDS THE APOSTLE, OR THE DUTY OF PRIVATE VISITATION. TO BE A PARTNER, COADJUTOR, OR JOINT WORKER WITH A PREACHER OF THE GOSPEL, MUST BE SOMETHING MORE THAN TO BE HIS WAITING-MAID.

* Greenfield.   † Dunbar.   ‡ Robinson.

WOMAN'S RIGHT TO PREACH THE GOSPEL. 19

Again, "Salute Tryphena and Tryphosa, who labour in the Lord. Salute the beloved Persis, which laboured much in the Lord" (Rom. xvi. 12). Dr. Clarke, on this verse, says, "Many have spent much useless labour in endeavouring to prove that these women did not preach. That there were prophetesses as well as prophets in the Church we learn, and that a woman might pray or prophesy provided that she had her head covered we know; and, according to St. Paul (1 Cor. xiv. 3), whoever prophesied spoke unto others to edification, exhortation, and comfort, and that no preacher can do more every person must acknowledge. Because, to edify exhort, and comfort, are the prime ends of the gospel ministry. If women thus prophesied, then women preached."

"There is neither Jew nor Greek, there is neither male nor female, for ye are all one in Christ Jesus" (Gal. iii. 28). If this passage does not teach that in the privileges, duties, and responsibilities of Christ's kingdom, all differences of nation, caste, and sex are abolished, we should like to know what it does teach, and wherefore it was written (see also 1 Cor. vii. 22).

As we have before observed, the text, Corinthians xiv. 34, 35, is the *only one* in the whole book of God which even by a false translation can be made prohibitory of female speaking in the Church; how comes it then, that by this one isolated passage, which, according to our best Greek authorities,* is wrongly rendered and wrongly applied, woman's lips have been sealed for centuries, and the "testimony of Jesus, which is the spirit of prophecy," silenced, when bestowed on her? How is it that this solitary text has been allowed to stand unexamined and unexplained, nay, that learned commentators who have *known* its true meaning as perfectly as either Robinson, Bloomfield, Greenfield, Scott, Parkhurst, or Locke have upheld the delusion, and enforced it as a Divine precept binding on all female disciples through all time? Surely there must have been some unfaithfulness, "craftiness," and "handling of the word of life deceitfully" somewhere. Surely the love of caste and unscriptural jealousy for a separated priesthood has had something to do with this anomaly. By this course divines and commentators have involved themselves in all sorts of inconsistencies and contradictions; and worse, they have nullified some of the most precious promises of God's word. They have set the most explicit predictions of prophecy at variance with apostolic injunctions, and the most immediate and wonderful operations of the Holy Ghost in direct opposition "to positive, explicit, and universal rules."

Notwithstanding however all this opposition to female ministry on the part of those deemed authorities in the

* Disinterested witnesses every one will allow.

Church, there have been some in all ages in whom the Holy Ghost has wrought so mightily, that at the sacrifice of reputation and all things most dear, they have been compelled to come out as witnesses for Jesus and ambassadors of His gospel. As a rule, these women have been amongst the most devoted and self-denying of the Lord's people, giving indisputable evidence by the purity and beauty of their lives that they were led by the Spirit of God. Now, if the word of God forbids female ministry, we would ask how it happens that so many of the most devoted handmaidens of the Lord have felt themselves constrained by the Holy Ghost to exercise it? Surely there must be some mistake somewhere, for the word and the Spirit cannot contradict each other. Either the word does not condemn women preaching, or these confessedly holy women have been deceived. Will any one venture to assert that such women as Mrs. Elizabeth Fry, Mrs. Fletcher of Madeley, and Mrs. Smith have been deceived with respect to their call to deliver the gospel messages to their fellow-creatures? If not, then God does call and qualify women to preach, and His word, rightly understood, cannot forbid what His Spirit enjoins. Further, it is a significant fact, which we commend to the consideration of all thoughtful Christians, that the public ministry of women has been eminently owned of God in the salvation of souls and the edification of His people. Paul refers to the *fruits* of his labours as evidence of his Divine commission (1 Cor. ix. 20). "If I am not an apostle unto others, yet doubtless I am to you: for the seal of mine apostleship are ye in the Lord." If this criterion be allowed to settle the question respecting woman's call to preach, we have no fear as to the result. A few examples of the blessing which has attended the ministrations of females, may help to throw some light on this matter of a Divine call.

At a missionary meeting held at Columbia, March 26th, 1824, the name of Mrs. Smith, of the Cape of Good Hope, was brought before the meeting, when Sir Richard Otley, the chairman, said, "The name of Mrs. Smith has been justly celebrated by the religious world and in the colony of the Cape of Good Hope. I heard a talented missionary state, that wherever he went in that colony, at 600 or 1000 miles from the principal seat of government, among the natives of Africa, and wherever he saw persons converted to Christianity, the name of Mrs. Smith was hailed as the person from whom they received their religious impressions; and although no less than ten missionaries, all men of piety and industry, were stationed in that settlement, the exertions of Mrs. Smith alone were more efficacious, and had been attended with greater success than the labours of those missionaries combined." The Rev. J. Campbell, missionary to Africa, says, " So extensive were the good effects of her pious exhortations, that on my first visit to the colony, wherever I met with persons of evangelical piety, I generally found that their first impressions of religion were ascribed to Mrs. Smith."

Mrs. Mary Taft, the talented lady of the Rev. Dr. Taft, was another eminently successful labourer in the Lord's vineyard. "If," says Mrs. Palmer, " the criterion by which we may judge of a Divine call to proclaim salvation be by the proportion of fruit gathered, then to the commission of Mrs. Taft is appended the Divine signature, to a degree pre-eminently unmistakable. In reviewing her diary, we are constrained to believe that not one minister in five hundred could produce so many seals to their ministry. An eminent minister informed us that of those who had been brought to Christ through her labours, over two hundred entered the ministry. She seldom opened her mouth in public assemblies, either in prayer or speaking, but the Holy Spirit accompanied her words in such a wonderful manner, that sinners were convicted, and, as in apostolic times, were constrained to cry out, 'What must we do to be saved?' She laboured under the sanction and was hailed as a fellow-helper in the gospel by the Revs. Messrs. Mather, Pawson, Hearnshaw, Blackborne, Marsden, Bramwell, Vasey, and many other equally distinguished ministers of her time." The Rev. Mr. Pawson, when President of the Wesleyan Conference, writes as follows to a circuit where Mrs. Taft was stationed with her husband, where she met with some gainsayers:—" It is well known that religion has been for some time at a very low ebb in Dover. I therefore could not help thinking that it was a kind providence that Mrs. Taft was stationed among you, and that, by the blessing of God, she might be the instrument of reviving the work of God among you. I seriously believe Mrs. Taft to be a deeply pious, prudent, modest woman. I believe the Lord hath owned and blessed her labours very much, and many, yea, very many souls have been brought to the saving knowledge of God by her preaching. Many have come to hear her out of curiosity, who would not have come to hear a man, and have been awakened and converted to God. I do assure you there is much fruit of her labours in many parts of our connection."

Mrs. Fletcher, the wife of the sainted vicar of Madeley, was another of the daughters of the Lord on whom was poured the spirit of prophecy. This eminently devoted lady opened an orphan house, and devoted her time, her heart, and her fortune, to the work of the Lord. The Rev. Mr. Hodson, in referring to her public labours, says, " Mrs.

Fletcher was not only luminous but truly eloquent—her discourses displayed much good sense, and were fraught with the riches of the gospel. She excelled in that poetry of an orator which can alone supply the place of all the rest —that eloquence which goes directly to the heart. She was the honoured instrument of doing much good; and the fruit of her labours is now manifest in the lives and tempers of numbers who will be her crown of rejoicing in the day of the Lord." The Rev. Henry Moore sums up a fine eulogium on her character and labours by saying, "May not every pious churchman say, Would to God all the Lord's people were such prophets and prophetesses!"

Miss Elizabeth Hurrell travelled through many counties in England, preaching the unsearchable riches of Christ; and very many were, through her instrumentality, brought to a knowledge of the truth, not a few of whom were afterwards called to fill very honourable stations in the Church. From the Methodist Conference, held at Manchester, 1787, Mr. Wesley wrote to Miss Sarah Mallett, whose labours, while very acceptable to the people, had been opposed by some of the preachers:—" We give the right hand of fellowship to Sarah Mallett, and have no objection to her being *a preacher in our connection*, so long as she preaches Methodist doctrine, and attends to our discipline."

Such are a few examples of the success attending the public labours of females in the gospel. We might give many more, but our space only admits of a bare mention of Mrs. Wesley, Mrs. Rogers, Mrs. President Edwards, Mrs. Elizabeth Fry, Mrs. Hall, Mrs. Gilbert, Miss Lawrence, Miss Newman, Miss Miller, Miss Tooth, and Miss Cutler, whose holy lives and zealous labours were owned of God in the conversion of thousands of souls, and the abundant edification of the Lord's people.

Nor are the instances of the spirit of prophecy bestowed on women confined to by-gone generations: the revival of this age, as well as of every other, has been marked by this endowment, and the labours of such pious and talented ladies as Mrs. Palmer, Mrs. Finney, Mrs. Wightman, Miss Marsh,* with numberless other Marys and Phebes, have contributed in no small degree to its extension and power.

We have endeavoured in the foregoing pages to establish, what we sincerely believe, that woman has a *right* to teach. Here the whole question hinges. If she has the *right*, she has it independently of any man-made restrictions which

* The record of this lady's labours has long been before the public. "*English Hearts and Hands*," in a truly fascinating manner, describes the wonderful success with which those labours have been attended. Well has it been for the spiritual interest of hundreds that no sacerdotal conclave has been able to place the seal of silence upon her lips, and assign her to "*privacy as her proper sphere.*"

do not equally refer to the opposite sex. If she has the right, and possesses the necessary qualifications, we maintain that, where the law of expediency does not prevent, she is at liberty to exercise it without any further pretensions to inspiration than those put forth by the male sex. If, on the other hand, it can be proved that she has *not* the right, but that imperative silence is imposed upon her by the word of God, we cannot see who has authority to relax or make exceptions to the law.

If commentators had dealt with the Bible on other subjects as they have dealt with it on this, taking isolated passages, separated from their explanatory connections, and insisting on a literal interpretation of the words of our version, what errors and contradictions would have been forced upon the acceptance of the Church, and what terrible results would have accrued to the world. On this principle the Universalist will have all men unconditionally saved, because the Bible says, " Christ is the Saviour of all men," etc. The Antinomian, according to this rule of interpretation, has most unquestionable foundation for his dead faith and hollow profession, seeing that St. Paul declares over and over again that men are " saved by faith and not by works." The Unitarian, also, in support of his soul-withering doctrine, triumphantly refers to numerous passages which, taken alone, teach only the humanity of Jesus. In short, "there is no end to the errors in faith and practice which have resulted from taking isolated passages, wrested from their proper connections, or the light thrown upon them by other Scriptures, and applying them to sustain a favourite theory." Judging from the blessed results which have almost invariably followed the ministrations of women in the cause of Christ, we fear it will be found, in the great day of account, that a mistaken and unjustifiable application of the passage, " Let your women keep silence in the Churches," has resulted in more loss to the Church, evil to the world, and dishonour to God, than any of the errors we have already referred to.

And feeling, as we have long felt, that this is a subject of vast importance to the interests of Christ's kingdom and the glory of God, we would most earnestly commend its consideration to those who have influence in the Churches. We think it a matter worthy of their consideration whether God intended woman to bury her talents and influence as she now does? And whether the circumscribed sphere of woman's religious labours may not have something to do with the comparative non-success of the gospel in these latter days.

Mrs Fannie McDowell Hunter

WOMEN PREACHERS.

MRS. FANNIE McDOWELL HUNTER,

FULTON, KENTUCKY.

INTRODUCED BY

DR. A. M. HILLS,

President Texas Holiness University.

PENIEL, TEXAS.

COPYRIGHTED 1905 BY THE AUTHOR.

PRICE 25 Cents.

STATION A, DALLAS, TEXAS:
BERACHAH PRINTING CO.,
RELIGIOUS PRINTERS AND PUBLISHERS.
1905.

TO
MY BELOVED SISTERS,

WHO ARE ANNOINTED BY THE HOLY SPIRIT AND COMMISSIONED, LIKE MARY OF OLD, TO TELL THE SORROWING OF THEIR RISEN LORD, AND WHO, AS THEY GO ON THEIR BLESSED MISSION FOR

THE MASTER,

OFTEN MEET THE OPPOSITION AND SCORN OF THEIR OPPONENTS, THESE PAGES ARE

Dedicated

BY THEIR SYMPATHIZING SISTER

THE AUTHOR.

PREFACE.

Like the Psalmist David, I may say: "I have believed, therefore have I spoken," in the pages of this little book. For it was born of profound conviction that the teaching set forth therein is in perfect harmony with the teachings of the Bible. And such conviction came from the prayerful study of the Bible.

"By what authority doest thou these things? And who gave thee this authority?" (Matt. 21: 23.) This is the question propounded by many when a woman enters the pulpit, takes a text and preaches a sermon. With a desire to prove from God's Word who gave her this authority, I have written these pages.

In my travels in the Evangelistic field, I have found that woman's right to preach is a much discussed subject. There are many views entertained concerning just what woman may or may not do in religious work.

I have reviewed the Scriptures carefully on this subject, consulting the best authorities for the original translation. I see no reason why it should not be considered as candidly as any other subject.

I ask a special favor of those who may have any prejudice against the public ministry of women and have decided not to agree with the position I have taken, that they will read before making any condemnatory remarks. I think the subject is worthy of patient and prayerful investigation.

The little book falls far below my ideal; but with all its defects, with an earnest desire to promote the glory of God, it is prayerfully sent forth on its mission of love.

MRS. FANNIE McD. HUNTER.

DECEMBER, 1904.

INTRODUCTION.

I have been greatly honored by the privilege of reading the manuscript of this little book, and also by being asked to write its introduction. I have read several books, and sermons, and essays on both sides of this subject. This is the best of all. The argument is unanswerable. It proves to a demonstration that women have as Scriptural a right to preach the Gospel as men have, and are often as truly called of God to do it.

It ought to make any reflecting Christian man blush with shame to think what persistent opposition holy women have had to encounter while like Deborah, and Huldah, and Priscilla, and Junia, and Tryphena, and Tryphosa, they have been laboring in the Lord, and what petty and contemptible arguments opponents have made to justify this opposition.

The author is herself a preacher of righteousness of extended usefulness, known in many States. The fragrance of her Christian influence "is like ointment poured forth." She knows what a woman called of God to ministerial service has to endure; but she does not forget that woman, who was last at the Cross and first at the Sepulchre, has a right, at the bidding of Jesus, to proclaim His love to sinful and perishing souls. May many saintly women be encouraged by the reading of these pages to be obedient to their Heavenly vision.

A. M. HILLS.

PENIEL, TEXAS, NOVEMBER 22d, 1904.

WOMEN PREACHERS.

CHAPTER I.

WOMEN PREACHERS—OLD TESTAMENT.

"The Lord giveth the word:
'The women that publish the tidings are a great host." —Psalms 68:11. (R. V.)

That women are to take a prominent part in evangelizing the world is clearly taught in the Old Testament. The first great prophecy concerning woman, declares that her seed "shall bruise the serpent's head;"—Gen. 3:15. It was by the "seed of the woman"—Christ—that our redemption was purchased.

It was predicted that woman was to have a part in publishing the glad tidings of salvation. "The Lord gave the word; great was the company of those that published it."—Psa. 68: 11. As this passage is rendered in the authorized version of the Bible, there does not appear anything out of the common order. Unfortunately our translators have covered up the gender in this verse. The Hebrew word is of feminine gender.

Dr. Adam Clarke, the world's greatest Commentator, says the original Hebrew reads: "The Lord gave the word: *Of the female preachers there was a great host.*" He says: "Such is the literal translation of this passage; the reader may make of it what he pleases."

We make of it a prediction that women were to preach the Gospel.

In the Revised Version a similar translation is given to Dr. Clarke's:—

"The Lord giveth the word:
The women that publish the tidings are a great host."

The Hebrew shows that the heralds are women, and that they are publishing or proclaiming God's Word. All through Jewish history, women were the ones chosen to announce good news or glad tidings. In Isa. 40: 9, we read:—

"O Zion, that bringest good tidings, get thee up into the high mountain; O Jerusalem, that bringest good tidings, lift up thy voice with strength; lift it up, be not afraid; say unto the cities of Judah, Behold your God!"

Dr. Adam Clarke says the Hebrew shows the herald here addressed is a woman, and should read: "O *daughter*, that bringest glad tidings to Zion, etc." God gives her the message He wants her to deliver: "Say unto the cities of Judah, Behold your God!"

The Gospel of Jesus Christ is the sweetest news ever brought to mortal ears—and why not woman, (whom God did not say was made a little lower than the angels) be allowed to bear the glad tidings of Jesus' power to save?

In Old Testament times it was no uncommon thing for woman to preach good tidings to the people. We have recorded instances, not a few, of those who acted in the capacity of prophetess in the days of Israel.

It really seems too bad, in this age of the world, that it becomes necessary to explain that a prophetess means a woman prophet—one who has the call of God for the sacred and responsible office of prophet.

We are not called upon to explain that a *queen* is a female king, duly vested with all his authority and functions of regal office. Nor are we called upon to explain that a priestess is a female priest, vested with all his authority and functions of priestly office.

Webster's definition of prophetess is: "A female prophet."

Robert Young, L. L. D., author of the "Analytical Concordance of the Bible," defines the Hebrew and Greek words translated *prophetess*, by the phrase, "female preachers." We are glad to cite such reputable authority on this translation.

Biblical and ecclesiastical literature gives us no warrant to make any distinction between the office and works of the male and female prophet. Some narrow the office of the prophet down to the foretelling of future events. In many instances we find it was no part of their work. Hodge, in his "Outlines of Theology," in answer to the question, "What is the scriptural sense of the word prophet?" says: "A prophet of God is one qualified and authorized to speak for God to men. *Foretelling future events is only incidental.*"

Geike, in "Life and Words of Christ," says: "A prophet, in the Jewish point of view, was less a seer than a *fearless preacher.*"

Sanballat said to Nehemiah: "Thou hast also appointed prophets to *preach* of thee at Jerusalem."—Neh. 6: 4.

Webster defines the word prophet: "A person illuminated, inspired, or instructed by God to speak in His name."

Smith, in "The Dictionary of the Bible," says: "The ordinary Hebrew word for prophet is nabi, derived from a verb signifying to "bubble forth" like a fountain. Hence the word means one who pours forth the declaration of God. He says: "The English word comes from the Greek Prophetes, which signifies, in classical Greek, one who speaks for another and interprets his will to man."

In Exo. 7: 1, 2, we have these words:—

"And the Lord said unto Moses, See, I have made thee a god to Pharaoh; and Aaron thy brother shall be thy prophet.

"Thou shalt speak all that I command thee; and Aaron thy brother shall speak unto Pharaoh, that he send the children of Israel out of his land."

The evident meaning of this passage is, that Aaron

as the prophet of Moses, declared the will of Moses, or delivered his message to Pharaoh. So a prophet or prophetess of God, is to declare His will, or deliver His message to the people. In other words, they are mouthpieces of Jehovah.

Moses said he wished that *all* the Lord's people were prophets:—

"Would God that all the Lord's people were prophets, and that the Lord would put his Spirit upon them." Num. 11: 29.

He did not except the women. Paul's wish accords with Moses' where he says in 1 Cor. 14: 5:—

"I would that ye all spake with tongues, but rather that ye prophesied: for greater is he that prophesieth than he that speaketh with tongues, except he interpret, that the church may receive edifying."

He gives us a definition of what it means to be a prophet, or what it means to prophesy. 1 Cor. 14: 3:—

"But he that prophesieth speaketh unto men to edification, and exhortation, and comfort."

He says in verse four: "He that prophesieth edifieth the church." The Apostle Paul further shows what the work of the prophet is.—Eph. 4: 11-12:—

"And he gave some, apostles; and some, prophets; and some, evangelists; and some, pastors and teachers;

"For the perfecting of the saints, for the work of the ministry, for the edifying of the body of Christ."

Not only for the "perfecting of the saints" and "the edifying of the church," but *"for the work of the ministry."* We see from this passage and 1 Cor. 12: 28, that prophets are ranked next to apostles:—

"And God hath set some in the church, first apostles, secondarily prophets, thirdly teachers, after that miracles, then gifts of healing, helps, governments, diversities of tongues."

This passage proves that they are an established order of ministers in the Church of Christ. So we are forced to the conclusion that prophets—male and female—are *preachers.* They are called of

WOMEN PREACHERS.

God, and inspired by His Spirit to preach the Gospel. We feel we are rich in Scripture references that accord with the meaning of the word prophetess.

The first prophetess mentioned in the Bible is Miriam. In Ex. 15:20, we find "Miriam, the prophetess," is the distinctive title given her. Dr. Young would style her a "female preacher."

She was the leader in a song of triumph over the destruction of Pharaoh's host at the crossing of the sea.

In matters pertaining to the prophetic office, Miriam claims equality with Moses and Aaron. In Num. 12:2, Miriam and Aaron ask the question: "Hath the Lord indeed spoken only by Moses? Hath He not spoken also by us?" The prophetical name and character had been bestowed upon them as well as Moses and they considered that for Moses to exercise an exclusive authority was an encroachment upon their rights. They shared with him the work of instructing Israel. In Micah 6:4, God sanctions this claim when He says to Israel:—

"For I brought thee up out of the land of Egypt, and redeemed thee out of the house of servants; and I sent before thee Moses, Aaron, and Miriam."

In this passage it is clearly seen that Miriam was by Divine appointment one of the three deliverers of Israel.

There is no way to escape the conclusion that she not only sustained an important official relation to the Israelitish movement, but that she was an inspired teacher and acted in the full capacity of prophetess—"woman prophet."

In the Book of Judges, 4th and 5th chapters, we have an account of Deborah, the prophetess, judge, and warrior.

Those who oppose woman's ministry and woman suffrage might do well to study this lesson from God's word.

14 WOMEN PREACHERS.

It is recorded in Judges 4: 4: "And Deborah, a prophetess, the wife of Lapidoth, she judged Israel at that time." "And the children of Israel came up to her for judgments."—Ver. 5. She became the animating spirit of the government and discharged all the special duties of a judge.

By Divine authority she appointed Barak as commander of the army. Although the place was assigned him, he refused to go unless she accompanied him, which she consented to do, but told him that the success of the expedition would be imputed to a *woman* and not to him.—Ver. 9.

Although Barak had ten thousand men at his command, Deborah, under God, planned the campaign and directed the movements of the army. She even gave the order when time came to fight and God gave her the victory and her prophecy was fulfilled. She told Barak: "The Lord shall sell Sisera (captain of Jabin's army) into the hand of a woman"—Ver. 9. He was killed by Jael.—Ver. 21.

We must accept the Bible record given of Deborah although we face the opposition of some theologians, who make an effort to prove that Barak and not Deborah was the real judge and ruler of Israel. The Bible record forces us to the conclusion that Deborah, as a prophetess in religious matters and as a judge in civil matters, had a God-given right to exercise all the duties and privileges of the offices. By virtue of her inspiration she was styled "a mother in Israel."

Following the record of the wonderful victory God gave her over Jabin, is her glorious triumphal ode in Judges, Fifth chapter, which is nothing less than a sermon. She said: "The Lord made me have dominion over the mighty."—Ver. 13.

She closed by saying: "So let all thine enemies perish, O Lord; but let them that love Him be as the sun when he goeth forth in his might."

WOMEN PREACHERS.

The next instance of a woman acting as a prophetess is that of Huldah recorded in 2 Kings 22: 14. In reading from the eighth verse we gather these facts: Josiah, who was king at this time, sent Shaphan, the scribe, to Hilkiah to look after the financial interests of the kingdom. After the settlement of their business matters, Hilkiah informed Shaphan that he had found the book of the law in the house of the Lord.—Ver. 8.

Hilkiah gave the book to Shaphan and he read it. He then took the book to the King and read it to him. The contents of the book so moved the king that he rent his clothes and commanded the priest, the scribe and servants as follows in Ver. 13:—

"Go ye inquire of the Lord for me, and for the people, and for all Judah, concerning the words of this book that is found."

They "went unto Huldah, the prophetess, and they communed with her."—Ver.14. Here we find the prime minister, the secretary of the State, and the High Priest consulting a woman to procure an authoritative opinion concerning the words of the book—and this in the time of Jeremiah and Zephaniah—both prophets of Judah, and she spoke to them with a "Thus saith the Lord."—Ver. 15. Her interpretation of the words is found in 2 Kings 22: 15-20. This shows plainly that Huldah, under Divine appointment, discharged the duties of a prophetess in delivering the message of God to not only the King, but to "the people" and to "all Judah" for the king included these with himself in the request he made.—Ver. 13.

In such veneration was this woman held by the Jewish nation that her sepulchre and those of the house of David were alone tolerated in the city of Jerusalem. ("Geike's Life of Christ.")

Mention is also made of the wife of Isaiah as a prophetess. (Isa. 8: 3.) Also Noadiah, the prophetess. (Neh. 6: 14.)

We conclude our review of the Old Testament by

reference to the fact that women *ministered* at the door of the Tent of meeting: "And he made the laver of brass, and the base thereof of brass, of the mirrors of the women which assembled to minister at the door of the tent of meeting."—Ex. 38: 8. (R. V. marginal reading.)

The word translated to "minister" or "serve" is used to designate two kinds of service—Military and Tabernacle or Temple service.

In the passage before us, it has reference to Tabernacle service and designates the service of but one class or order of Tabernacle attaches—the Levites. In Num. 8: 24, it is said of them:—

"They shall go in to *wait upon the service* of the tabernacle of the congregation." Hebrew scholars give the literal translation as follows: "*They warred the warfare* of the Tent of meeting." We conclude that these women who "*ministered*" at the door of the Tabernacle, belonged to the order of the Levites, because the original word translated "to minister," aside from its military sense, is used only of the Levites in connection with their Tabernacle service. They were Levite women and had some part in the Tabernacle service. The Levites were ordained to service. We find in the Eighth chapter of Numbers that they were inducted into office with prescribed ceremonies.

It is urged that women were never admitted to the priesthood. We quote from Rev. Anna Starr, of the M. P. Church, regarding the women not being admitted to the priesthood. She says: "We answer that this fact would afford no just ground for discriminating against women in the present dispensation:—

"FIRST.—Because the priest was typical of Christ in His *humanity*. His incarnation was in the form of man.

"SECOND.—Because the office of priest was done away in Christ." See Hodge's Outlines of Theology, page 398. There is now, "One Mediator between God and men, the man Christ Jesus."—1 Tim. 2: 5. Hodge says: "No priestly function is ever attributed to any New Testament officer, inspired or uninspired, extraordinary or ordinary." There is no office in the Christian church to-day corresponding to the office of priest. The minister of the Christian dispensation corresponds with the Levite and with the prophets of the Levitical dispensation, and both of these offices were open to women.

Under the Old Testament economy, a woman could be a Nazarite. "And the Lord spake unto Moses saying, speak unto the children of Israel, and say unto them, when either man or woman shall separate themselves to vow a vow of a Nazarite, to separate themselves unto the Lord."—Num. 6: 1-2. Geike affirms that "the life-long Nazarite *stood on an equality with the priest and could enter the Holy Place.*"

Woman may have been debarred from the priesthood, but not from exercising the *higher office* of prophet. The prophet was God's representative and as such declared His will to man. The priest was man's representative and officiated in man's behalf. The prophet was God's spokesman and the priest was man's spokesman. Geike says of John the Baptist, that though a hereditary priest, he chose the "higher mission of prophet." The highest office in the Old Testament church was that of prophet and we find where they rebuked, instructed and commanded the priests.

It can be demonstrated in perfect accord with the views of the best Biblical authorities that, "so far as plenary authority in the church is concerned, the prophetic office ranks above that of priest, and as the greater includes the lesser, it by right includes all that belongs to him; so it can but rationally follow that God has thought proper to bestow the *highest office in His Church upon a woman.*

CHAPTER II.

WOMEN PREACHERS—NEW TESTAMENT.

"And there was one Anna, a prophetess."—Luke 2:36.

We come now to the New Testament where in Lu. 2: 36-38, we find an account of Anna, a prophetess. She was prophetess in Jerusalem at the time of our Lord's presentation in the temple and just after Simeon had blessed the Babe, she "*spake* of Him to all them that looked for redemption in Jerusalem." She preached Jesus as the actual Saviour of all, to those who like herself and Simeon, were devoutly waiting for the promised Redeemer. Thus woman was the first to preach Jesus to the Jews as the real Messiah.

The probabilities are that Anna was a Nazarite. She "departed not from the Temple, worshipping with fastings and supplications night and day." Dr. Godbey says: "She was no backwoods preacher, but a metropolitan enjoying a settled pastorate at Jerusalem."

Woman was also first to preach Jesus to the Samaritans.—Jno. 4: 28.

It is instructive to read the whole account of this woman coming in contact with Jesus, which resulted in Him using her to overcome the deeply rooted prejudice of the Samaritans. Christ especially honored women. It was to this Samaritan woman that He, for the first time, explicitly declared Himself to be the Messiah. She at once and fully believed upon Him. In spite of her past unsavory record, impelled by love, she at once dared to proclaim Christ *in public to men*. She was so filled with the joy of the

Living Water that she forgot her original errand. "She left her water-pot." Dr. Steele says: "She came for a pitcher of water and took a whole well away with her."

She "*saith to the men*, Come, see a man which told me all things that ever I did: is not this the Christ."— Ver. 29.

She aroused the whole city and the inhabitants came pouring out to welcome the Messiah whom this woman preached.

"And many of the Samaritans of that city believed on him for the saying of the woman, which testified, He told me all that ever I did."—Jno. 4: 39.

She publicly proclaimed Christ to a congregation of men and He had no word of rebuke to offer. In all that we have ever read against woman's right to preach the Gospel, we have never read a single quotation from the words of Jesus against this right. This is significant.

Women accompanied Jesus on His tours through Palestine.

"And it came to pass afterward, that he went throughout every city and village, preaching and shewing the glad tidings of the kingdom of God: and the twelve were with him.

"And certain women, which had been healed of evil spirits and infirmities, Mary called Magdalene, out of whom went seven devils."—Luke 8: 1-2.

These women not only accompanied Jesus on His preaching tours through cities and villages, but they followed Him from Galilee to Calvary.

"There were also women looking on afar off: among whom was Mary Magdalene, and Mary the mother of James the less and of Joses, and Salome;

("Who also, when he was in Galilee, followed him, and ministered unto him); and many other women which came up with him unto Jerusalem."—Mark 15: 40-41.

They beheld where He was laid, showing they

were last at the cross.—Mark 15: 47.

They were first at the sepulchre.

"And very early in the morning, the first day of the week, they came unto the sepulchre at the rising of the sun."—Mark 16: 2.

"*At the rising of the sun.*"

We have no record of Jesus disapproving of their conduct or telling them "to stay at home and learn of their husbands." On the other hand, He appeared to them *first* after the resurrection and appointed them to first announce to men His resurrection.

"Then said Jesus unto them, Be not afraid: go tell my brethren that they go into Galilee, and there shall they see me."—Matt. 28: 10.

"Jesus saith unto her, Touch me not; for I am not yet ascended to my Father: but go to my brethren, and say unto them, I ascend unto my Father, and your Father; and to my God, and your God.

"Mary Magdalene came and told the disciples that she had seen the Lord, and that he had spoken these things unto her."—Jno. 20: 17-18.

And so at last all the band of devoted women unite in proclaiming the risen Jesus to the incredulous apostles.

"It was Mary Magdalene, and Joanna, and Mary the mother of James, and other women that were with them, which told these things unto the apostles."—Luke 24: 10.

They were the *first* to tell of the risen Lord.

When Christ appeared to the disciples on the way to Emmaus, after the resurrection, they designate these women as "certain women also of our company."

"Yea, and certain women also of our company made us astonished, which were early at the sepulchre;

"And when they found not his body, they came, saying, that they had also seen a vision of angels, which said that he was alive."—Luke 24: 22-23.

Afterwards Peter was preaching in the house of Cornelius, at Cæsarea and in his sermon he said: "Him God raised up the third day, and gave Him to be made

WOMEN PREACHERS. 21

manifest, not to all the people, but *unto witnesses chosen before of God.*"—Acts. 10: 40-41. Were not these women who "had come with Him out of Galilee" and were first to meet Him after the resurrection, "Witnesses chosen before of God?"

Paul says in Acts 13: 30-31:—

"But God raised him from the dead:
"And he was seen many days of them which came up with him from Galilee to Jerusalem, who are his witnesses unto the people."

Now Jesus said to Mary:—"Go to my brethren,"—Jno. 20: 17—and to the women, (the names of some are given) He said: "Fear not: go tell my brethren that they depart into Galilee, and there shall they see Me."—Matt. 28: 10.

That He did not merely refer to the Apostles is evident from the recorded fact that He appeared to them that *same night in Jerusalem.*—Jno. 20: 19. But His "brethren" were to depart *into Galilee* and *there see Him.* We find that Christ used the term "Brethren" in a very broad sense and to include the entire body of believers.

"Then came to him *his* mother and his brethren, and could not come at him for the press.

"And it was told him *by certain* which said, Thy mother and thy brethren stand without, desiring to see thee.

"And he answered and said unto them, My mother and my brethren are these which hear the word of God, and do it."—Luke 8: 19-21.

The angel said to the women:

"And go quickly, and tell His disciples that He is risen from the dead; and, behold, He goeth before you into Galilee; there shall ye see Him: lo, I have told you."—Matt. 28: 7.

In this passage the term *disciples* is used and is generally limited to the Apostles. To thus limit the term is not Scriptural. The Apostles were usually

called "The Twelve," "The Eleven," "The Apostles." "And when it was day, he called unto him his disciples: and of them he chose twelve, whom also he named apostles."—Luke 6: 13.
Joseph of Arimathea was called a Disciple.—Matt. 27: 57; Jno. 19: 38. Tabitha, Timothy, Ananias, and Mnason were called disciples and none of them were of the Twelve.—Acts 9: 36; 16: 1; 21: 16.

So we see from the Word, that the women were Divinely commissioned to proclaim the resurrected Christ to the "brethren" and to the "disciples". They were first to receive this commission from the lips of the Saviour. In Luke 24: 9, it is recorded of the women: "And returned from the sepulchre, and told all these things unto the Eleven, and to *all the rest.*"

They were in that assemblage that met in Galilee, for the angel had said to them: "He goeth before you into Galilee; there shall ye see Him: lo, I have told you." —Matt. 28: 7.

The evening after the resurrection, Jesus appeared to the Apostles "and them that were with them." —Luke 24: 35-36. Jno. 20: 19-23, and He said to them: "Peace be unto you: as my Father hath sent me, even so send I you." He breathed on them and said unto them, "Receive ye the Holy Ghost." "Then opened He their understanding, that they might understand the scriptures."—Luke 24: 45. He then commissioned them—the Apostles and "them that were with them"—to preach repentance and remission of sins in His Name among all nations, beginning at Jerusalem. He said: "And ye are witnesses of these things."—Luke 24: 48. He commanded them what to do in order to be fitted for this service: "Tarry ye in the city of Jerusalem, until ye be endued with power from on high."—Luke 24: 49. Although the atonement was complete, the sacrifice had been offered and the lost world was waiting for the message of the

Gospel, they were commanded to "tarry." This command was renewed at the time of the ascension.—Acts 1: 4-5.

While it is not in so many words recorded that the women were present the night after the resurrection when Jesus appeared to the Apostles "and them that were with them," but we believe *they* were included among "them that were with them." They may or may not have been present at the Ascension. But we do know that they were among the number who assembled themselves in that upper room in Jerusalem. "These all continued with one accord in prayer and supplication, with the women, and Mary the mother of Jesus, and with His brethren."—Acts 1: 14.

Someone has said: "Woman truly rocked the cradle of the Pentecostal Church." The women were in the majority of the company of those gathered in the upper room. The company numbered about one hundred and twenty.—Acts 1: 15. In verses thirteen and fourteen we find them classified and enumerated. The names of the eleven disciples are mentioned, the four brethren of Jesus, (Matt. 13: 55.) Mary the mother of Jesus, and the women. Anyone with the least mathematical turn can see that the eleven disciples and four brethren taken from one hundred and twenty leaves one hundred and five women who received "The promise of the Father" (Acts 1: 4.) and were fitted to be witnesses unto Jesus "unto the uttermost part of the earth."—Acts 1: 8.

The following facts occur in the history of Pentecost:

FIRST.—The *women* and Mary the mother of Jesus were present with the Apostles and His brethren, praying for "The Promise of the Father."

SECOND.—"When the day of Pentecost was fully come, they were all with one accord in one place."—Acts 2: 1. The *"all"* includes the women of Acts 1: 14.

THIRD.—"And suddenly there came a sound from

Heaven as of a rushing mighty wind, and it filled all the house where they were sitting," and "cloven tongues like as of fire" appeared, and "it sat upon *each* of them." "And they were *all* filled with the Holy Ghost and began to speak with other tongues as the Spirit gave them utterance."—Acts 2: 1-4. The foregoing facts prove that the men and women bear the same relation to the day of Pentecost. They were ALL, (women as well as men) filled with the Holy Ghost and began to SPEAK (women as well as men) with other tongues as the Spirit gave them utterance. It is a mistake to assume that Peter was the only preacher on that occasion, for the pen of inspiration records that *"all"* began to speak. *All* (women as well as men) were fitted to tell out to the lost world of the crucified Saviour—that marvelous story of matchless love— and the story of His resurrection. The *women* as well as the men had tongues of fire—God's weapons for the spread of the Gospel.

It is recorded in Acts 2: 7, that "they were all amazed and marvelled" at this Pentecostal demonstration—just as the people are to-day—especially if a woman begins to speak as the Spirit gives utterance. The old-time inquiry is made: "What meaneth this?" (Acts 2: 12.) "Who gave thee this authority?" (Matt. 21: 23.) Thank God! The great host of women that are publishing the tidings can answer the question as Peter did in Acts 2: 16-18:—

"But this is that which was spoken by the prophet Joel;

"And it shall come to pass in the last days, saith God, I will pour out of my Spirit upon all flesh: and your sons and your daughters shall prophesy, and your young men shall see visions, and your old men shall dream dreams:

"And on my servants and on my handmaidens I will pour out in those days of my Spirit; and they shall prophesy."

"*All flesh* shows that the pouring out of the Spirit

WOMEN PREACHERS. 25

is not limited to either rank, sex, office, or nationality. "Your sons and your *daughters* shall prophesy." Now Peter says that Joel's prophecy was fulfilled on the day of Pentecost. It was not fulfilled unless the "daughters" and "hand-maidens" prophesied, i. e., spoke to "men to edification, and exhortation, and to comfort." (1 Cor. 14: 3.) The real meaning of prophesy is to "bubble-forth"—to be so filled with the Spirit that the gospel message will literally "bubble forth" from the heart. In 1 Cor. 12: 7, (R. V.) we read: "To each one is given the manifestation of the Spirit *to profit* withal." The question naturally arises, why, on the day of Pentecost, did the Holy Ghost bestow on these women the gift of tongues if they were not to "profit withal?" The assumption that they exercised their gifts in private and that the men exercised their gifts in public, is contrary to the teaching of God's Word. It might be well to note here, that these women were not "fortune-tellers." They did not foretell of future events as that has been proven is not the meaning of New Testament prophesying.

Following the outpouring of the Spirit, the "sons and daughters," "servants and hand-maidens" went forth as heralds of mercy and truth.

In Acts 8: 3-4, we have an account of their being "scattered abroad went everywhere preaching the word." This was the result of the Sauline persecutions. "Saul made havoc of the church, entering into every house, and haling men and women, committed them to prison." —Ver. 3. These were not the *Apostles* as some would have us believe, but *men and women* of the church which was at Jerusalem. —Ver. 1. *Men and women* "were scattered abroad went every where preaching the word." They preached Jesus as faithfully as the Apostles had. —Acts 5: 28.

In Acts 21: 9, we find that Philip, the evangelist. "had four daughters, virgins, which did prophesy."

Paul tarried "many days" with Philip, but Luke does not record that he rebuked these daughters or in any way disapproved of their public ministry. We read of no "resolutions" against their efforts to "speak unto men to edification."

We call attention next to the account of Priscilla, whose name occurs five times in the New Testament; three times her name precedes that of her husband indicating no doubt that she was the chief actor—probably being of the two, the more prominent and helpful to the Church. In Acts 18: 24-26, we read: "And a certain Jew named Apollos, born at Alexandria, an eloquent man, and mighty in the Scriptures, came to Ephesus. This man was instructed in the way of the Lord; and being fervent in the Spirit, he spake and taught diligently the things of the Lord, knowing only the baptism of John. And he began to speak boldly in the synagogue: whom when Aquilla and Priscilla had heard, they took him unto them, and expounded unto him the way of God more perfectly." In the Revised Version, Priscilla's name stands first, Both Paul and Luke bestow this honor upon her. Here we have a woman, not only teaching, but *expounding to a man* the way of God more perfectly. Note that it was to an "eloquent man and mighty in the Scriptures." She had, previous to this, abundant opportunity to know Paul's views on "Woman's Right," for he had resided in her home at Corinth eighteen months. This passage is an example of not only *lay* ministry, but woman ministry of the highest type. Priscilla is an example of what a married woman may do in conjunction with home duties and not separate from her husband.

In Rom. 16: 1-15, Paul mentions the names of several women preachers. He says of Phebe, "I commend unto you Phebe our sister, which is a servant of the church which is at Cenchrea: That ye receive her in the Lord, as becometh Saints, and that ye assist her in

WOMEN PREACHERS. 27

whatsoever business she hath used of you; for she hath been a succourrer of many and of myself also."—Vers. 1-2. Binney says: "The correct translation of this passage shows that Phebe was a *deaconess* of the church and a succourrer or patron of many—the original of *patron* being radically the same as is rendered 'he that ruleth,' in chapter 12: 8." Dr. Godbey says: "In Methodism the deacons are all ordained preachers of the Gospel. So you see I prove by Paul that she was a preacher and by the Methodist church that she was an ordained preacher." In his translation of the New Testament, he renders this passage as follows: "Phebe, our sister, who is a *minister* of the church, etc."

The word translated "servant" occurs twenty times in Paul's writings. Sixteen times it is translated "ministers." Three times it is translated "deacon." Only once is it translated "servant" and it is rather singular that the single exception is where the word is used in reference to Phebe. The same Greek word is used where it is said of Paul that he was made a minister. "Whereof I, Paul, am made a minister" (in the original, deacon.)—Col. 1: 23, and Eph. 3: 7. "Who then is Paul, and who is Apollos, but ministers" (deacons) "by whom ye believed."—1 Cor. 3: 5. "Who hath also made us able ministers (deacons) of the New Testament." 2 Cor. 3: 6.

It is also used where it is said of Tychicus that he was a "beloved brother and faithful minister."—Eph. 6: 21, and Col. 4: 7; of "Epaphras our dear fellow-servant, who is for you a faithful minister of Christ."—Col. 1: 7; of "Timotheus, our brother and minister of God."—1 Thess. 3: 2. And the *same* Greek word is used where it is said of Phebe that she was a *"servant."* In both our common and Revised Version it is uniformly translated *minister*, except in this one solitary instance *where it refers to a woman.*

We can but complain of the unfair treatment of

woman at the hands of the King James' Translators and can plainly see the power of prejudice in even learned and pious men. It seems, the fact that Phebe was a woman, determined them to make this departure in the Authorized Version of the Scriptures.

Paul when called a *deacon*, our translators call a *minister;* but Phebe, when called a *deacon* they make a *servant.*

The Bible record shows that the churches of that day were poor and hence had no *servants*, in the ordinary sense of the word servant. They had no church edifices in which to conduct religious services, but held them in private houses.

Of this passage (Rom. 16: 1,) Dr. Gordon says: "'Deaconesses' has timidly crept into the margin of the Revised Version, thus adding prejudice to slight by the association which this name has with High Church sisterhoods and orders."

Some scholars object to the translation "deaconess" because they assert that the Greek language has no such word. It is a fact that the Greek word translated "minister" in so many passages and "servant" when reference is made to Phebe, is of *common gender* and applies to either male or female.

Webster's definition of the word "deaconess" is a "female deacon."

We find nowhere in the New Testament the slightest intimation that the work of a "female deacon" was *in any respect different from that of the male deacons.* The office was one—the functions the same. So Phebe possessed the functions and discharged the duties of a deacon.

Granting that her work was the same as a deacon, does not prove that she was not a *minister* of the church and as such did not preach, for deacons not only ministered unto the sick and needy, but they preached and discharged other spiritual functions.

It is said that Philip, the evangelist, was "one of the seven" who was appointed as assistants of the Apostles.—Acts 6: 1-6. Philip performed the work of a preacher of the Gospel. "Then Philip went down to the city of Samaria, and preached Christ to them."—Acts 8: 5. He also baptized the Eunuch.—Acts 8: 38. Stephen was also one of the seven, and following is the record we have of his labors: "And Stephen, full of faith and power, did great wonders and miracles among the people. And they were not able to resist the wisdom and the spirit by which he spake."—Acts 6: 8, 10.

It is generally assumed the seven who were appointed over the business of seeing that the widows were not neglected in the daily ministration were deacons. However it is a noticeable fact that they are never called deacons. The New Testament teaching, that deacons were preachers, is very clear. They were one order of the ministry. Paul addresses one of his epistles, "To all the saints in Christ Jesus which are at Philippi, with the bishops and deacons." It is true they did other things, but these were incidental to the preaching.

So with the light we have on the Bible concerning this subject, we can but enter our protest against the partiality shown by the Church to the men who fill this office.

We insist that the duties of a woman filling the office should be the same. It is unfair to clothe the men deacons with ministerial dignity to preach in the pulpit and to help administer the sacraments and yet refuse these prerogatives to the women deacons and give to them only the drudgery in hunting up the deeply depraved in the slums of our cities and administer to the needs of the destitute and dying. We recognize this as being Christ-like work, and it is a work that all Christians and preachers should take part. But why give to a woman an office with an honorable name and not allow her the full functions of same?

Junia is the name of another woman preacher mentioned by Paul in this Sixteenth chapter of Romans. "Salute Andronicus and Junia, my kinsmen and fellow-prisoners, who are of note among the Apostles."— Ver. 7. The Syriac Version renders this verse as follows: "Salute Andronicus and Junia, my relatives, etc." We quote Dr. Gordon's comment on this passage: "Is Junia a feminine name? So it has been commonly held. But the words with which it stands connected, has led some to conclude that it is Junias, the name of a man. This is not impossible. Yet Chrysostom, who is a Greek Father, *ought to be taken as high authority*, makes this frank and unequivocal comment on this passage: 'How great is the devotion of this woman, that she should be counted worthy of the name of an apostle.'" Chrysostom lived in the Fourth Century and he was a man of great learning: the Greek was his native language and he declared Junia to be a woman.

Bishop Lightfoot says: "It is doubtful if there was such a name as Junias, while Junia was a common name among the women of Rome."

Olshausen, in his comment on this verse says: "Junia appears to have been the wife of Andronicus."

Luther, in his German Bible, translates this clause as follows: "welche sind bernhmte Apostele"—*who are renowned apostles.*

On examination of the term apostle we find it is not confined to the Twelve. Barnabas was not of the Twelve, but was called an apostle. (Acts 14:14.) In Gal. 1:19, James, the Lord's brother, is called an apostle. Matthias was chosen as an apostle. (Acts 1:26.) In Phil. 2:25, Epaphroditus is called *messenger* in our version, but an *apostle* in the original. In 2 Cor. 8:23, it is said of certain brethren, that they were apostles. Paul says he was "ordained both a preacher and an apostle."—1 Tim. 2: 7.

That God has placed apostles in the highest rank in His Church can not be disputed. In proof that they are the highest order of the ministry, we quote from Eph. 4: 11-12: "And he gave some, apostles; and some, prophets; and some, evangelists; and some, pastors and teachers; For the perfecting of the saints, for the work of the ministry, for the edifying of the body of Christ." In this passage Paul states that God gives them "for the work of the ministry." The apostolical office did not expire with the Twelve Apostles.

If God chooses and sends a woman out to do the work of an apostle, should she not be recognized as such, and should there be any hesitation in giving the Scriptural name to the office she is fitted and qualified to fill?

With Paul, we recognize Junia as an "apostle of note" and as he was *ordained* to fill the apostolical office, (1 Tim. 2: 7) we believe she was also.

Paul sent his salutations to several other women. "Salute Tryphena and Tryphosa, who labor in the Lord. Salute the beloved Persis, which labored much in the Lord."—Ver. 12. We quote Dr. Clarke's comment on this verse: "We learn from this, that Christian *women* as well as *men*, labored in the ministry of the Word. Many have spent much useless labor in endeavoring to prove that these women did not *preach*. That there were some *prophetesses* as well as *prophets* in the Christian church, we learn; and that a woman might *pray* or *prophesy*, provided she had her *head covered* we know and that whosoever *prophesied* spoke unto others to *edification, exhortation,* and comfort, St. Paul declares. —1 Cor. 14: 3. And that no preacher can *do more*, every person must acknowledge; because to *edify, exhort* and *comfort* are the prime ends of the Gospel ministry. If *women* thus *prophesied*, then women *preached.*"

Paul also sent greetings to Mary (Ver. 6) and to the mother of Rufus, and the sister of Nerens.—Ver. 13. We do not believe that Paul disposed of these women as some would in these days by making them deaconesses in some Church and then divesting that office of the functions that belong to it when filled by a man. It is a glaring imposition that women ought to refuse to submit to.

CHAPTER III.

OBJECTIONS ANSWERED.

"Let your women keep silence in the churches."—1 Corinthians 14: 34.

We come now to the Pauline Epistles and will take up two passages which have been used so long by the opponents of the equality of women. "Let your women keep silence in the churches: for it is not permitted unto them to speak; but they are commanded to be under obedience, as also saith the law. And if they will learn anything, let them ask their husbands at home: for it is a shame for women to speak in the church."—1 Cor. 14: 34-35. "But I suffer not a woman to teach, nor to usurp authority over the man, but to be in silence."—1 Tim. 2:12.

This is the favorite battle-ground of the opponents, and where their batteries of opposition are planted and from every side they belch forth their shot and shell with the hope of putting a "padlock" on the mouths of women. In many instances they have effectually closed the mouths of godly women by teaching them to believe that the public ministry of the Word by themselves is committing a sin against God and that it is even a *shame* for a woman to *speak* in the churches. This teaching has silenced many a talented woman so she would not even witness to the saving power of Jesus, much less present herself to God to go forth bearing precious seeds of Gospel Truth for the salvation of the lost.

Some years ago the writer was assisting in a revival meeting in Kentucky. The Holy Spirit descended upon the congregation in a most marvelous manner during one afternoon service. A middle-aged woman arose with shining face, clapping her hands and said: "I *must* praise God although my church has taught me that a woman *must keep* silent in the church, and that it is a *shame* for her to speak. But the Spirit of God is upon me and my heart is so filled with praises, I *must* speak." She talked and shouted as any old-time Methodist would have done. Thank God! In this Holy Ghost dispensation, minds that have been beclouded by the fogs of superstition from mediaeval errors are being cleared and as the Spirit touches the heart, *liberty* is given: "Where the Spirit of the Lord is, there is liberty."

Opposition to women preaching has largely grown out of ideas based on tradition, prejudice and misunderstanding and misapplying these two passages of Scripture found in Paul's writings. We face the difficulty of truth finding its way out of the jungles of prejudice and ignorance. Many persons who are blinded by prejudice, simply refuse to open their eyes. They remind us of the man of whom we heard a woman evangelist tell. It illustrates why some fail to get the right meaning to these texts.

"A man told John he would give him five dollars if he could not show him fifty rats in five minutes. So he took him to the stable and instructed him where to stand to see the rats run out as he would be inside to scare them out. The man asked John if he saw the rats, to which John replied in the negative. After repeating the question several times and receiving the same reply, he stepped outside and to his amazement found that John had his eyes *closed tight* and of course could see no rats." So many of our opponents are doing just as John did. Simply *will not* see the truth because they allow prejudice to close their eyes to it.

By carefully examining these two passages before us, we can make Paul harmonize with the Scriptural teaching we have already presented and thus the supposed mountain in the way of women speaking for Jesus in the churches will have been removed. It is only made a *phantom* mountain from a mole-hill that never existed, and yet, it has afforded our opponents much consolation.

At the time Paul gave these directions for women to "keep silence," the greatest disorder prevailed in the Corinthian Church. There were factions, divisions, drunkenness, etc.—1 Cor. 1: 11-12; 5: 1-2; 6: 1; 11: 18-21. Such confusion prevailed in their public services that it was not possible to celebrate the Lord's Supper. Paul showed them in plain words what was expected of them when they came together.—1 Cor. 11: 20-34.

In the Fourteenth chapter and the 26th verse he is trying to restore order and exhorts them as follows: "Let all things be done unto edifying." Each one had a psalm, a doctrine, a tongue, a revelation, or an interpretation, and all were trying to take part in the service at once.

Paul took in the situation and gave three commands to silence. We notice in every case it is *conditional*. "Let *him* keep silence in the church."—1 Cor. 14: 28. This was the command to those who spoke in an unknown tongue. But it is on condition that "there be no interpreter present." He directs even that they speak in turn if an interpreter is present.

He next reproves the prophets and the command given is: "Let the first hold his peace."—Ver. 30. It is to the prophets "speaking by two or three," but it is on *condition* that "a revelation be made to another sitting by."

The third command to silence is to women who have been disturbing the service by asking questions and he commands them also to "keep silence in the churches," but it is *on condition* of their interruptions of the service by asking questions, for the Apostle adds:

"For it is not permitted unto them to speak" and "if they will *learn anything*" to "ask their husbands at home." Eastern women are exceedingly loquacious and their united talk (all at once) made great confusion and he rebuked this unseemly confusion and babblings in the churches. He says in Ver. 33: "For God is not the author of confusion, but of peace." To maintain peace and quiet, Paul tells women to stop asking questions publicly and if there was anything they wished to know they were to ask their husbands at home.

We notice that the larger part of this 14th chapter of 1 Corinthians is devoted to regulations for the men. When the command is given to women it is not in general terms, but *your women*—the women who *abused* the liberty of the Gospel, as the men also did, by yielding to a disorderly spirit. Paul's prohibition—34th verse—was for that local church and was only temporary.

We state emphatically the Apostle did not rebuke those women because they had made an effort *to teach* or *preach*, but for their effort to *learn*. "If they would *learn* anything," he said. If he meant to debar women from praying or prophesying (preaching) his command is not at all applicable. The directions he gives would be perfectly meaningless.

From the Gospel record we find that Christ was often interrupted in His public discourses by persons asking questions. Missionaries tell us that the same annoying custom prevails in the Oriental lands to-day. Rev. R. L. Harris (deceased) said that he never knew the meaning of 1 Cor. 14: 34, until he went as a missionary to Africa. He said that women are kept in ignorance, but that the men are educated. He also said it was considered a disgrace for a girl when she reaches womanhood not to get married. As soon as they are grown they enter into the marriage relation.

When he began conducting religious services, many of them would attend with their husbands. They were

WOMEN PREACHERS. 37

so very ignorant they could not comprehend even his plain preaching of the Gospel. So they would interrupt him by asking questions while he was giving the Gospel message.

One woman would rise to her feet to ask questions. Sometimes several would be asking questions at the same time, which caused great confusion. In order to maintain order he finally would command them to be seated and when at home to ask their husbands for an explanation of what he was preaching.

If Paul meant literally for women not to prophesy or speak in the churches he certainly was self-contradictory. He not only permitted but encouraged the public ministry of women as he gives directions how they are to pray and prophesy. 1 Cor. 11: 5, 6:—

"But every woman that prayeth or prophesieth with *her* head uncovered dishonoureth her head: for that is even all one as if she were shaven.

"For if the woman be not covered let her also be shorn: but if it be a shame for a woman to be shorn or shaven let her be covered."

What man was allowed to do with *his head uncovered*, woman was allowed to do with her *head covered*. This was enjoined upon them in conformity to the custom of the age. So the Holy Ghost, through Paul authorizes women to pray and prophesy. Again we call attention to the Bible definition of prophesying in 1 Cor. 14: 3:—

"But he that prophesieth speaketh unto men to edification, and exhortation, and comfort."

Women may prophesy unto men *not to "confusion"* but "to edification, exhortation and to comfort."

By noting his careful directions as to woman's apparel when engaged in religious services, it seems anyone would be convinced that Paul did not exclude women from praying or prophesying (preaching). He gives the following directions: "I will therefore that the men pray everywhere, lifting up holy hands, without wrath and doubting. In like manner also, that the women adorn themselves in modest apparel with shamefacedness (*"shamefastness"* in Revised Version) and sobriety, not with braided hair or gold, or pearls, or costly array; but which becometh women professing godliness with good works.—1 Tim. 2: 8-10. The meaning of this passage is very plain. He wills "that men pray everywhere, lifting up holy hands, etc." "In like manner" he wills "that women pray in modest apparel, etc." Chrysostom and most commentators supply the Greek word meaning "to pray" in order to complete the sense. "In like manner" compels them to this course.

We will now examine the other passage our opponents use against woman's right to preach.—1 Tim. 2: 11, 12:—

"Let the woman learn in silence with all subjection.

"But I suffer not a woman to teach, nor to usurp authority over the man, but to be in silence."

The Revised Version renders it as follows: "Let a woman learn in quietness with all subjection. But I permit not a woman to teach, nor to have dominion over a man." *"In quietness."* That is in a decorous, orderly manner. Dr. Gordon says: "Let a woman learn in quietness," an admonition not at all inconsistent with decorous praying and witnessing in the Christian assemblies. When *men* are admonished, the King James' translators give the right rendering to the same word: "That with *quietness* they work and eat their own bread (1 Thess. 3: 12), an injunction which no reader would construe to mean that they refrain from speaking during their labor and eating." The Greek word which these Translators have rendered *silence* occurs in three others passages and is rendered *"quiet."*—1 Pet. 3: 4; 1 Thess. 4: 11; 1 Tim. 2: 2. Well may we wonder that they render-

ed the passage in reference to women differently.
In this passage it is a noticeable fact that preaching or speaking in church is not under consideration. Women preachers are often accused of having no regard for this injunction and the opposers hurl the passage into their faces as if they were trying to "usurp authority over man" by engaging in ministerial work. Women have no such desire. "To exercise authority with which one is *lawfully invested*, is not to *usurp* authority." The Queens of different countries exercise authority over men, but no one considers them as usurpers.

Greek scholars say that the word "usurp" is not in the Greek. Dean Alford translates this passage, *"nor to lord it over."* In the original, the word is *authentein*, *"to be a despot."* The men are exhorted not to be *"lords over God's heritage."*—1 Pet. 5: 3.

We feel assured if our opponents will do as Daniel Webster advised: *"Conquer our prejudices,"* they will decide that Paul did not intend to prohibit women from taking any part in religious services, or even from preaching. In proof that he permitted and encouraged the public ministry of women, both in teaching and preaching, we have referred to several cases. The case of Priscilla, the "teacher of teachers" someone has styled her, to whom he sent greetings and commended her as a fellow-worker and places her name before her husband.—Rom. 16: 3, 4; 2 Tim. 4: 19.

He commended Phebe as a minister of the church at Cenchrea and instead of rebuking her for "usurping authority" he urged that they "receive her in the Lord as becometh saints, and that ye assist her in whatsoever business she hath need of you."—Rom. 16: 1.

In Phil. 4: 3, Paul further mentions woman's work: "And I entreat thee also, true yoke-fellow, help those women which labored with me in the Gospel, with Clement, also, and with other my fellow-laborers, whose names are in the Book of Life." The word here translated *labored with* means to *strive along with one, on his side, to help vigorously.*

It is a mistake to assume these women merely labored in the kitchen to cook for Paul, for he says, "labored with me *in the Gospel.*" This is explanatory. They gave him the same assistance that Clement did, "Helped him to preach," Dr. Godbey says. Rev. W. K. Brown, D. D., ex-President of the Cincinnati Wesleyan College, says: "The expression, 'Help those women' indicates a leadership on the part of the women. The term also indicates a similarity in the labors of the males and females. And the charge is, help those women, which being given to a man, fully confirms the associate labor of men and women."

In Titus 2: 3, 4, we find Paul's exhortation to women to be "teachers of good things." Dr. Brown renders this passage as follows: "That the *women* elders likewise be reverent in demeanor—teachers of that which is good." No doubt they were teachers in the direct personal application of the Gospel truths. "Teachers of good things," indicate this meaning.

So, evidently Paul's frequent mention of the merits and prerogatives of women fully acquits him of the false charge, that he wished to relegate them to the background and thus debar them from the office of the ministry.

We conclude this chapter by calling attention to one more quotation from Paul's writings that brings the apparent conflict to an end and removes the fetters from woman and leaves her free to serve Christ in any position she may be called to fill.

"There is neither Jew nor Greek, there is neither bond nor free, there is neither male nor female, for ye are all one in Christ Jesus."—Gal. 3: 28.

We quote Dr. Godbey's comment on this verse: "This brief and terse statement of the Holy Ghost forever sweeps from the field all the world-wide controversy relative to woman's Gospel rights, by simply annihilating sexhood in the Kingdom of Grace and Glory. This affirmation establishes the conclusion irrefutable that sexual distinction is unknown in the Kingdom of Grace and Glory." We are in full agreement with these comments.

In his comment on this verse, Dr. Adam Clarke says: "Under the blessed spirit of Christianity women have equal *rights*, equal *privileges*, and equal blessings, and, let me add, they are equally *useful.*"

This is all we contend for—perfect equality of all under the Gospel, in rights and privileges, without respect to nationality or condition or sex.

"The woman was made," says Matthew Henry, "of a rib out of the side of man; not made out of his head to lord it over him, nor from his feet to be trampled upon by him, but out of his *side to be equal* with him, under his arm to be protected by him, and near his heart to be loved by him." Yes, *equal,* but *not* to have dominion over him. "*Let them* have dominion."—Gen. 1: 26. The dominion which God gave to man at creation was a *joint* dominion—given to woman equally as to man. Woman was not relegated to the background. Dr. C. C. Harrah says: "Where the Golden Rule is true, the subordination of woman is a lie." Before the fall she had all the rights of man and nothing was said of her subjection until after the fall. She had to suffer because of her transgression and as a part of her punishment it was said to her: "Thy desire shall be to thy husband and he shall rule over thee."—Gen. 3: 16. On this verse Dr. Adam Clarke says: "*And he shall rule over thee*, though at their creation both were formed with equal rights, and the woman had probably as much right to *rule* as the man; but subjection to the will of her husband is one part of her curse; and so very capricious is this *will* often, that a sorer punishment no human being can well have, to be at all in a state of liberty, and under the protection of wise and equal laws." But there is an encouraging promise: "And I will put enmity between thee and the woman, and between thy seed and her seed; it *shall bruise thy (serpent's) head,* etc."—Gen. 3: 15. On this verse B. T. Roberts in his book, "Ordaining Women," says: "Christ was the seed of the woman. Woman gave to the world man's Redeemer. If she was first in the fall, she was first in the restoration. 'Christ hath redeemed us from the curse of the law, being made a curse for us.'—Gal. 3: 13. The *us* includes *woman.* Christ came to repair the ruin wrought by the fall."

The Pharisees asked Christ: "Is it lawful for a man to put away his wife for every cause?" In His answer He did not appeal to existing laws, or long established sermons. He based His answer on the *state of things that existed before the fall.* "Have ye not read, that he which made them at the beginning made them male and female?"—Matt. 19: 4. Why this appeal to *the beginning?* It was *to re-enact the law enacted then.* "FOR THIS CAUSE SHALL A MAN LEAVE FATHER AND MOTHER, AND SHALL CLEAVE TO HIS WIFE: AND THEY TWAIN SHALL BE ONE FLESH." Thus Christ restored *the primitive law.* He said nothing about *the subjection of woman—not one word.* According to the teaching of God's Word, we conclude that woman is not excluded from enjoying equal privileges and rights, under the blessed spirit of Christianity.

CHAPTER IV.
MODERN WOMEN PREACHERS.

"And it shall come to pass in the last days, saith God, I will pour out of my Spirit upon all flesh: and your sons and daughters shall prophesy."--Acts 2: 10.

Joel's prediction was not exhausted on the day of Pentecost but was to continue to be fulfilled throughout the entire Christian dispensation. This is implied in the words, "in the last days." "Sons and daughters," "servants and handmaidens," under the influence of the Holy Spirit, continue to preach the crucified and risen Christ.

Consecrated women ever and anon, in obedience to a Divine call have taken upon themselves all the essential functions (many have taken *all* the functions) of the ministry in so far as prayer, exhortation, and preaching are concerned.

Early Methodism was blessed with the labors of such women. They acted as class leaders, held prayer meetings, did house-to-house visitation, exhorted, read sermons, and, in the true sense, preached. Notable among these was Susanna Wesley, the mother of nineteen children, among whom were John and Charles Wesley. She commenced with her own children in the absence of her husband, and her congregations increased until she had between two and three hundred present. Her ministry was remarkably fruitful. Her husband approved of her course, although he was cautious and conservative in the main. Her opponents were only two or three curates, whose ministry was unsuccessful and fruitless.

Another remarkable instance was that of Mary Bosanquit, afterwards Mrs. Fletcher. She was of a wealthy, cultured family. They desired her to be a woman of pleasure and fashion, but she was weaned from such in her life devoted to God and His service. Early in life she founded an orphanage which, under her care, was a center of spiritual influence. She was also a class and band leader and preacher. The latter work was not of her own choosing, but was providentially thrust upon her. She appeared before many large audiences made up of all classes of society. Her public ministry covered a period of forty-five years. Mr. Wesley was favorably impressed with her preaching. To her he wrote: "I think the case rests here; in your having an extraordinary call."

Jno. Wesley approved the public ministry of other godly women, but he was conservative and had due regard for the prejudices of education. He authorized Miss Mallett to become a traveling preacher. She became Mrs. Bryce at the Manchester Conference of 1787. He gave authority to this godly woman in the following terms: "We give the right hand of fellowship to Sarah Mallett and have no objections to her being a preacher in our connection so long as she preaches Methodist doctrine and attends to our discipline."

Not only was early Methodism blessed by the public ministry of women, but other denominations, not a few, have shared in the blessing. John Bunyan attended the meetings conducted by women who were members of the Baptist congregation at Bedford, where he received the first elements of spiritual instruction. He was particularly struck with the fact that they conversed "as if joy did make them speak." The world knows the result of Bunyan's conversion through the ministry of those godly Baptist women.

The Friend's Church has been greatly blessed by woman's ministry. For over two hundred years, woman has been accorded by the Quakers the *same rights* as man in the work of the ministry, and has been given the same opportunity for advancement. She is allowed perfect freedom in exercising the gifts and graces God has given her. A long list of women preachers of this denomination could be given. We mention the name of one of their women preachers whom God honored greatly—Hulda A. Rees (deceased.) She was styled the "Pentecostal Prophetess." Esther T. Pritchard said of her: "She was a minister of the Gospel of God's own making. She was not the product of a theological course nor of a parental choice, though her theology was wonderfully clear and her heredity of devout and priestly lineage. She was divinely elected to her calling, annointed with the Holy Ghost, and developed in the actual service. The steady growth of her ministerial gift was after the divine law of spiritual increase, viz: 'To him that hath shall be given, and he shall have in abundance.' She put her talent out to usury, and for a score of years traded with it until it multiplied many fold."

The Salvation Army have about five thousand women preachers among their ranks. The immortal Catherine Booth, who was called "Mother" of the Salvation Army, gave a thrilling experience of when she was called to preach after she was the mother of four children. It looked like an inopportune time to begin to preach, but she said: "God gave me grace and strength and enabled me to do it; and while nursing my baby, many a time I was thinking of what I was going to say next Sunday, and between times noted down with a pencil the thoughts as they struck me." She said: "He never allowed me to open my mouth without giving me signs of His presence and blessing."— ("Aggressive Christianity.") She preached a number of years and during her ministry led about twenty-five thousand souls to Christ and reared nine children, who preached the Gospel of Christ.

WOMEN PREACHERS.

Dr. Daniel Steel, a "Methodist D. D.," speaking of Mrs. Booth, through his Church paper (New York) several years ago, said: "He had listened to all the celebrities in London, not excepting Spurgeon and Parker, but had heard no speaker who had moved him so deeply as a woman preaching in a hall in the West End of London. That woman was Mrs. Booth."

Cooper in the "History of Our Country" in giving an account of the settlement of Massachusetts Bay Colony (1628) mentions the fact that Mrs. Anne Hutchinson delivered public lectures in the colony, in which she urged, among other doctrines, that not an upright life but a direct inward revelation proved a person to be saved, and that anyone "justified" and "sanctified" was free from sin. Her teachings caused great excitement and gained many adherents. Because of her teaching, she was banished from the colony, but was kindly received in Rhode Island by Roger Williams.

Mrs. Howard Taylor tells of a most degraded woman in a city in the heart of China who was converted and became an Evangelist. She was so anxious to travel with Mrs. Taylor that she said: "I am going with you, and will do your washing and make shoes. I love you and your Jesus." Mrs. Taylor gives the following statement concerning her ministry:

"There came a day when there was a great fair and hundreds of women crowded to see us. While I was speaking to them I lost my voice and could not go on talking. The room was full and this woman was sitting near me. She had been a Christian two or three months and turning to her, I said, "You see I cannot speak any more, will you try and just tell the women the rest." She said, "I cannot preach, don't ask me to do such a thing." "Well," I said, "if you don't, they will have to go without hearing and perhaps never come again. The Holy Spirit can help you and make you tell them far better than I can. Won't you ask Him?"

She bent her head in prayer for a moment, and I sat praying for her with intense earnestness, feeling that it was a crisis in her life and might prove such for many souls. Presently she raised her head, looked around, and I saw what had happened. Never shall I forget the light which shone upon her face and she began to try to tell the certainty of those things that she herself had known about Jesus. She forgot me, the time, everything, and just poured out her heart before these women.

If ever I saw anybody filled with the Spirit of God it was that woman that day. She went on for an hour or two without a pause and nobody moved. Many of them were in tears, many of them had never heard of Jesus. They had never had a missionary until two weeks before. A woman sitting in the room gave her heart to God and still lives a consistent Christian life.

Best of all, the preacher was saved from herself and filled with the Spirit and became from that time such a teacher of the Gospel that I never thought of speaking when she was there."

Amanda Smith, who was born in Southern slavery, was called of God from the wash-tub and ironing-board to the front of the Gospel ministry. The writer had the privilege of hearing her preach to a large audience in Los Angeles, California. With her simple Gospel message she held the people spell-bound. Her ministry in America, Europe, Asia, and Africa has been wonderfully owned of God and blessed to the good of her hearers.

The names of *many* other women whose labors God has blest and is blessing could be mentioned.

Dr. Talmage said that Mrs. Phebe Palmer (woman preacher of New York), won for Christ, by her direct influence, one hundred thousand persons.

The writer heard Mrs. Maggie Van Cott say she had held by the hand seventy-five thousand who had

48   WOMEN PREACHERS.

been saved in her meetings and promised to meet her in Heaven.

Mrs. C. T. Boyce, Mrs. E. E. Williams, Mrs. Hattie Livingstone, and a great host of other women are laboring successfully in the Master's vineyard, winning many souls to Him. They, with many other women, are allowed perfect freedom in preaching the Gospel by the denominations to which they belong.

The Friend's Church, the Free Methodist Church, the Methodist Protestant Church, the Church of Christ, and other churches, not a few, approve of the *ordained* ministry of women.

* * * * *

SOME OF GOD'S LEADINGS.

AN AUTOBIOGRAPHICAL SKETCH.
MRS. FANNIE McD. HUNTER.

My parents are of Scotch descent and are natives of Missouri, which is my native State also.

To my precious mother, who has never ceased to pray for the first little one God gave her to train, and to my dear father who, from earliest childhood, has encouraged me in all that is good and true, I owe, under God, what I am to-day.

One of my first recollections is of being taught to kneel at mother's knee and lisp, "Now, I lay me," and "Our Father, who art in Heaven." Quite well do I recall how the Sabbath afternoons were spent. She devoted that time to teaching my brother, sister and myself, the "Sunday School Catechism," and reading to us and having us to read good books. Such training wielded a wonderful influence over me and led me early to have a decided drawing to and preference for the Christian life. The reading of one book especially made a profound impression upon my childish heart. The title of it was, "Vinny Leal's Trip to the Golden

The Author's Childhood Home.

Shore." My heart was melted and softened as I poured over its pages, and I longed to be as good as *Vinny* was, so I might at last gain the Golden Shore to dwell with God and the angels forever.

Although I was of a bright and merry temperament and was truly a fun-loving child, I was capable of the deepest religious feeling. I recall distinctly religious play-meetings which in innocent fun I conducted with keen enjoyment. But many times in my youth I would have very serious thoughts of devoting my life to God's service. As I would hear my mother relate incidents connected with the missionary labors of my grandfather, a Methodist preacher among the Indians, I would think that perhaps sometime in the future I would be *good enough* to teach the heathen.

As a child I frequently felt the promptings of the Holy Spirit and was thus influenced at times not to do wrong and not to yield to my sinful inclinations. The first motto I remember of adopting, was, "In God we trust." When danger of any kind threatened me, I would repeat this with an upward look to the skies, and such sweet assurance of God's care would come to me that all fear was banished. One time when sent to the pasture for the cow I lost my way, and in those hours of loneliness my heart was comforted by repeating this motto. I really believed God's eye was upon me and that I would reach home safely.

At the age of twelve, I attended a revival meeting in Fulton, Kentucky, (the town of my childhood days) under the direction of a God-honored preacher of the Methodist Church, and for the first time, I sought God at a public altar of prayer. I felt a great softness of heart and as there flashed over me the memory of sins I had been guilty of, I longed to have them forgiven and have my heart changed so I would be a good girl. I was ignorant of what steps to take. Unfortunately when at the altar seeking God, a dear woman urged me to profess an experience when I really did not possess it. She said to me: "Why you love Jesus do you not?" Of course with the training I had, I replied, "Yes, I do." She said: "That is religion, all you have to do is to stand up and confess that you love Jesus." And thus I was persuaded into making a profession of religion without any change of heart. I was counted among the fruits of that revival and with quite a number, united with the Church. I resolved now that as I had become a Church member, I would be good and not yield to any sinful inclinations. I soon discovered that to try to lead a Christian life without a change of heart was a most difficult task, in fact it could not be done.

As the years drifted by, and sometime after entering my teens, my soul was distracted by the attractions of the world to the extent that I became thoughtless and God-forgetting. I had a proud heart and worldly ambitions.

I dreamed dreams and wove wondrous plans for the future. Many air-castles did I build. Among my society friends I courted admiration. At times, I would become dissatisfied with the emptiness, frivolity, and littleness of such a life and I would resolve I would be a Christian. I would try to engage heartily in the things I *thought* would make me so—such as reading my Bible and religious books, and a strict attendance upon all the ordinances of the Church. But in spite of this and good resolutions, I would indulge in amusements one evening and religiously attend prayer-meeting the next, vainly trying to serve God and the world. This experience was totally unsatisfactory and brought me no real happiness.

I then began to seek happiness at different sources. As I think of the passing fancies I took in those days, when love was changeable, as fickle girlhood ever is, it reminds me of a butterfly flitting from flower to flower. So I sought to be happy "in scenes and friendships new." But new scenes and faces and all the rest did not satisfy the longings of my soul.

Time passed quickly on. The day came that I was to be wedded to the man I loved and who loved me devotedly—Prof. W. W. Hunter, graduate of Lebanon University, Lebanon, Tenn. That autumn day the skies seemed to have had a tenderer blue, and as the leaves nodded to the whisperings of the autumn breeze, it seemed I could hear the sweetest melody. I thought *now*, that true happiness had come to my life. My mind was filled only with the brightest thoughts. 'T was mercy's hand that screened from my view the sorrow awaiting me in the near future. That dreaded disease, tuberculosis, had marked my husband as its victim, and not quite three years after our marriage, he exchanged the sorrows and sufferings and trials of earth for the peace, joy, and triumph of Heaven. My heart lay crushed with grief, and as I was not a Christian, I was deprived the comforts of salvation. God alone knows the depths of sorrow and loneliness I passed through.

This greatest sorrow of my life, God used to turn all of my high and worldly ambitions into a channel of glorifying Him and blessing Christless people. It firmly set my heart upon devoting myself to the service of God's cause. It was the means of weaning me from the world. Although only twenty-two years of age, I never again entered worldly society.

Brightest plans, cherished ambitions, sweetest hopes, and fondest dreams were made to stand still. The pain of my crushed hopes and disappointments, at times would almost seem greater than I could bear, but my heart was not rebellious nor hardened, but was softened and made sympathetic by this great sorrow.

I was greatly disquieted on account of my lack of spirituality. I longed to have the assurance that I was a child of God. I mentioned the fact of my determination to seek the Lord to my sister and a dear friend, and because I was a Church member, a Sabbath School teacher, and was consistent so far as my outward life was concerned, they said if I was not a Christian then none of the Church members were. I knew my heart better than they did. As there was no opportunity afforded me to attend revival meetings, I had an altar of prayer alone in my room. I sought with neither light nor comfort from any Christian, but was full of determination to press on and pray until I *knew* I was a child of God. I went through many a melancholy and apparently fruitless struggle, and for a *long* time was utterly discouraged, I shed many a bitter tear. The sin of unbelief prevented me realizing the pardoning favor of God.

Above the discordant noises of earth, I heard the clear, sweet words of my Master, "Come unto me all ye that labor and are heavy laden and I will give you rest." —Matt. 11: 28. How tired and weary of the struggle my poor heart was. After such a *long* struggle, at last a peace and rest stole into my soul that I had never experienced before. It was so sweet and strangely blissful. The melting power of the Spirit was upon me. I burst into tears and one of the first utterances that fell from my lips was: "'T is so sweet to trust in Jesus," and I sang lustily the old-time hymn, "Happy day when Jesus washed my sins away." Every longing of my soul was met in Jesus. I had tried to love Him and His Word, but now the love of God was shed abroad in my heart by the Holy Ghost. "For love is of God and every one that loveth is born of God and knoweth God." —1 Jno. 4: 7. My soul was fairly flooded with love and joy. I knew it was the witness to my salvation and adoption into the family of God. "The Spirit Himself beareth witness with our spirit that we are the children of God."—Rom. 8: 16.

I no longer would read the Bible hastily in order to read some other book I relished; but I simply devoured it, and Oh! how *sweet* the words to me! I was melted to tears as I would read the gracious words of Jesus. Prayer, instead of being the perfunctory offering of petitions to God at the bedside night and morning, was a constant, burning interview with Him.

The world looked very little, and its honors and rewards seemed almost contemptible. "For whatsoever is born of God overcometh the world."—1 Jno. 5: 4. This was another evidence that I was a child of God. "If any man love the world, the love of the Father is not in him."—1 Jno. 2: 16.

I could sing from my heart:—

"I am drinking at the fountain
  Where I ever would abide,
For I've tasted life's pure river,
  And my soul is satisfied.
There's no thirsting for life's pleasures,
  Nor adorning rich and gay,
For I've found a richer treasure,
  One that fadeth not away."

With this sweet experience came a love for perishing souls. They were constantly before me, helpless, sunken deeply in sin and vice. Their woes appealed to my heart. The voice of human need stirred me.

Not only that, but I heard the sweet, confiding voice of the resurrected Christ to women saying: "Go tell."

Various leadings of Providence brought me into my my Master's vineyards to labor for souls.

My entrance upon the Evangelistic field was at the instance of an evangelist and wife of Kentucky, who were constantly engaged in revival meetings. They discovered that God had given me a musical talent that had been sufficiently cultivated to fill the position of organist. They felt impressed that He would use me in the ministry of song, and so, invited me to assist them in revival work.

I rejoiced to go on this great and glorious mission. Most tender ties bound me to my home, but stronger ties of love and duty bound me to the service of my Master. With joy did I hail the privilege of throwing my entire being into sacrifice and service for Him and mankind.

Being separated from loved ones, of course was a deprivation for me; but having the smile and approval of my Master gave me great joy. The glory of being in His will enabled me to say, I can go:—

"Any where Jesus needs me,
Any where Jesus leads me."

"Thou wilt keep him in perfect peace whose mind is stayed on Thee."—Isa. 26: 3.

"Peace, perfect peace, with loved ones far away,
In Jesus' keeping we are safe and they."

I can still say from my heart these words I have written on the fly-leaf of my Bible:—

"Put any burden upon me, only sustain me;
Send me anywhere, only go with me,
Sever any tie; but the one that binds me
To Thy service and to Thy heart."

So my first Christian work was to sing the Gospel. I soon found that God had entrusted me with a key that unlocked many hearts that were impervious to all other appeals. Few hearts are such impregnable fortresses that they will not yield to assaults of love through the ministry of song. God has used me in this way to cheer many sad hearts and to brighten lives for Him and to rescue lives from the service of Satan.

For the glory of God, I relate the following incident. When assisting in a revival meeting in Tennessee, six or eight years ago, on one Sabbath afternoon I sang a solo with accompaniment on my guitar, leaving the result with God, resting upon the promise: "He shall multiply your seed sown." Two years afterwards, I visited a Missionary Training Home in St. Louis.

WOMEN PREACHERS. 55

There I met a young lady I remembered quite well as having been converted in the above mentioned revival meeting.

In conversation with her one day, she said to me: "Do you know what led me to Jesus?" I replied: "No, but I recall the Sabbath afternoon that you were converted." She said: "It was that solo you sang with your guitar that Sabbath afternoon." Together we praised God and gave Him the glory.

She was being trained for the foreign field, but it was Heaven for her instead of India.

The day I received the news of her promotion to Heaven, I faced an audience to sing, not having her in mind at all. As I arose to sing, I had a vision of her bending over from the skies, robed in white and face lighted with the glory of Heaven, and it seemed I heard her sweet voice say: "Go on Sister Hunter, and sing the Gospel and bring many more souls to Jesus."

The reader may imagine how my soul was melted and thrilled as I thought of the joy that awaits us in Heaven where many shall tell us that we were the instruments that God used to lead them to Himself.

Singing with the guitar has opened many doors to me. It has been an assistance to me in gaining entrance into and holding services in saloons and other places run by the devil.

When on my second trip to California, the first evening just after supper, a party began playing a game of cards in the sleeper, I commenced singing salvation songs with guitar accompaniment and God used it to break up the game. The crowd gathered around me and soon all of them joined me in singing, "Home, Sweet Home," "Nearer my God to Thee, etc." That was the last of the card playing. When I observed that the crowd was getting restless and I thought it was time for them to play a game, I would get the guitar and thus I would get ahead of the devil. Opportunity was afforded me also to give them Gospel messages.

And so, in all of my religious work, I have kept before me this exhortation: "As we have therefore opportunity, let us do good unto all men."—Gal. 6: 10. God has led me to sow the seed in the congregation, in the home, on the street, in the cars, in the temperance hall, anywhere, everywhere. He has blessed me in the distribution of tracts. This is one way of preaching the Gospel and I truly believe many hearts have been reached by these silent little messengers. It takes special grace to distribute tobacco tracts in a smoking car, but God always has on hand a good supply of grace to furnish. Of course, some will scoff, but occasionally someone will say: "God bless you and speed you on in this good work."

God has also given me evidence of His approval of Gospel messages given in open air meetings. I recall one incident of an infidel saloon keeper being reached in this way. After having talked from the text, "The eyes of the Lord are in every place, beholding the evil and the good,"—(Prov. 15: 3,) I approached this man and talked to him about his soul's salvation and requested him to pray for himself before coming to the next service in the evening. After supper he retired to a secret place in the garden. When he knelt, he said: "Lord you know I don't know how to pray. Will you please excuse me for all the sins I've committed against you?" The sins of years were blotted out in answer to his petition offered in penitence.

One line of Christian work in which God has specially used me has been in conducting children's meetings. He has allowed me to witness many conversions among them.

If I have any one thing more than another to be thankful for, it is that I am a mother and that God made me a blessing to the two children He committed into my hands to train for Him.

WOMEN PREACHERS. 57

R. W. Hunter.

My step-son, Robert W. Hunter, was four years of age at the time of my marriage. God gave me a mother's love for the precious boy, and it was with interest that I watched and assisted him in cultivating the good qualities of head and heart that caused him to develop into a noble man. He was happily married to Miss Callahan of Kentucky.

In the year 1882, as a sweet pledge of God's love, my precious daughter Anita, was given me. She was endowed with talents that have been cultivated and she has developed into a true, beautiful and noble woman.

Mrs. A.C. Bell.

She married Rev. A. C. Bell of Virginia. Unitedly God blesses their efforts to advance His cause.

The highest compliments ever paid me were by these two children. In conversation with my son one day we were talking of our separation for a time after his father's death. I remarked to him that perhaps the influence of certain ones during that time made him a good boy. He said: "No, mamma, your letters did it." He continued to say: "Often as I was tempted to do wrong, I would go to my trunk and get a letter of yours to read and all desire to do wrong would be gone."

The compliment my daughter paid me, was when she was a mere child at the altar of prayer in a camp-meeting. She said to some one instructing her: "Go tell my mamma to come and pray for me and I'll get saved." To my Heavenly Father be *all* the glory!

After a time the call of the Lord to greater labors came clearly and distinctly, and the personal influence of an evangelist of Kentucky led me to conduct afternoon services in a revival meeting. When he asked me to do this, I hesitated and said: "I do not think I can, for I've only sung the Gospel and done other little things for God." He replied: "Yes, you can. God is going to make a preacher of you." While standing there in the depot ready to take the train, the Spirit brought these words to me: "*I can do all things through Christ which strengtheneth me.*"—Phil. 4: 13. As the train pulled out, it seemed as the wheels turned, they said: "*I can, can, can,*" and I say to the glory of God, I *did, did, did*. I did not even consider the fact that I had never been specially trained for public speaking and that my advantages had been very limited to gain knowledge of the teachings of God's Word, at least I had not improved the advantages afforded. But with open Bible on my knees, I plead with God for texts and thoughts and He had regard for my pleadings and put His seal upon the messages. I had never conducted an altar service, so He spared me an embarrassment in the presence of several preachers, and sanctified one of their wives in the midst of the congregation. God honored me with souls in this meeting. He continued to push me out where I had to stir up the gift that was in me and accept providential openings for service.

I realized my unworthiness, but more did I realize my need of the Baptism of the Holy Ghost for service I felt I must obey the command: "Tarry ye * * until ye be endued with power from on high."—Lu. 1: 49. I was encouraged by the promise in Acts 1: 8: "But ye shall receive power, after that the Holy Ghost is come upon you." My cry to God was to be fully fitted and qualified for the work He had called me to do. One day all alone in my room after a season of agonizing prayer, I lifted my hands and eyes toward Heaven and said: "Welcome in, blessed Holy Ghost, make my heart your home." Then and there I received the Baptism of the Holy Ghost, which came in purifying (sanctifying) power, removing every discordant element in my soul, and gave a fitness for work.—Acts 15: 8, 9.

With this anointing came an *intense* desire to do what this verse says: "How beautiful upon the mountains are the feet of him that bringeth good tidings, that publisheth peace; that bringeth good tidings of good, that publisheth salvation; that saith unto Zion, Thy God reigneth."—Isa. 52: 7. This desire was accompanied with sweet, divine touches of the Spirit upon my soul. I did not reason against nor resist God's call to preach "good tidings of good" and to "publish salvation." "I thank Christ Jesus our Lord, who hath enabled me, for that He counted me faithful, putting me into the ministry."—1 Tim. 1: 12. He has led me by His loving Hand and called me to different fields and I have joyfully gone forward to do His will in proclaiming a full Gospel. I have welcomed the life of the evangelist with the ever ceaseless travel, living in a "trunk," body often so weary and worn that a garret would seem inviting to get alone for a rest. Many times on this battlefield I have had to wrestle with giants of difficulty, and I have met with opposition and persecution; but what matters if devils rage and human opposition be felt, so long as we have the smile and approval of our Master. The joy of bringing the lost to Jesus outweighs all the toil, privations, and suffering.

Often-times I have been tempted to discouragement, and when the body was almost exhausted, the suggestion would come to give up the work.

One time after an apparent fruitless effort in a revival meeting, I almost yielded to the suggestion. There was much opposition to the public ministry of women, and the hindrances to our having a successful meeting were many. I did not know of a soul being influenced by my ministry. When about decided to give it up, my Heavenly Father gave me a dose of encouragement from His Word: "For consider Him that endured such contradiction of sinners against Himself, lest ye be wearied and faint in your minds."—Heb. 12: 3. Two years after the time the above revival was held, I took the train to go to a camp meeting, and I was being tempted again to discouragement. It was like our Father to teach His discouraged child a lesson so gently. I had not been seated long in the car when a preacher of my acquaintance spoke to me. He told me a gentleman friend of his desired to become acquainted with me. I assured him I would be pleased to meet his friend. After being introduced, the friend said: "Do you remember the meeting you assisted in, in the town of ———— —, Kentucky?" I replied, "Yes, quite well." "Well," he said, "I will tell you for the glory of God, that as you sang a consecration hymn on your knees the last night of the meeting, I fully consecrated myself to God and He sanctified me. Since then I have been licensed to preach and am now preaching a Gospel of full salvation." I lifted my heart in thankfulness to God and promised Him that if ever discouragement should dare to step into my life, I would quickly send it away and press on in the work He called me to. I feel that such results prove ample compensation for all self-denying toil. Truly the King's service has its rewards. Roses and lilies have kissed my feet as I would stoop to lift the fallen. The realization of the wonderful strengthening and girding power of the words: "Lo I am with you" has cheered me and brought me out of trials that seemed like prison walls, to be, "more than conqueror."

I shall be fully repaid if I can only be permitted to bear golden fruit from my field of labor to the feet of my Master and hear Him speak in loving appreciation of my services as He did Mary's: "She hath done what she could."

Will not the reader join me in a prayer that many precious souls may be won to Him as a result of the work that still remains for me to do?

CHRISTIAN EXPERIENCE AND CALL TO PREACH.

MRS. WM. E. FISHER.

MRS. WM. E. FISHER.

I am of Swedish parentage and I shall forever praise the Lord for the training of godly parents.

When about fourteen years of age I was truly regenerated by the power of the Holy Ghost. Very soon after this I was impressed that God would have me spend my life in His vineyard in a special work.

I had never heard of a woman preacher. Did not know that any woman had ever given her life to the work of the ministry. I thought that her only field of usefulness, so far as public Christian work was concerned, was in the foreign field. So I thought that some time in the future my life work would be across the briny deep.

In my spirit, I would strive to be submissive to God's will, and in prayer would say to Him: "I am willing to do anything you would have me do."

In the mean time, I felt that I must be busily engaged in some kind of work for my Master. I was very enthusiastic in Sabbath School work and in prayer meeting. He graciously blessed me and my efforts to do good. Constantly did the Holy Spirit assure me that I must spend my life in His service. Sometimes I would rejoice that God would thus honor me and counted it as a great privilege. At other times, as I would consider my inability, a feeling of regret would possess me.

I was influenced by circumstances to the extent that I lost the joys of salvation. But in the year 1895, in a meeting conducted by Mrs. Mary Lee Cagle near my home on the prairies of Western Texas, I was reclaimed and my heart flooded again with the joy of the Lord. In this same meeting, after hearing the doctrine of sanctification preached as a second work of grace, I sought and obtained the experience by faith.—Acts 15: 8, 9. Immediately the call to God's work pressed upon me, and as never before I had the burden for lost souls. The burden was so great I could scarcely rest day or night.

I promised God I would follow His leadings. I looked to Him for Divine guidance. I soon had providential openings for soul-saving work. I entered the pulpit with His commission to preach the Gospel and the anointing of the Spirit was upon me.

Numerous calls came for me to conduct revival meetings, and as I answered them I realized God was back of them. As I said "*yes*" to these calls, how the Holy Spirit would descend upon me in power and blessing!

God graciously honored my work in the salvation of precious souls. His seal was upon my efforts to bring the lost to the feet of my Christ.

My conviction has been from the time I realized what work He would have me to do, that I must obey or lose my soul. "Woe is me if I preach not the Gospel!"

Oftentimes, in the hour of physical suffering, the enemy of my soul has made this suggestion: "It is best for you to give up the work and not try to preach any more." I praise God I am not ignorant of his devices. I do not waste any time in arguing the matter with him for I feel assured if I should entertain the thought of doing so, my Lord would hide His face from me.

Since my marriage, my husband (who is a preacher) and I have been greatly blessed in the evangelistic field. Our united ministry has been very fruitful. We realize it is true, that "*one* can chase a thousand, but *two* can put to flight ten thousand." We are grateful to God for the sweet privilege of telling the story of Jesus' love and power to save. As we witness precious souls coming into the Kingdom of God, we feel that we are rewarded for the sacrifice we made of the comforts of a home life, the separation from loved ones, etc.

I crave no greater joy than to be permitted to stand at last before the throne of God among the host of my precious sisters who have told the sorrowing of our risen Lord and there lay our trophies at His feet and hear Him commend us for being faithful to our call.

MY CALL TO PREACH.

MRS. ELIZA J. RUTHERFORD.

An Ordained Preacher of the Methodist Protestant Church.

I was convicted of my sins by the Holy Ghost and when I truly repented of them and met God's conditions of salvation, He powerfully converted my soul.

Afterwards, I heard the doctrine of sanctification as a second work of grace preached. When God revealed to my heart the need of it, I sought and obtained the experience.

Mrs. Eliza J. Rutherford.

Both my conversion and sanctification was distinct, definite, and clear. The Holy Spirit witnessed to the work wrought in my soul.

On Jan. 10th, 1892, God called me to preach the Gospel. He plainly revealed to me that I was to do the work of an Evangelist.

When I recognized His voice calling me to this work, I answered: "Here am I Lord! I am wholly consecrated to Thee. I belong to Thee to go where and when you want to send me and by your power will do your whole will."

At this time I was attending a revival meeting which was being held in a large tent in my home town, Ennis, Texas.

The night after I received the call to preach, I was invited to conduct the service in this revival meeting. The Lord gave me the text: "Worship God."—Rev. 22: 9. His Everlasting Arms were beneath me and I

66   WOMEN PREACHERS.

could say with the Apostle Paul: "I can do all things through Christ which strengtheneth me."—Phil. 4: 13. God graciously put His seal upon the service. My soul was so fired with the love of God that my one desire was to bring precious lost souls to the feet of my Saviour.

My husband at this time was unsaved. He was engaged in the sale of liquor. He was bound by the iron chains of sin. He was one of the most inveterate users of tobacco I ever knew.

Strange to say, he was so blinded by prejudice against the public ministry of women, that he thought for me to obey the call to preach was to disgrace the name of Rutherford.

He had been a very kind husband although he was a great sinner. I had such regard for his wishes that I disliked to displease him, but during all the time he so bitterly opposed me in answering the call to preach, God enabled me to be patient and kind, but *determined* to follow as He might lead. This spirit I manifested conquered him.

In July 1893, a little more than a year after I was called to preach, my husband was gloriously converted. Soon after this he was wholly sanctified. He was endued with power from on high and thus fitted and qualified by the Holy Ghost for soul saving work, he entered the Evangelistic field with me.

Unitedly we pressed the battle against sin. God made our ministry most fruitful, which was our reward for all of the toils and hardships connected with the work of an Evangelist.

On the 29th of June of this year, (1904) my precious husband was called home to Heaven to receive his reward and I have no doubt that the first words he heard our loving Master say, was, "Well done thou good and faithful servant."

While he is greatly missed at my side, God does not release me from the call to preach His Word. The call still rings in my soul and with the help of God I will continue to lead precious souls to Him and will be true to Him to the end of life, so that when my life's labors are ended, I will be permitted to join my husband in laying many sheaves at our Master's feet and we will praise Him throughout all eternity.

EXPERIENCE AND CALL TO THE MINISTRY.
MISS LILLIAN POOL.

I had religious impressions when quite young. When ten years of age the Holy Ghost convicted me of my sins. I realized I had displeased God by yielding to actions prompted by a sinful heart. I knew I was a sinner and needed a change of heart although I was so very young.

My heart was thus seized with conviction while attending a revival meeting. I went to the altar of prayer and there, truly repented of my sins, confessing them to God, and I found His Word to be true: "If we confess our sins, He is faithful and just to forgive us our sins and to cleanse us from all unrighteousness."—1 Jno. 1: 9.

I was truly converted to God and my soul was so flooded with His love and joy that I shouted His praises. Oh! what peace came to me. "Therefore being justified by faith we have peace with God."—Rom. 5: 1.

It was not long after this, until I realized there was an inward trouble which caused me to have a struggle to gain the victory when I would meet with vexatious things in my every day life.

I was often overcome by a man-fearing spirit to the extent that I would fail to testify to the work that God had so graciously wrought in my soul. This also hindered me from having freedom in Christian work. I would shrink from doing what God was calling me to do.

Under the preaching of an Evangelist on the subject of sanctification the Holy Spirit revealed to me my need. I plainly saw I had the remains of carnality in my heart and I saw the only remedy that could bring me perfect deliverance, "If we walk in the light as He is in the light, we have fellowship one with another, and the blood of Jesus Christ His Son cleanseth us from all sin."—1 Jno. 1: 7. So by faith in the cleansing Blood of Jesus, after having consecrated my ransomed powers to God, I realized I was cleansed from *all* sin. There was not a doubt in my mind about the work wrought in my soul, for the Holy Ghost witnessed to it. "For by one offering He hath perfected forever them that are sanctified. Whereof the Holy Ghost is also a witness to us."—Heb. 10: 14, 15.

"Why need we struggle on in self,
 We cannot make one black spot white,
'T is Christ's own blood and that alone
 Can change and cleanse the heart aright."

How I rejoiced to find that this cleansing delivered me from the inward struggle.

This blessed experience of sanctification I find makes *"religion easy."* Two years after I obtained this experience, God very clearly called me to preach the Gospel. The struggle I had over this was terrible. I had no doubt about it being a call from God, for I recognized His voice saying: "Lillian, go preach My Word to the lost." These words were whispered to my heart time and again.

I began to fast and pray, and at night, while others slept, I was awake spending the time in prayer trying to settle this question. The only answer from God to my prayer was: "Go preach My Word." It seemed I could not say *"yes"* to God's will.

My argument against yielding to the call, was, that I was too young and had been deprived of educational advantages. And, too, the thought of leaving home and being separated from loved ones harassed me until at times it seemed I could never consent to do so. But sweet promises from God's Word were whispered to me by His Spirit: "Lo, I am with you alway, etc., etc." The words found in Matt. 10: 37, came to me with great force: "He that loveth father or mother more than Me is not worthy of Me." And with these words came the sweet assurance that if I would leave *all* for Jesus' sake, and the Gospel's, that I should receive an hundred-fold now in this time, and in the world to come eternal life.—Mark 10: 29, 30.

At last the struggle was ended, and I said: "Here am I, send me." He opened the way for me to have advantages in attending school.

For six years I have been preaching His Word to the very best of my ability, and I have witnessed many souls coming to Christ and being saved and sanctified.

To Him be *all* the glory.

MY CALL TO THE MINISTRY.

MRS. MARY LEE CAGLE.
Ordained Preacher in the Church of Christ.

Mrs. Mary Lee Cagle.

Early in life I had a longing desire to be a blessing to the world.

When fifteen years of age I was truly converted to God and with this change of heart, the longing to carry gladness and sunshine to darkened hearts and homes became more intense. I felt assured of a Divine call to engage in Christian work. On account of the teachings of that time regarding woman's ministry, I decided there would be no opening for me in my home-land. I came to the conclusion that my call was to the foreign field where I supposed a woman would have freedom in preaching Christ to the heathen. Many dreams I had of crossing the waters and preaching to them.

I opened up my heart to my mother, telling her of my call and of my intention to obey it. She gave me no encouragement, but on the contrary bitterly opposed me, saying she would rather have me go to my grave than to the foreign field as a missionary.

Finally I became discouraged and a spirit to disobey the call came into my heart and thus I lost the joys of salvation. Although backslidden in heart my outward life was consistent and I kept up the form of religion but without power. My name was on the church record and my pastor considered me a true, loyal Christian.

WOMEN PREACHERS. 71

While in this backslidden condition, a preacher filled with the Holy Ghost came to our Church to conduct a revival meeting. Holy Ghost conviction seized my heart and the former joyful experience was restored to me. With the restoration came the old-time call to preach; but God by His Holy Spirit revealed to me that my work was not across the waters, but here in my home-land. What a struggle I had. I plead with God to release me from the call. It seemed it would have been so easy for me to say "Good-bye" to loved ones and native land and pour out my life among the heathen. The thought of remaining at home to preach the Gospel brought trouble to my heart. I knew there was not so much reproach attached to going as a missionary.

On my face before God, with tears, I would plead to be released. I knew to go out in this country as a woman preacher would mean to face bitter opposition, prejudice, slanderous tongues, my name cast out as evil, my motives misconstrued and to be looked upon with suspicion.

Besides this, I was so conscious of my inability. My educational advantages had been very limited. I was reared a timid, country girl and had never been out in the world—in fact until twenty-seven years of age, had never been outside of my native county in the State of Alabama. It seemed very strange God would call me when all these things were considered.

So often as I would plead my inability, the following verses of Scripture would be presented to my mind: "Then said I, Ah Lord God! behold I cannot speak: for I am a child. But the Lord said unto me, Say not I am a child: for thou shalt go to all that I shall send thee, and whatsoever I command thee thou shalt speak. Be not afraid of their faces: for I am with thee to deliver thee, saith the Lord. Then the Lord put forth His hand, and touched my mouth. And the Lord said unto me, Behold, I have put My words in thy mouth."—Jer. 1: 6-9. Many times, as I would take my Bible to read it, it seemed it would open where this passage is, I wished in my heart it was torn out of my Bible.

During this struggle I am thankful I did not say, "*I will not preach*"—but I said, "*I can not preach.*"

While debating in my mind about the call, I became engaged to and married Rev. R. L. Harris, the Texas Cow-Boy Preacher. I married him thinking that by becoming a preacher's wife, I could more easily do the work God called me to. But instead of this, I found it so easy to shift the work upon him, and I thought by so doing that God would release me and I would conduct the singing and women's prayer meetings and would assist in the altar work in our revival meetings.

During all this time my heart was not satisfied. God still pressed upon my heart *the call to preach.*

After three short years of married life, my husband was seized with that dreadful disease—consumption of the lungs. It was a great source of grief to me.

After some months of suffering he told me his work was done and that God was going to take him to his home in Heaven.

I refused to entertain such a thought. We were so devoted to each other, I felt that I could not submit to such a separation.

One day I went all alone with God to have a season of secret prayer. In my desperation I said: "Lord, if you will heal my husband, I will preach," and God answered me with these words: "Will you do what I want you to do whether I heal your husband or not?" These words came as a thunder clap to my soul.

There on my knees the inward struggle was long and heated. Finally by the help of God I was enabled to say from my heart: "Yes Lord, whether my husband lives or dies, I will do what you want me to do."

WOMEN PREACHERS. 73

What joy flooded my soul! From that hour to this, that question has been settled.

About two months after this my husband was promoted to Heaven. At the time of his departure God did a most gracious work in my soul. He sanctified me wholly, thus fitting me to go out on the battlefield as an Evangelist to win souls.

Shortly after husband's death I entered the open doors in Kentucky, Tennessee, Alabama, and Arkansas. God graciously put His seal upon my ministry in rewarding my efforts with many precious souls brought into His Kingdom.

Then came a call to West Texas in which field God has enabled me to carry the Gospel message across the Plains into New Mexico.

Mrs. J. W. Waldrop.

For several years in this field, I was assisted by Miss Trena Platt, now Mrs. Waldrop of California.

In many a hard battle she stood faithfully at my side. With joy we endured privations, hardships and persecutions. We were fully repaid by precious souls of all classes of people being saved.

She naturally possessed a fine musical talent and she had been afforded the best advantages in her musical education. But best of all her talent was consecrated to God.

God put His seal upon her ministry of song and with that consecrated talent she reached many hearts that were impervious to all other appeals. Eternity alone will reveal the number of souls she was instrumental in bringing to God.

About four years ago I was united in marriage to Rev. H. C. Cagle. Our united ministry is being blessed of God. We are engaged in the battle against sin until our Heavenly Father shall say that our work on earth is done.

To God, the Father, Son, and Holy Ghost, be glory now and forever.

MY CHRISTIAN EXPERIENCE.

MRS. R. B. MITCHUM.

Mrs. R. B. Mitchum.

My early religious impressions were due to the prayers and influence of a godly mother.

Very well do I remember how the Holy Spirit would visit my childish heart in convicting power and as a result, I had a longing desire to be a Christian.

My heart was very tender and as I would realize that I was a sinner, I oftentimes would cry myself to sleep after mother had tucked me away in my trundle-bed. I feared I might die and be lost.

How easily then could I have been led to accept Christ as my Saviour. With no special instructions as to *how* to become a Christian, I still struggled on with Holy Ghost conviction upon my heart, until I was twelve years of age. At this time I was privileged to attend a series of revival meetings being conducted in the Presbyterian Church, in Purdy, Tenn. I went to the altar of prayer to seek God for the pardon of my sins, but found relief and rest to my soul in my room where no one was near but God. I surrendered all to Him and the Holy Spirit witnessed that I was His child. I rejoiced in a Saviour's love.

For some years I enjoyed this sweet experience. Many happy hours I had in communion with my Lord privately at a sacred spot in the garden of our country home. There He would fill my heart to overflowing with Divine love and praises to Him for what He had done for me.

As time passed, not having clear and definite teaching as to how Christians should live, being thrown among worldly associates I awoke to the fact that the love of the world and its pleasures had crept into my heart and crowded out the precious love of Jesus. "Love not the world neither the things that are in the world. If any man love the world, the love of the Father is not in Him."—1 Jno. 1: 15.

Although I was aware of my lack of spirituality, I continued a zealous worker in the Methodist Church. Was teacher of a class in the Sabbath School and was leader in several of the societies of the Church. I was a regular attendant of all the Church services. Was an enthusiastic worker in Church suppers and entertainments.

But when the Holy Ghost revealed to me the fact that I was void of saving grace and only had the form of religion without any power, I confessed it to the Church and went to the altar of prayer and heartily repented. To me repentance meant restitution and confession to those I had wronged in any way. God enabled me to fully meet the conditions of salvation.

While on my knees in my room alone I surrendered fully to God and He graciously restored me to His favor. I realized my back-slidings were healed and I was made a new creature. Certainly old things had passed away and behold all things became new.—2 Cor. 5: 17. I shouted the praises of God because the joy of salvation had been restored to my heart.

By the Holy Spirit, through His Word, it was revealed to me that it was better to "obey than to sacrifice." For Jesus' sake, I laid aside my jewelry and worldly attire, to adorn myself in modest apparel and not with gold or pearls, or costly array, thus heeding the exhortation found in 1 Tim. 2: 10.

From this time on, God gave me victory over sin and enabled me to overcome the world, and I had sweet fellowship with Jesus. But under the clear teaching of sanctification as a second work of grace, the Holy Spirit revealed to me my need of being cleansed from the carnal mind. I saw hid away in my inmost nature the depths of pride, anger, jealousy, impatience, etc., —all of which I knew were traits of carnality. The sainted Fletcher expressed such a condition of the heart as follows: "The sins that crucified my Lord."

In studying the word of God I found that it was His will that I should be sanctified—"For this is the will of God even your sanctification."—1 Thess. 4: 3.

I found also that without the experience of Holiness I could not enter Heaven. "Follow peace with all men, and Holiness without which no man shall see the Lord."—Heb. 12: 14. "Blessed are the pure in heart for they shall see God."—Matt. 5: 8.

I also read the command: "Be ye holy for I am holy."—1 Pet. 1: 16. I felt assured God would not require an impossibility of His children. I hungered and thirsted after this precious experience.

I began to cry to God in faith:—

"Oh, how I hate these lusts of mine
  That crucified my Lord,
That sin that pierced and nailed His flesh
  Fast to the fatal wood!

"Yes, my Redeemer, it shall die,
  My heart hath so decreed;
Nor will I spare that inward sin
  That made my Saviour bleed.

"While with a melting, broken heart,
  My murdered Lord I view
I'll raise revenge against the sin
  And slay the murderers too."

For three days I fasted and prayed, confessing the carnality in my heart, at the same time making an entire consecration of my ransomed powers to God. As I plead His promises, the Holy Ghost witnessed to my heart the that work was done. These words came very forcibly to me: "The King's daughter is all glorious within, her clothing is of wrought gold." · I searched to see if these words were in the Bible. I found them penned by the Psalmist David in Psa. 45: 13.

The sweet rest from in-dwelling sin came to my heart, and I knew the suggestion from the Evil One that I could never be released from this body of sin was untrue.

With this great deliverance came an intense desire to be used of God in bringing lost souls to Him.

Ten happy years have passed since God called me to work for Him. He has blessed my labors in the salvation of sinners and sanctification of believers. To Him be all the glory!

God has honored my work in my own home. He has enabled me to rear four children for Him. I deem it a work an angel might envy.

Not only has God justified, sanctified, and fitted me for His work, but He has healed me of acute rheumatism and the suffering has never returned.

"What a wonderful Saviour is Jesus my Lord,
   He taketh my burdens away,
He holdeth me up and I shall not be moved.
   He giveth me strength as my day.

"With numberless blessings each moment He crowns
   And filled with His fulness Divine
I sing in my rapture, O, glory to God,
   For such a Redeemer as mine.

"When clothed in His brightness, transported I rise
   To meet Him in clouds of the sky,
His perfect salvation, His wonderful love,
   I'll shout with the millions on high."

MY CALL TO GOD'S WORK.
MRS. JONNIE JERNIGAN.

Mrs. Jonnie Jernigan.

The days of my childhood were not without tokens of the character of my future life and work.

Very early in life I felt impressions from the Holy Spirit upon my spiritual nature. An intense longing to tell the lost world of Jesus' love possessed my soul.

I was reared by Methodist parents, and any suggestion to them that a woman might be called of God to preach, was promptly pronounced un-Methodistic, so I kept the longing a secret from everyone.

In my girlhood days I was thrown with some Catholics, who told me the story of devoted Nuns and Sisters of Charity, who lived a life of seclusion in order that they might live holy, and give their lives to the ministry of the suffering and helping the needy. Stories of their devoted lives in plague-stricken districts fell into my hands. They were fascinating to my young, girlish heart. As I repeated them to my parents, my heart fairly burned with the desire to take the Catholic veil, thinking that I might be thus fitted to bear the story of the "Man of Sorrows" to suffering hearts. But my parents promptly gave me to understand that

Roman Catholicism was a delusion, and only a snare to trap fickle-minded women.

I was utterly discouraged and my heart crushed, as it seemed no way was open to me to give my life to the service of God. The Methodist Church would not recognize a woman preacher, and to join the Catholics meant to disgrace my family name of which I was proud, and so, broken-hearted and discouraged, I sought relief by going to a solitary place in the orchard of our home place where I wept bitterly before God.

These conditions prevented me being converted until after I was a grown woman. All of the time I was resisting the call of God until my heart became hardened. My heart was filled with pride, although I was a poor girl. I became a devotee of fashion, and my occupation was that of a milliner and fashionable dressmaker. I bent every energy to please my customers; but many times as they walked away attired in the latest styles, assuring me that they were pleased with my work, there would steal into my heart an intense longing to polish the soul of the woman and make it shine for God as I had adorned her body to shine for the gaze of worldlings.

This awful struggle in my heart continued unknown to anyone but God and myself, until one day I read a thrilling story of a missionary who braved many dangers to carry the Gospel to China's forbidden soil. The Holy Spirit again impressed the call to Gospel work upon my spiritual nature.

I reasoned as follows: "If the Methodist Church will not allow a woman to preach the Gospel in America, I will give my heart to God and go as a foreign missionary to China where they will allow a woman to preach."

I wondered why they would allow her to preach in China and not in America; and why the Church would have a grand missionary rally on the return of a woman missionary from China and allow her freedom in the Churches to tell of her foreign work, but would refuse the pulpit to a woman of America to preach the Gospel.

Soon after this I yielded to God and was gloriously converted.

Not long after this occurred, I was married; and to my surprise soon discovered that my husband too, had a call to preach and was not obeying it, under the delusion that the best thing for him to do was to take a course in a medical college to fit himself for a physician.

The pride in my heart soon led me to imagine that I was a rich doctor's wife, driving fine horses, helping to minister to the needs of suffering humanity.

We built many "air castles" only for God to sweep away at one stroke and leave us with blasted hopes.

One bright Monday evening, my husband came home from his work with face all aglow, as he told me that he had obtained the experience of sanctification. He told me of his *entire consecration* to God. He was so filled with the Spirit that he looked like a new man and the change in him affected me as I felt the fire to begin to burn in my own heart.

He looked at me with such a radiant face as he said: "I told God that I would preach the Gospel and I am ready to begin immediately." I said in my heart: *"There it is again—a call to preach."*

All of the bright prospects of being a rich doctor's wife vanished immediately and I meditated thus: "I will be troubled again with that call to preach and no Church will want a woman preacher."

I turned away from my husband with a sad, heavy heart. For two weeks I fasted and prayed until I was physically weak. At last I yielded to God, saying: "Here am I, send me. I am ready to report for orders, dear Master. Summon me and I will go on any errand of love for Thee." From that time I have done my best for Him who has done so much for me.

I felt that my call was to the ones no one else seemed to care for. I longed to tell the unfortunate girl the story of Mary Magdalene, who washed the feet of my Lord with her tears of penitence, while He washed her sins away with His own precious blood and commissioned her to preach the first sermon of the Resurrection.

I desired to go to the homes of poverty and tell them of the Babe born in an ox-stall and cradled in a manger. Of Him who had no place to lay His head and no money to pay His taxes.

I longed to tell the broken-hearted of the "Man of Sorrows" who was acquainted with grief—who wept with those who wept—who offered garments of praise for a spirit of heaviness.

I desired to tell all who were bound with the chains of sin, that Jesus came to set at liberty the captives, and to open the prison doors and set free the prisoners of sin.

I desired to tell the nameless child of one who "made Himself of no reputation," who was conceived of the Holy Ghost and born of a virgin.

I deem it a great privilege to carry the Gospel to the despised and neglected of earth and it affords me great joy to watch the joy of God's salvation flood their souls. The united ministry of my husband and myself is honored of God in the salvation of precious, immortal souls.

I am so grateful to God for not only endowing me with the gift of preaching, but also with a love for home and children. I feel that I am honored to be the mother of six children—all of whom are with us but Baby Rachel, who went to Heaven a few months ago.

Home duties, the care of my precious children, and of an invalid mother, I have not neglected. God has enabled me to meet these obligations cheerfully. While I have recognized my first duty was to home and children, this has not lessened my zeal for lost souls, nor has it been a hindrance to my obeying the call to the ministry. When my presence has been required at home so that I was prevented going into the highways and hedges, God has sent the erring ones to my home to receive spiritual help. In my own home there have been precious, erring girls redeemed from a life of sin. To God be all the glory!

I often preach on rescue work and as a result more than a score of erring girls have been brought to Jesus.

God has also given me a message for mothers and wives. Many sad hearts have been comforted by this message.

By the grace of God I expect to continue in this work, so that I may at last hear Him say, "Well done!"

CHRISTIAN EXPERIENCE AND CALL TO PREACH.

MRS. E. J. SHEEKS.

Ordained Preacher of the Church of Christ.

Mrs. E. J. Sheeks.

My religious impressions date from childhood. I do not owe them nor my call to the ministry to any home training, for my parents were not spiritual although they were Church members. There was no family altar erected in my home until I was seventeen years of age, and I never heard my father and mother pray until that time.

When eleven years of age I was converted while attending an old-fashioned revival in Kentucky, in which penitents found pardon for their sins at the "mourner's bench."

For lack of spiritual help and training, I lost the joys of salvation after having led a Christian life for some time. I drifted along backslidden in heart, although my outward life was consistent in the main. My pastor and the Church members considered me an exemplary Christian.

When seventeen years of age I attended a revival where the doctrine of sanctification was preached. I had never heard it preached, and the very first sermon I heard on the subject drove conviction to my heart. I confessed my back-slidings, consecrated my life to God, made vows to Him, and He blessed me wonderfully. Had the teaching been clear, I would not have professed the experience of Holiness at this time, but only as having been reclaimed from a back-slidden condition.

WOMEN PREACHERS.

God gave me great victory over sin and used me in leading souls to Him.

Previous to this time I had never prayed in public nor conducted a public service. Not only was it the teaching of the denomination to which I belonged that women must keep silence in the Church and must not speak in public, but my mother was bitterly opposed to women speaking in public. I was fourteen years of age before I ever heard a woman pray in public.

Soon after I was so wonderfully reclaimed, I was called upon to conduct a prayer meeting. As I was about to decide to refuse the remembrance of the promise I made to God when at the altar of prayer that I would do *any* thing He wanted me to, led me to decide that I would do the best I could. So with the help of God I conducted it. God gave me evidence that He was pleased with the effort and I returned home with victory in my soul.

My elder sister had reached home and informed my mother that I had conducted the prayer meeting. She rebuked me sharply, telling me I was very much out of my place and she forbade me ever doing such a thing again. I went to my room with a discouraged heart, but I fell upon my knees and had a "little talk with Jesus," and Oh! He comforted me, and I received such help from Him that I continued my work for Him. He gave me grace to erect a family altar in my father's home, and my parents became spiritual so that they assisted me in family worship.

I was very happy in doing for God whatsoever my hands found to do. The early impression in childhood days that I was to labor in my Master's vineyard, still lingered with me, but I thought of course it meant to be a missionary across the ocean for I did not think that a woman would be allowed to preach the Gospel here in Christian America. So everything I could find to read about missionaries I devoured with eagerness.

I was eighteen years of age when I heard the first sermon preached by a woman—Mrs. M. L. Woosley of the Cumberland Presbyterian Church. She was conducting an annual camp meeting. My mother was privileged to attend and she was convinced that a woman under the leadership of the Holy Ghost had the right to preach or speak in religious services. Many times since have I heard her pray, testify, and even shout the praises of God.

I married a short time before my twentieth birthday, and as my husband was a traveling man, I traveled with him the first two years of my married life. This kind of life threw me into worldly company and I was so influenced that I soon became worldly and gradually lost my religious zeal. It is with regret I mention as thus having been drawn away from my Lord and His service. Strange to say, I tried to hold on to an empty profession, and we even continued to have family prayers, but my soul was so very barren and I realized that I did not have the former sweet experience. My teaching "once in grace, always in grace," led me to hold on to the outward form of religion.

We located in Memphis, Tenn., where my husband and I united with a denomination which worshiped in one of the finest Churches in the city and I was very enthusiastic in what is commonly called "Church work," but that did not restore to me my lost joy and peace. I led a very fashionable life. My chief desire was to dress as stylishly as the wealthiest members of that city Church. My husband spared no means to gratify this desire and to live in luxury in an elegant home.

I shall always praise God for giving me one more chance to get right with Him. I was afforded the opportunity to attend a meeting in Tennessee conducted by Rev. R. L. Harris. Under his searching sermons, I humbled myself before God, gave up all worldliness, took the plain pilgrim way, and God restored to me the former peace and joy. Two years afterwards, while reading Wesley's five sermons on "Sin in Believers," I was deeply convicted for the need of the experience of sanctification. I sought and obtained it in my own room with no one present but God and my husband.

I confessed the traits of carnality to God and thoroughly tested my consecration to Him, I really *let go* of everything and person—home, friends, loved ones, husband, and self, and I desired the whole will of God.

I even consecrated to go to India that night, as I had an impression that possibly sometime in the future God might call me to go. I certainly will do so if God should at any time whisper "*Go.*"

I shall never forget that night. It seemed that the windows of Heaven were opened and glory flooded my soul. This testimony came to me: "The King's daughter is all glorious within, her garments are of wrought gold."

Soon after this God called me to preach His Gospel. It was the voice of God and naught else. Yet I would not acknowledge it to anyone else—not even to those who had told me that they felt that God's hand was upon me for the work.

In my prayers this call was before me, and as I would listen to others preach I would really tremble as I felt it was only a question of time when I would have to do the same thing or lose my soul.

I was so very conscious of my inability, so I offered many excuses to the Lord. But He continued to press the call upon me.

I was willing to continue conducting prayer and jail meetings, and to give messages to the girls of the Rescue Home and to talk in Epworth League meetings.

The conflict in my mind about this matter was fierce, I had a comfortable home, my husband received a handsome salary and never stinted me. I never knew what it was to lack for anything. I knew to accept the call to preach meant sacrifice, self-denial, reproach, opposition and persecutions. A very dark picture was before me. In my imagination I saw my husband opposing me and refusing to have a wife who was not a keeper at home. I could see myself a "grass widow" going from place to place with satchel and Bible in hand. I felt going that way, I would forever be disgraced.

For days I struggled and prayed over this matter. In desperation I cried to God and He gave me the following verse of Scripture: "In an acceptable time have I heard thee, and in a day of salvation have I helped thee; and I will preserve thee and give thee a covenant of the people to establish the earth, to cause to inherit the desolate heritages: That thou mayest say to the prisoners go forth; to them that are in darkness shew yourselves."—Isa. 49: 8, 9.

After spending the whole night in prayer, I said: "Lord, if it takes husband and everything else on earth, I'll preach, for I am assured the call is from Thee." Such rest and peace came to my soul. The old-time song, "How Firm a Foundation," began to ring through the corridors of my soul. So the matter was *settled* and I had the assurance the call was not a human impression, but a Divine call. This gave me courage to tell my husband, who previous to this time had not had the slightest intimation of the call or the struggle I had passed through.

I opened up my heart to him and I was greatly surprised to find he had not an objection to offer. He at once bought me a nice Gospel tent in which to conduct revival meetings.

For nine years I have been constantly engaged in Evangelistic, City Mission, and pastoral work. God has given me many souls for my hire, for which I praise Him.

I've met with great opposition and persecution. I've had experiences that took me to the lion's den and into fiery furnaces, but my blessed Saviour has always stood by and brought me out with a shout of triumph. I expect to be true to Him and do His will.

It is with a grateful heart I mention the faithfulness of Mrs. E. A. Masterman, the sweet Gospel singer, who has labored with me in my Evangelistic meetings. She has a Christ-love for perishing souls out of Christ. God has wonderfully put His seal upon her ministry of song and prayer. Heaven alone can declare the harvest of this precious woman.

Mrs. E. A. Masterman.

MY CALL TO THE MINISTRY AFTER YEARS OF SERVICE IN THE MASTER'S VINEYARD.

MRS. FANNIE E. SUDDARTH.

Mrs. Fannie E. Suddarth.

Having been reared by parents of the Old School Presbyterian faith, it seems but natural that I should become a zealous advocate of the Calvinistic doctrine. In accordance with this predilection, after attending the altar exercises in a revival meeting in the Presbyterian Church, at the urgent request of my honored father, I united with that Church in my native town of Harrodsburg, Mercer County, Kentucky, at the early age of twelve years. Although I did not realize any change of heart at this time, I was an earnest seeker after the "truth as it was in Christ Jesus," and my father being my spiritual guide, I feel that it was just and right that I should follow his advice and heed his counsel.

After the death of my dear parents in the year 1860, I united with the Episcopal Church, having been attracted by its ritual and imposing forms of worship. Some years after this, when I was a wife and mother, God spoke to me that I should consecrate my precious babe to Him in baptism as I had been dedicated in infancy. I immediately obeyed the "still, small voice," that like a monitor reminded me of the baptismal vows made for me by my precious parents in my infancy. Not having the convenience of the Episcopal Church, I united with the M. E. Church South at Franklin, Kentucky, and dedicated my babe in baptism at the same time.

Upon the afternoon of that memorable Lord's Day, I attended, for the first time in my life, an *old-fashioned Class meeting.* I must confess to an inborn prejudice against all attempts on the part of any woman to be heard speaking or praying in a public congregation. My prudent and decorous mother had given me timely lectures on the gross impropriety of violating Paul's command: "Let your women keep silence in the Churches." However, I feel it was through a special providence that I was permitted to attend that Class meeting, where I heard the rapturous testimonies of my pupils and their parents, with whose consistent lives I was well acquainted. As I listened, my interest increased, and the result was, that I stated my own convictions that this mode of public worship and liberty of speech allowed to all regardless of sex, the the blending of *head and heart* in religion, was *the perfection of religious systems.* There in that Class meeting I found soul-rest and peace after long years of futile efforts in *trying* to be a Christian. I felt in my heart that I had been truly converted. I was truly devoted to this new faith, which was a quick transition from the stern doctrine of

Calvin to the high and holy creed of the Wesleys.

I learned to love the doctrines of my adopted Church-home. I saw the truth and beauty of the sanctified life, which after three years of halting between *more than two opinions*, I met the conditions in order to obtain the experience. After three weeks of earnest prayer and three days of awful soul agony, I was enabled to consecrate my redeemed powers to God and by faith received the Baptism of the Holy Ghost.

In due time the call to preach was whispered to my heart by the Holy Spirit, but I dared not call myself a minister. I gave numberless lectures and exhortations, but I shrank from calling them sermons until the summer of 1903, while attending a Camp meeting at Rising Star, Texas. While in the pulpit conducting a service, I realized the presence of God and felt His power upon me in an unusual way. At the close of the service I returned to the home of Dr. Gibson, where I was being entertained, and the words came direct to me from the Lord: "*You ought to preach.*" With the assurance that these words were the revelation of God's will, from that moment I have been His willing servant to preach His Word. My continual heart-cry to Him is to give me souls for my hire. He blesses my efforts and I am content to "spend and be spent" in His blessed service, trusting to gather many golden sheaves to lay at my Master's feet at the feast of ingathering in the skies.

I rejoice that the first sermon on the Resurrection was preached by a timid, trembling woman, and ever since women have obeyed the Master's command to them, "*Go tell.*" And now in these last days when the rumbling of the chariot wheels that shall bring the Christ to earth again are heard, I rejoice that many women, with uplifted hand, are proclaiming that in Jesus there is liberty to the captives of sin.

I also rejoice to stand in my humble place with my

saintly sisters and with them bring precious souls to our Christ.

God grant that every woman called of Him may prove faithful unto death and that the world-wide Revival may find many precious souls brought to Christ through the ministry of woman, who, with her brethren in the ministry, shall by the grace of God, hear their welcome from the lips of Him who hath anointed them to preach the Everlasting Gospel.

CHAPTER V.

CONCLUSION.

"There is neither Jew nor Greek, there is neither bond nor free, there is neither male nor female: for ye are all one in Christ Jesus."

—Galatians 3: 28.

In the preceding pages we have given the Bible teaching on the equality of man and woman.

FIRST:—That woman was not created as a *servant* of man, but as his *companion*, his *equal*. "I will make him an help-meet for him."—Gen. 2: 18. Nothing was said of the subjection of woman before the fall.

SECOND:—That at the fall, as she was first in the transgression, it was said to her as a part of her punishment: "Thy desire shall be to thy husband and he shall rule over thee."—Gen. 3: 16.

THIRD:—That Christ re-enacted the primitive law (Matt. 19: 4, 5) thus restoring to woman under the blessed spirit of Christianity equal *rights* and equal *privileges*.

FOURTH:—That Joel's prediction, that "your sons and *daughters* shall prophesy," (Joel 2: 28) was not exhausted on the day of Pentecost, but was to continue to be fulfilled throughout the entire Christian dispensation.

FIFTH:—That the objections to the equality of man and woman in the Christian Church are based upon the misinterpretation and misapplying of a few passages of Scripture.

SIXTH:—That God thought proper to bestow upon woman the highest office in His Church. She filled the office of Apostle, Prophet, Deacon or Preacher, and Pastor.

WOMEN PREACHERS. 95

In the face of the Bible teaching on the ministry of women, who would presume to silence *one* of the thousands of modest, Christian women, who are in homes, the Church, school, or in the W. C. T. U., and other organizations, being blest of God in using their voices in His service? And yet there are some ecclesiastics who form resolutions against their efforts to preach the Gospel.

The writer was once present when a large body of preachers were in annual session. During that year, one of their pastors had invited a woman preacher to assist him in the revival services on his charge. She was greatly used of God in bringing the lost to Him. This body of preachers were in very plain terms expressing their disapproval of his course and of a woman being allowed to fill any pulpit within "their bounds." Different suggestions and resolutions were offered in order to prevent the repetition of such a course. At last it was settled in this way: "It is the *sense* (?) of this body that no woman be allowed to fill any pulpit within our bounds." Later on, before the session closed, the Presiding Officer introduces his wife to the audience, who, *standing in the pulpit,* proceeds to make a speech in favor of the "——— Society" of the Church, and from the pulpit very pathetically pleads with men and women to support it with their means and prayers. She met with the approval and applause of every member of that body. She was allowed perfect freedom to explain from the pulpit, *the plan of their society* (organization.) But a woman preacher must not be allowed the privilege of explaining the *plan of salvation* and plead with lost men and women to yield to Christ. This same body of men approve of women going as missionaries, for their Board of Missions is supporting some in the foreign field. "Consistency thou art a jewel."

While men meet to discuss, "How to reach the masses," women with Divine authority are going down to the masses. Miss Jane Addams was recently introduced to an audience, as "a woman who has done more for the down-trodden and oppressed in Chicago than any one man or set of men."

This may be well called woman's age. She moves up and the world feels her power. She is invading every line of employment. The census of 1900 makes returns for 303 separate occupations, and only in eight of these do women workers fail to appear. If she has freedom to engage in secular employment, why not allow her freedom to engage her time and talents in telling the story of Jesus and His love?

It is true she was first in the transgression and thus opened the flood-gates of damnation and brought the curse of sin, misery, and woe upon us. If she, under the influence of the Evil One, could do so much damage, why not allow her, under the influence of the Holy Spirit, to do all she can to rescue us from the curse?

Dr. Adam Clarke said: "An ass reproved Balaam, a cock reproved Peter, and why not woman reprove sin?"

It is a well known fact that she has done more to advance the cause of temperance in the last twenty-five years than the men had done in a hundred years previous. When our country is sufficiently advanced in thought to give women the ballot, prohibition will soon be a settled question. She would soon abolish laws licensing saloons.

Truly Jesus is the woman's Friend. He conferred on her the right, to think, to worship and act—honored her specially. She was the first He turned aside from the Jews to give His benedictions. He knew what she would be to the world.

Rev. Herrick Johnson says: "The best example of self-denying liberality in the Bible is recorded of woman. The best example of loving service in the Bible

WOMEN PREACHERS. 97

is recorded of woman. The best example of conquering prayer in the Bible is recorded of woman. The gift was a widow's mite; the service was the anointing of Jesus with a box of ointment; the prayer was a mother's prayer for a daughter possessed with the devil. Jesus never let fall such words of royal commendation as concerning these women. Of the poor widow He said, 'She has cast in more than they all.' Of Mary He said, 'She hath done what she could.' And to the Canaanitish mother He said: 'O woman, great is thy faith! Be it unto thee even as thou wilt.'"

A heathen woman on reading the Bible said: "This Book must have been written by a woman. It says so many good things about her." We know without it and without the Saviour, whom it teaches, the lot of woman is pitiable in the extreme.

Where Christ is preached, woman's sphere is not one of deep degradation as it is where He is not preached and as it was among the numerous kingdoms of ancient paganism. In this Christian land she is honored. Woman, representing the highest place in the civilization of the world, is placed on the dome of the Capitol of Washington, holding in one hand the sword representing justice, and in the other, the Olive branch, representing Peace.

She is also the money-controlling power. You will find her image stamped on every piece of silver.

In New York Harbor, which is the gateway for the commerce of the world to America, there stands the tower of Bartholdi, which is about four hundred feet high, and on the top of it is a *woman*—"The Goddess of Liberty"—representing this nation as the land of the free and the light of the world. She has one arm nine feet long lifted aloft, lighted by electricity, which throws its light far out on the ocean, thus lighting the vessels into port.

Since woman owes her elevation to Christianity,

may she show her appreciation by rallying around the Cross and may the careless daughters hear God's call to *arouse* and His warning of the consequences of being careless: "Rise up, ye women that are at ease; hear my voice, ye careless daughters: give ear unto my speech. Tremble ye women that are at ease; be troubled, ye careless ones, etc."—Isa. 32: 9-11. O, that many more of our Christian women would say with Phebe Palmer: "When I consecrated myself to God, my lips and voice were included."

"Rise up ye women," and do the bidding of your Master, although some of His disciples may become indignant and say: "To what purpose is this waste?" Let Jesus reply to them: "Why trouble ye the woman? for she hath wrought a good work upon me."—Matt. 26: 10.

We come now to this final conclusion: That we women preachers will adopt the glorious motto given by Peter: "We ought to obey God rather than men."—Acts 5: 29.

" 'T WAS WOMAN."
WITH REPLY.

On the fly leaf of an old book the following was written:—

Who hailed the first appearance of pride,
And listened while the serpent lied,
Consented to be deified?
    'T was woman!

Who by the tempter first betrayed,
Infringed the laws that God had made,
And all the world in ruin laid?
    'T was woman!
    'T was woman!
  —From Charity and Children, 1891.

REPLY.
By N. B. C.

Who failed to tell his new made bride
How Satan basely, foully lied
About their being deified?
    'T was Adam!

Who joined his wife in sinful pride,
Altho' he knew the serpent lied
About their being deified?
    'T was Adam!

Who tried to charge upon his wife
The blame of his own sinful life
When God and man were set at strife?
    "Old Adam!"

Who ever since has laid the blame
Of his own follies, sin and shame
Upon the wife who bears his name?
    "Old Adam!"

Who viler than the serpent's hiss,
Betrayed his Savior with a kiss
And shipwrecked every hope of bliss?
    "Not woman!"

Who vowed that he would sooner die
Than Lord and Master he'd deny,
And on that eve did curse and lie?
    "Not woman!"

Who urged the rabble to deride
The Son of God, and crucified
Their Lord with thieves on either side?
    "Not woman!"

Who nailed his Savior to a tree
And mocked His dying agony
When He expired to set man free?
    "Not woman!"

Who used her place as ruler's wife
To intercede for Jesus' life,
When plots of enemies were rife,
    "'T was woman!"

Who, when her plea could not avail,
Stood near the cross to weep and wail
While murderers drove the cruel nail?
    "'T was woman!"

And when he bruised the serpent's head
And rose triumphant from the dead
What was the first word Jesus said?
    "'T was woman!"

When John on Patmos saw the sights
And glories of celestial heights,
Whom saw he 'mid the heavenly lights?
    "'T was woman!"
Now, everybody say amen!

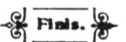

TITLES in THIS SERIES

1. THE HIGHER CHRISTIAN LIFE; A BIBLIOGRAPHICAL OVERVIEW. Donald W. Dayton, *THE AMERICAN HOLINESS MOVEMENT: A BIBLIOGRAPHICAL INTRODUCTION*. (Wilmore, Ky., 1971) *bound with* David W. Faupel, *THE AMERICAN PENTECOSTAL MOVEMENT: A BIBLIOGRAPHICAL ESSAY*. (Wilmore, Ky., 1972) *bound with* David D. Bundy, *Keswick: A BIBLIOGRAPHIC INTRODUCTION TO THE HIGHER LIFE MOVEMENTS*. (Wilmore, Ky., 1975)

2. *ACCOUNT OF THE UNION MEETING FOR THE PROMOTION OF SCRIPTURAL HOLINESS, HELD AT OXFORD, AUGUST 29 TO SEPTEMBER 7, 1874*. (Boston, n. d.)

3. Baker, Elizabeth V., and Co-workers, *CHRONICLES OF A FAITH LIFE*.

4. THE WORK OF T. B. BARRATT. T. B. Barratt, *IN THE DAYS OF THE LATTER RAIN*. (London, 1909) *WHEN THE FIRE FELL AND AN OUTLINE OF MY LIFE*, (Oslo, 1927)

5. WITNESS TO PENTECOST: THE LIFE OF FRANK BARTLEMAN. Frank Bartleman, *FROM PLOW TO PULPIT—FROM MAINE TO CALIFORNIA* (Los Angeles, n. d.), *HOW PENTECOST CAME TO LOS ANGELES* (Los Angeles, 1925), *AROUND THE WORLD BY FAITH, WITH SIX WEEKS IN THE HOLY LAND* (Los Angeles, n. d.), *TWO YEARS MISSION WORK IN EUROPE JUST BEFORE THE WORLD WAR, 1912-14* (Los Angeles, [1926])

6. Boardman, W. E., *THE HIGHER CHRISTIAN LIFE* (Boston, 1858)

7. Girvin, E. A., *PHINEAS F. BRESEE: A PRINCE IN ISRAEL* (Kansas City, Mo., [1916])

8. Brooks, John P., *THE DIVINE CHURCH* (Columbia, Mo., 1891)

9. RUSSELL KELSO CARTER ON "FAITH HEALING." R. Kelso Carter, THE ATONEMENT FOR SIN AND SICKNESS (Boston, 1884) "FAITH HEALING" REVIEWED AFTER TWENTY YEARS (Boston, 1897)

10. Daniels, W. H., DR. CULLIS AND HIS WORK (Boston, [1885])

11. HOLINESS TRACTS DEFENDING THE MINISTRY OF WOMEN. Luther Lee, "WOMAN'S RIGHT TO PREACH THE GOSPEL; A SERMON, AT THE ORDINATION OF REV. MISS ANTOINETTE L. BROWN, AT SOUTH BUTLER, WAYNE COUNTY, N. Y., SEPT. 15, 1853" (Syracuse, 1853) bound with B. T. Roberts, ORDAINING WOMEN (Rochester, 1891) bound with Catherine (Mumford) Booth, "FEMALE MINISTRY; OR, WOMAN'S RIGHT TO PREACH THE GOSPEL . . ." (London, n. d.) bound with Fannie (McDowell) Hunter, WOMEN PREACHERS (Dallas, 1905)

12. LATE NINETEENTH CENTURY REVIVALIST TEACHINGS ON THE HOLY SPIRIT. D. L. Moody, SECRET POWER OR THE SECRET OF SUCCESS IN CHRISTIAN LIFE AND WORK (New York, [1881]) bound with J. Wilbur Chapman, RECEIVED YE THE HOLY GHOST? (New York, [1894]) bound with R. A. Torrey, THE BAPTISM WITH THE HOLY SPIRIT (New York, 1895 & 1897)

13. SEVEN "JESUS ONLY" TRACTS. Andrew D. Urshan, THE DOCTRINE OF THE NEW BIRTH, OR, THE PERFECT WAY TO ETERNAL LIFE (Cochrane, Wis., 1921) bound with Andrew Urshan, THE ALMIGHTY GOD IN THE LORD JESUS CHRIST (Los Angeles, 1919) bound with Frank J. Ewart, THE REVELATION OF JESUS CHRIST (St. Louis, n. d.) bound with G. T. Haywood, THE BIRTH OF THE SPIRIT IN THE DAYS OF THE APOSTLES (Indianapolis, n. d.) DIVINE NAMES AND TITLES OF JEHOVAH (Indianapolis, n. d.) THE FINEST OF THE WHEAT (Indianapolis, n. d.) THE VICTIM OF THE FLAMING SWORD (Indianapolis, n. d.)

14. THREE EARLY PENTECOSTAL TRACTS. D. Wesley Myland, THE LATTER RAIN COVENANT AND PENTECOSTAL POWER (Chicago, 1910) bound with G. F. Taylor, THE SPIRIT AND THE BRIDE (n. p., [1907?]) bound with B. F. Laurence, THE APOSTOLIC FAITH RESTORED (St. Louis, 1916)

15. Fairchild, James H., OBERLIN: THE COLONY AND THE COLLEGE, 1833-1883 (Oberlin, 1883)

16. Figgis, John B., KESWICK FROM WITHIN (London, [1914])

17. Finney, Charles G., *Lectures to Professing Christians* (New York, 1837)

18. Fleisch, Paul, *Die Moderne Gemeinschaftsbewegung in Deutschland* (Leipzig, 1912)

19. Six Tracts by W. B. Godbey. *Spiritual Gifts and Graces* (Cincinnati, [1895]) *The Return of Jesus* (Cincinnati, [1899?]) *Work of the Holy Spirit* (Louisville, [1902]) *Church—Bride—Kingdom* (Cincinnati, [1905]) *Divine Healing* (Greensboro, [1909]) *Tongue Movement, Satanic* (Zarephath, N. J., 1918)

20. Gordon, Earnest B., *Adoniram Judson Gordon* (New York, [1896])

21. Hills, A. M., *Holiness and Power for the Church and the Ministry* (Cincinnati, [1897])

22. Horner, Ralph C., *From the Altar to the Upper Room* (Toronto, [1891])

23. McDonald, William and John E. Searles, *The Life of Rev. John S. Inskip* (Boston, [1885])

24. LaBerge, Agnes N. O., *What God Hath Wrought* (Chicago, n. d.)

25. Lee, Luther, *Autobiography of the Rev. Luther Lee* (New York, 1882)

26. McLean, A. and J. W. Easton, *Penuel; or, Face to Face with God* (New York, 1869)

27. McPherson, Aimee Semple, *This Is That: Personal Experiences Sermons and Writings* (Los Angeles, [1919])

28. Mahan, Asa, *Out of Darkness into Light* (London, 1877)

29. *The Life and Teaching of Carrie Judd Montgomery* Carrie Judd Montgomery, *"Under His Wings": The Story of My Life* (Oakland, [1936]) Carrie F. Judd, *The Prayer of Faith* (New York, 1880)

30. *The Devotional Writings of Phoebe Palmer* Phoebe Palmer, *The Way of Holiness* (52nd ed., New York, 1867) *Faith and Its Effects* (27th ed., New York, n. d., orig. pub. 1854)

31. Wheatley, Richard, *The Life and Letters of Mrs. Phoebe Palmer* (New York, 1881)

32. Palmer, Phoebe, ed., *Pioneer Experiences* (New York, 1868)

33. Palmer, Phoebe, *The Promise of the Father* (Boston, 1859)

34. Pardington, G. P., *Twenty-five Wonderful Years, 1889-1914: A Popular Sketch of the Christian and Missionary Alliance* (New York, [1914])

35. Parham, Sarah E., *The Life of Charles F. Parham, Founder of the Apostolic Faith Movement* (Joplin, [1930])

36. *The Sermons of Charles F. Parham*. Charles F. Parham, *A Voice Crying in the Wilderness* (4th ed., Baxter Springs, Kan., 1944, orig. pub. 1902) *The Everlasting Gospel* (n.p., n.d., orig. pub. 1911)

37. Pierson, Arthur Tappan, *Forward Movements of the Last Half Century* (New York, 1905)

38. *Proceedings of Holiness Conferences, Held at Cincinnati, November 26th, 1877, and at New York, December 17th, 1877* (Philadelphia, 1878)

39. *Record of the Convention for the Promotion of Scriptural Holiness Held at Brighton, May 29th, to June 7th, 1875* (Brighton, [1896?])

40. Rees, Seth Cook, *Miracles in the Slums* (Chicago, [1905?])

41. Roberts, B. T., *Why Another Sect* (Rochester, 1879)

42. Shaw, S. B., ed., *Echoes of the General Holiness Assembly* (Chicago, [1901])

43. *The Devotional Writings of Robert Pearsall Smith and Hannah Whitall Smith*. [R]obert [P]earsall [S]mith, *Holiness Through Faith: Light on the Way of Holiness* (New York, [1870]) [H]annah [W]hitall [S]mith, *The Christian's Secret of a Happy Life,* (Boston and Chicago, [1885])

44. [S]mith, [H]annah [W]hitall, *The Unselfishness of God and How I Discovered It* (New York, [1903])

45. Steele, Daniel, *A Substitute for Holiness; or, Antinomianism Revived* (Chicago and Boston, [1899])

46. Tomlinson, A. J., *The Last Great Conflict* (Cleveland, 1913)

47. Upham, Thomas C., *The Life of Faith* (Boston, 1845)

48. Washburn, Josephine M., *History and Reminiscences of the Holiness Church Work in Southern California and Arizona* (South Pasadena, [1912?])